Social Change in the United States,
1945–1983

SOCIAL CHANGE IN THE UNITED STATES, 1945–1983

William Issel

Schocken Books · New York

140317

First Schocken paperback edition 1987
First American edition published by Schocken Books 1985
10 9 8 7 6 5 4 3 2   87 88

Copyright © William Issel 1985
Published by agreement with Macmillan Publishers Ltd, London and Basingstoke

Library of Congress Cataloging in Publication Data
Issel, William.
Social change in the United States, 1945–1983.
(The Contemporary United States)
Bibliography: p.
Includes index.
1. United States—Social conditions—1945–
2. United States—Economic conditions—1945–
3. United States—Government and politics—1945–
I. Title.   II. Series.
HN59.179   1985   306'.0973   84–16297

Manufactured in the United States of America
ISBN 0–8052–3956–1 (hardcover)
ISBN 0–8052–0844–5 (paperback)

For Zenobia

Contents

Preface

DURING the past two decades, historians of the United States have turned increasingly to narrowly defined studies in order to advance the reliability and refine the elegance of their generalisations. These studies have advanced the discipline of history in many ways. The quality of evidence has increased due to more scrupulous attention to research methodology. More and better information is available on long-term trends because historians have moved away from preoccupation with single events. Heretofore ignored social groups, the poor, women and ethnic minorities, can be located in the history of their communities now that case-studies of the 'underside' of American life have become available. This 'new history', by its very success in counteracting an older narrative tradition, has created a demand for works of synthesis that address our need to understand the influence of the past on our present situation.

This book is intended to occupy a middle ground between specialised case-studies of particular aspects of post-war social change and general surveys of post-1945 United States history. Drawing on recent historical and social science research, the book has more in common with the historical essay than the definitive social history. Impressed by instances of continuity between the pre- and post-Second World War years, I have frequently included details from earlier years intended to provide background information. Convinced that the South and the West have marked post-war history in distinct ways, I have tried to give these important regions the attention they deserve. The introduction describes the federal system of government, the geography of the United States, and population trends. Readers familiar with this material can go directly to Chapter 1.

Social change and continuity are examined in this book in the context of the dominant influence of capitalism on American life. Both creative and destructive, capable of opening new horizons of economic growth as well as setting limits on individual and group opportunity, American capitalism enjoyed unprecedented success between 1945 and 1974 only to suffer setbacks thereafter. Throughout the entire post-war period, the business system and the federal government shaped American life to a greater degree than ever before in American history. I have sought to describe how the period can be understood more fully when studied in relation to the political economy. Tensions, conflicts and crises associated with class, racial, ethnic, cultural and regional competition over resources, power and prestige have also shaped American history since 1945. Most of these conflicts have been fought out within the boundaries of the constitutional government system. The economic, social and political inequalities that prompted conflict have by no means disappeared. Yet millions of individuals and families from all social and economic backgrounds have improved their living standards, and millions more have maintained their hope in such progress. This hopefulness, as much as its counterpart of frustration, emerges as a distinctive feature of post-war American history.

Many people have contributed to this book. They deserve credit for its strengths, but I alone am responsible for errors or omissions. Collective thanks go to the authors of the countless books, articles and government reports whose research I have depended upon; those whose ideas have especially influenced me receive credit in the notes and the bibliography. Conversations with Christopher Brookeman started me thinking about the need for a book of this kind. Richard Crockatt read drafts of several chapters and gave me good advice on the differences between an historical essay and a guide book. Marjorie P. Lasky took time from her own research and writing, and from her vacation, to read the first draft of the book. Her detailed criticisms and suggestions saved me from errors in fact and cautioned me against dubious interpretations; her editorial remarks helped me to strengthen the writing considerably. Some of our discussions provoked me to an appreciation of the complexity of my material that would have escaped me otherwise. Peter N. Carroll also read the entire manuscript, and his comments helped me to make numerous stylistic improvements. Discussions with Robert W. Cherny and Jules Tygiel helped me clarify various issues raised by my reading. Karen Gilbert turned a first draft of dubious legibility into typed pages, and she deserves a special word of thanks. Sarah Mahaffy and Vanessa Peerless of Macmillan provided encouragement, support and patience in just the right combination despite what must have been annoying delays.

My wife, Zenobia Grusky Issel, while immersed in her own career, nonetheless contributed immensely to my book by listening to my ideas, criticising my prose, and reminding me that I could do better. She knows how much her support has meant to me, just as I know there is no way to express my appreciation in words.

WILLIAM ISSEL

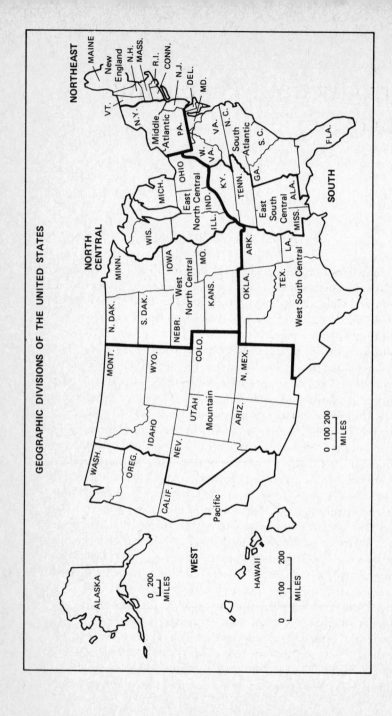

MAP 1

SOURCE: US Dept. of Commerce, Bureau of the Census, *Annual Survey of Manufactures, 1975–1976* (1979). Appendix E, p. E-11

Introduction. People and Place

REGIONS AND RESOURCES

THE United States contains 3,615,200 square miles. This total area puts the nation in fourth place in the world, for only the Soviet Union, Canada and China have larger territories. The 1980 official census counted 226,504,825 residents, and only China, India and the Soviet Union contain higher populations.

Political authority in the United States, because the nation is a federal republic, is divided between the federal and the state governments. The 50 state governments, like the federal, have executive, legislative and judicial branches. The states (Alaska and Hawaii are 'new' states that joined the union in 1959) vary greatly in territory and population. States contain local government units called counties, and the counties also vary greatly in number, residents and size from the 3 in Delaware to the 254 in Texas. In Louisiana the units of local government are called 'parishes'. In Virginia, Maryland, Missouri and Nevada, some cities are independent of any county government and exist as political units in their own right. Alaska's settled areas are divided into boroughs. The United States contains some 3,100 counties or their equivalents. In addition to the counties, there are over 18,000 municipalities and almost 17,000 townships, making a total of over 38,000 general local governments. Special governmental districts for various purposes from pest control to garbage collection number close to 40,000, thereby raising the number of all types of local government to nearly 80,000.

The federal capital of the United States is located in the District of Columbia, on territory that the state of Maryland ceded to the nation in the eighteenth century. The United States governs a number of Caribbean islands, Puerto Rico being the most important, as well as territory in the Pacific Ocean, including hundreds of small islands in Micronesia.

The United States, like all continental temperate zone countries, is hot in summer and cold in winter. Along the Pacific coast, where westerly winds blow off the ocean and keep winters mild and summers relatively cool, the ocean tempers the climate. All of the United States east of the Rocky Mountains receives most of its rain in summer, but the Pacific coast has a different rainfall pattern. Coastal parts of California, Washington and Oregon receive little or no rain in summer, but they have damp winters. Except for the coastal strip extending north from San Francisco, the western half of the nation is generally too dry for farming without irrigation, whereas the eastern half is humid enough to grow crops.

By the Second World War, the United States had differentiated itself into a number of relatively distinct regions, areas where particular types of environment had encouraged the evolution of an identifiable economic life. The Pacific coast region had its eastern boundary at the north-south wall formed by the Cascade and the Sierra Nevada mountain ranges. On the other side of this barrier, an arid inter-mountain plateau region extended eastward to the base of the Rocky Mountains and south to the Mexican border. Lack of rainfall inhibited the economic development of this region prior to the 1940s. East of the Rocky Mountains, no significant climatic barriers interfered with development. Land use related to qualities of the soil, precipitation, length of the growing season and location of minerals. The Great Plains region stood immediately east of the Rockies and extended eastward to a line where grazing and wheat-growing shifted to corn, cotton and dairy-farming activities of the more humid eastern area. The Great Plains suffered from rainfall deficiency and its eastern boundary shifted with the rainfall cycle and relative prices of the products grown on the eastern margins. This eastern boundary separated the dry-climate agriculture of western United States from the humid-climate types in the east.

East of the Great Plains, the regional boundaries followed an east-west direction. In the north, a forest and lake region comprising much of Wisconsin and Minnesota cultivated dairying. South of this area, the Corn Belt extended from eastern South Dakota, Nebraska and Kansas through Iowa, northern Missouri, Illinois, Indiana and Ohio. South of the Corn Belt, in an area marked by highly diversified physical and economic characteristics, the Appalachian-Ozark region stretched from western Virginia and North Carolina to Missouri in the West. The Cotton Belt, just to the south, covered the humid subtropical areas that ran from South Carolina westward through Georgia, Alabama, Mississippi, southern Arkansas, northern Louisiana, eastern Texas and southern Oklahoma. In 1940, this area produced half of the world's cotton crop.

Along the coasts of the Atlantic Ocean and the Gulf of Mexico, a seacoast region had developed by the Second World War that stretched from New York Harbor to Corpus Christi Bay in Texas. This area served as the seacoast for almost half of the nation and provided the shipping for the great cotton, wheat, coal and petroleum producing regions of the interior. Almost all of the large cities of this coastal strip depended upon commerce between distant world ports and the American interior. In the northeastern United States, a manufacturing belt extended westward from New England, New York and Pennsylvania to northeastern Ohio, southern Michigan, and northern Indiana and Illinois. Good transportation and easy access to raw materials had attracted more than half of the manufacturing of the continent to this region by 1940, the cities of the area constituted the centre of its livelihood, and agriculture played a secondary role.

After the land in these ten regions of the United States was pried away from the various Indian tribes whose vastly different concepts of ownership made them easy marks for European and American settlers, it was then owned by some unit of government, kingdom, colony, state or their colonising agent. The federal government once owned three-fourths of this land, and about two-thirds of that has been disposed of to individuals, states, railroad companies or other purchasers or grantees. Nearly a third of the nation's land has been retained under federal ownership. In 1974 individual Indians or Indian tribes owned 51 million acres.

Throughout American history, Congress has passed laws designed to cover the disposal of farmland, mineral lands or other special types of territory such as swampland, but pressure by developers has typically led to modifications in these laws. The United States had developed a system of mixed resource ownership by 1945. Federal, state and local governments owned some lands fully (39.6 per cent of the total by 1974) and exercised control over private lands and water rights. At the same time, individuals, corporations and other private bodies owned land or rights to land such as the right to extract gas and oil.

The United States possessed abundant supplies of water, timber, fish and game in the eastern half of the country during the eighteenth and nineteenth centuries. Many areas, including California, Nevada, Colorado and Idaho, possessed minerals in deposits rich enough for exploitation – copper, iron, silver and gold. In the late nineteenth century, almost half of the gross national product (the market value of all final goods and services produced by the economy in a year) came from natural resource commodities. The proportion in the late 1970s had fallen to about 10 per cent. Once the nation exported more raw materials than it imported, with surpluses of exports over imports for agricultural materials before 1920, and surpluses for minerals, including fuels, in the 1920s. Since 1960, the agricultural surplus of exports over imports has returned, but the country has become much more dependent on imports of minerals, especially oil.

The population has increased more than five times since 1870, and agricultural output has kept pace, so per capita consumption of food has remained quite steady. Farm acreage expanded from 1870 to around 1920, and output per unit of farm area has increased since about 1940 to produce a rising total agricultural output at relatively stable prices. Americans have changed the composition of their diet and consume more fresh fruits and vegetables while relying less on grains. The United States has more than half of the world's exportable agricultural surpluses, though it has less than half of total world production.

Shifts away from agriculture towards industrial and urban living conditions show up in the increases in American consumption of energy and physical-structure materials. Per capita energy consumption has more than doubled since 1900 with sharp rises in prices since the 1930s: $86 in 1937; $99.7 in 1956; $121.1 in 1969; $136 in 1977 (in constant 1972 dollars). Per capita consumption of physical-structure materials has risen by more than half since the 1930s at lower rates of price increase.

Expansion in the output of natural resource commodities came without proportionate increases in the workforce producing them. Labour productivity increases in these industries have been due partly to increases in capital per worker, but have also depended upon technological improvements.

POPULATION GROWTH

The total population of the United States doubled five times between 1790 and 1950, rising from less than 4 million persons to over 150 million. Between 1960 and 1980, total resident population climbed from 178,464,236 to 226,504,825. Between the first census and 1850, the annual increase of population stayed above 3 per cent, whereas the rest of the nineteenth century and the first ten years of this century saw annual increases that ranged from 2.7 to 2.1 per cent. Between 1910 and 1930, population growth fell to 1.5 per cent and 1.6 per cent per decade, and during the depressed 1930s it fell to 0.7 per cent. After the 1930s, growth increased, reaching a high of 1.9 per cent during the 1950s post-Second World War baby boom. Birth rates dropped sharply after 1960, and population growth declined to an average of 1.0 per cent per annum during the 1970s.

Changes in the size and composition of the population depend upon birth rates, the excess of births over deaths, and the net effect of immigration and emigration. The birth rate began to decline early in the nineteenth century from its high point of around 55 (births per thousand persons per year). The rate dropped to 18 during the depression years of the 1930s, but the return of prosperity after 1945 and the baby boom that followed demobilisation pushed the birth rate up to an average of 25 between 1947 and 1950. After 1958 the rate decreased, but the number of births per year still exceeded 4 million, the baby boom level, until 1965. During the early 1970s, the birth rate dropped further, reaching an all time low of 14.8 in 1975 and 1976, but as the baby boom generation reached reproductive age, the birth rate began to rise, reaching 15.2 in 1978 and 16.1 in 1980.

The fertility rate – the number of children born per women of child-bearing age – reached a post-1945 peak of 3.7 children per woman between 1955 and 1959, but it dropped to 1.8 in 1976. This trend away from large families had been under way between 1920 and 1950, but it speeded up after 1965. For white women, and probably non-white also, the decrease came entirely from the decline in births of three or more children. The rate per 1,000 women aged 15 to 44 for first and second births rose from 46 to 47, but for third or higher it dropped from 28 to 15. Numerous explanations have been offered for the upsurge of population growth during the late 1940s and 1950s and the population 'bust' that followed the baby boom. The increasing sense after 1965 that the social, economic and political conditions at home and abroad limited opportunities for future income probably contributed as much to the decline as improved birth control technology, changes in women's attitude towards their roles, and increases in employment opportunities for women. At the same time, increases in public awareness of problems caused by excessive population growth rates reinforced the other factors that contributed to limitations on family size. Oddly enough, at the time that fertility has been generally decreasing, there has been a rise in the birth rate for unmarried women of all ages. Rare in 1950, these births accounted for 8 per cent of white births and almost one of every two non-white births at the end of the 1970s. Only a tiny part of this increase could be attributed to the rising proportion of births to women under the age of 20 who have historically had the highest percentages of out-of-wedlock births.

Death rates in the United States, at all ages, for both sexes, and despite race, stood lower in 1980 than they had in 1950. Females had greater rates of decline than males and non-whites greater rates of decline than whites. Between 1940 and the mid-1950s, the spread of various new antibiotic drugs brought an unprecedented improvement, then the death rate levelled off until the late 1960s. Since about 1968 a new decline began in mortality rates, unusually rapid for the older ages of all race and sex groups, and it was accompanied by a rapid decline in infant and child mortality. The mortality improvements since the 1940s add up to an average increase in life expectancy at birth of almost fifteen years, from 58.5 years in 1936 to 73.2 in 1977. Although the white life expectancy is still higher than all other races, the gap (after a widening in the 1954–68 period) has been more than halved (from 10.8 years to 5 years). The death rate from diseases of the circulatory system has declined rapidly since 1965, although heart disease and cancer account for more than half of all deaths. Accidents, and violence, began to emerge as the greatest contributor to health costs by the end of the 1970s. In 1975, the economic cost of accidents and violence stood 62 per cent higher than the cost of cancer and was 17 per cent below the cost of all cardiovascular diseases.

Despite its reputation as 'the melting pot' of the world, most of the 50 million persons who have entered the United States since 1820 originated in Europe, and most of them came from places in northern and western Europe (95 per cent up to 1860 and 68 per cent between 1861 and 1900); 58 per cent of the 1901–30 immigration derived from southern and eastern Europe, but prejudice against these groups prompted Congress to pass restrictive legislation with national origins quotas in the early 1920s. Even before the First World War, restrictive Congressional legislation and treaties aimed at stopping the so-called 'Yellow Peril' reduced Asian immigration to only 3 per cent in the 1901–30 period. During the restriction period up to 1960, northern and western Europe together with northern America and Latin America provided 77 per cent of all immigrants, and the average annual number admitted was about 132,000. From the 1920s to the 1950s, the racial make-up and the national origins of the population remained essentially stable, and the restrictions led to large reductions in the total immigration, especially in relation to population.

During the 1960s and 1970s, significant changes took place in immigration to the United States. In large part, these changes followed the passage of the Immigration Act of 1965 which abolished national origins as the basis for quotas in favour of criteria such as labour skills and humanitarian concerns. Persons of Asian and Latin American origin accounted for over half of the legal immigrants in the 1960s and nearly three-fourths of the 1971–4 period. From 1972 to 1976, Mexico, the Philippines, Korea, Cuba, India, Taiwan and the Dominican Republic sent the highest numbers of immigrants to the United States in that order. By 1977, the 462,000 net annual immigration amounted to 2.1 per thousand population, and in 1980 the number rose to 654,000 (2.9 per thousand) due to the Cuban and Haitian refugees admitted that year.

The illegal immigration of the post-1965 period received widespread attention in the press and stimulated Congressional debate over changes in federal immigration policy. Estimates of the number of illegal aliens in the United States have ranged from 1 to 8 million. Official estimates made by the Immigration and Naturalization Service (INS) during the middle 1970s put the number at over 7 million, and the INS reported arresting and deporting between 600,000 and 800,000 per year during the same period. The Population and Reference Bureau, a private research organisation, estimated in 1982 that of the projected 795,000 to 970,000 net annual immigration during the 1980s, half would enter illegally, primarily from Latin America.

Although hardly a new social phenomenon (the 'wetback' issue became prominent in the 1950s), the illegal immigration of the 1970s and 1980s appears to differ in several respects from the earlier period.

The recent growth appears to be occurring in urban-industrial areas throughout the nation, not merely in agricultural areas along the Mexican border. Midwestern, and eastern, cities have begun to attract illegal aliens, and on the east coast, the largest group comes from Haiti and the Dominican Republic.

POPULATION COMPOSITION

Fertility, mortality and immigration have contributed to the growth patterns of the United States population. Important changes have also occurred in the age and sex characteristics of the population and its racial and ethnic composition. Improvements in life expectancy and changes in fertility have led to the aging of the population. While the age distribution in 1980 was not much different from what it had been in 1950, large changes took place in the years between. From 1800 to 1950 the median age (half the population was older and half younger) had risen from 16 years old to 30.2 years old. By 1970, because of the post-war baby boom, the median age had declined to 28 years old, but by 1980 it had risen again to 30. The percentage of the population 65 years of age and over has increased significantly, from 3.1 million (4.1 per cent of the population) in 1940 to 25.5 million (11.3 per cent) in 1980. In 1970–80 the number of persons in each ten-year age group above the mid-50s increased at rates above the 11.4 per cent for the total population. The proportion of females in the 65 years old and over population was higher than that of males, and the gap has increased in the post-war period because of the higher life expectancy of women. Although all racial groups have participated in the 'aging' of the population, the percentage of persons under 15 years old is lower among whites compared to blacks and other races, and the proportion 65 years old and over is higher among whites.

In 1850, when the census first recorded birthplaces, the 2.2 million foreign-born persons accounted for 10 per cent of the total United States population. During the period 1890–1910, some 14 per cent of the population claimed overseas birthplaces, but from then on the proportion of foreign-born declined to 4.7 per cent in 1970 and 5.1 per cent in 1980. Persons of mixed or foreign parentage made up 14.8 per cent of the population when they were first counted in 1870. This 'second generation' population rose to its highest point in 1920, when such persons amounted to 21.5 per cent, but by 1970 their numbers had declined to 11 per cent. According to a Census Bureau survey made in 1979, more Americans traced their ancestry to Germany than to any other country. About 52 million considered themselves partly German (28.8 per cent of the population), followed by 44 million of Irish ancestry (24.4 per cent) and those of English background (22.3 per cent). Some 14.2 million counted themselves Scots, and 2.6 million declared a Welsh background, so the total for the British Isles would make it the nation's largest ancestral group.

Although the proportion of the foreign-born has declined during the twentieth century, the non-white population has experienced a marked increase since 1945. Blacks counted for one of every five persons in the United States at the time of the first census in 1790. By 1870, after the end of slavery and with continued immigration of whites, the black share of the population had dropped to 12.6 per cent of the total. Further declines, down to 9.7 per cent, showed in the 1930 and 1940 census figures. Then white fertility began to decline significantly faster than black, and non-white immigration increased relative to white. The black population reached 22.6 million (11.1 per cent) in 1970 and 26.5 million (11.7 per cent) in 1980.

Persons of Hispanic origin or descent comprised the second largest ethnic minority group in the United States by 1980. During the 1950s, 319,000 immigrants came from Mexico and 72,000 from South America. During the 1960s the figures were 443,000 and 228,000. In addition, the 1960s saw a movement of 519,000 from the West Indies (256,769 from Cuba alone). By 1980, 1 of every 16 persons in the United States claimed such origin or descent; 60 per cent were of Mexican origin. This population had a lower median age: 22 years old compared to 25 years for blacks, 30 for the total population, and 31.3 years for whites. Spanish was the most common language other than English spoken in the home, and of the 2.6 million children (8 per cent of the population) who spoke languages other than English at home, two out of three spoke Spanish. Those who claimed Hispanic ancestry amounted to 12.5 million in 1979, slightly more than the 11.7 million who considered themselves of Italian background. The dramatic expansion of the Spanish-origin population created a rise to 14.6 million in 1980, a 61 per cent increase since 1970.

The Asian and Pacific Island population likewise increased in the post-war period. Only 157,000 immigrants came to the United States from Asia during the 1950s, but the altered quota system contributed to the entry of 445,000 between 1961 and 1970. The census recorded 591,000 of Japanese ancestry, 435,000 of Chinese ancestry, and 343,000 of Filipino ancestry in 1970. All told the Asian population amounted to 1.5 million in that year. By 1980 the figure had increased to 3.5 million and 60 per cent lived on the Pacific Coast and in Hawaii.

POPULATION DISTRIBUTION

Until about 1945, the American population had carried out a significant long-term migration from rural to urban areas, including central cities of 500,000 or more. Since the end of the Second World War, the relative decline of the rural areas has continued, but the large central cities have experienced slower growth or in some cases decline. Suburban growth, though a familiar feature of American life long before the 1940s, assumed greater significance thereafter, as both smaller cities and urban areas outside city limits began to account for all of the relative growth of metropolitan places. Non-whites, however, kept moving to the central cities. Some 80 per cent of the Mexican-American population made the shift from farms to central cities by 1970. (By 1980, 83 per cent of the Spanish-origin population lived in urban areas, including over 1 million Puerto Ricans in New York City alone.) During the 1940s, 43 cities outside the South doubled their black population, compared to only 2 in the South, and during the 1950s 1,457,000 non-whites moved out of the South. The 1960 census showed that for the first time more than half of American blacks lived outside the South.

Central cities showed a 48 per cent increase in black population during the 1940s, compared to an increase of only 10 per cent for whites. The non-white population of central cities rose from 10 per cent in 1940 to 33 per cent in 1950, and the black proportion increased to 58 per cent in 1970. In 1980, because of a small increase in the proportion of blacks living in suburbs (black suburbanites still amounted to only 21 per cent compared to 40 per cent of the total population), 56 per cent of the black population lived in central cities. The vast magnitude of this urban migration by black Americans led one demographer to conclude in 1964 that next to the worldwide population explosion 'the movement of Negroes from the southern part of the United States has without a doubt been the greatest and most significant sociological event of our country's recent history'.

The American population as a whole became more urban, specifically metropolitan (living in places with central cities of 50,000 or more and their surrounding counties) between 1945 and 1970. In 1940 some 168 such places existed, with 52.8 per cent of the total population, and by 1970 their number had grown to 243 and they contained 73 per cent of the population. During the 1970s non-metropolitan areas grew faster than metropolitan areas. Due partly to the decentralisation of manufacturing, this widely discussed 'decon-centration' of the population also resulted from the development of recreation and retirement areas for the growing elder population, the environmental movement, and the spread of the interstate highway network. Probably one-third to one-fourth of non-metropolitan growth can be attributed to suburban developments outside the official metropolitan boundaries used by the census takers. Non-metropolitan population increases took place almost entirely in non-farm areas, so the phenomenon did not represent a 'back to the farm' movement. The magnitude of the trend can be seen in a comparison of 1960s metropolitan growth rates with those of the 1970s. In the 1960s the metropolitan areas increased by 17 per cent compared with 4 per cent for non-metropolitan areas. During the 1970s the metropolitan areas experienced only a 9.5 per cent growth, whereas the non-metropolitan areas grew by 15 per cent and the country as a whole by 11 per cent. Whereas two-thirds of the nation's total population growth during the 1970s occurred in metropolitan areas, during the 1960s these same areas had accounted for fully 92 per cent of United States growth. Despite the decline in the metropolitan growth *rate*, the nation continued to be metropolitan in 1980, with 165 million people, 73 per cent of the population, in metropolitan areas.

Changes in the regional distribution of the population, historically an important consequence of the tendency of people to follow jobs, housing, retail shops and roads, continued to shape the nation's development after 1945. Table I shows that the relative shift from the Northeast and the North Central regions to the West (see Map 2) had become a familiar story even before the Second World War. Between 1940 and 1970 the industrial expansion and urbanisation of the West doubled its population and raised its proportion of the population from 11 to 17 per cent. By 1980 the West contained 19 per cent of the

TABLE I   US population by region: 1790 to 1980
(in millions)

Year	Northeast	North Central	South	West
1790	2.0	—	2.0	—
1800	2.6	—	2.6	—
1810	3.5	0.3	3.5	—
1820	4.4	0.9	4.4	—
1830	5.5	1.6	5.7	—
1840	6.8	3.4	7.0	—
1850	8.6	5.4	9.0	—
1860	10.6	9.1	11.1	0.6
1870	12.3	13.0	12.3	1.0
1880	14.5	17.4	16.5	1.8
1890	17.4	22.4	20.0	3.1
1900	21.0	26.3	24.5	4.3
1910	25.9	29.9	29.4	7.1
1920	29.7	34.0	33.1	9.2
1930	34.4	38.6	37.9	12.3
1940	36.0	40.1	41.7	14.4
1950	39.5	44.5	47.2	20.2
1960	44.7	51.6	55.0	28.1
1970	49.0	56.6	62.8	34.8
1980	49.1	58.9	75.3	43.2

population, compared to the South's 33.3 per cent (its largest share of the total since 1860), the Northeast's 21.7 per cent, and the North Central region's 26 per cent.

As birthrates began their decline after the end of the post-war baby boom, the importance of interregional migration as a factor in regional growth rates increased. Even in the early 1950s, migration accounted for 50 per cent of the West's population growth, and in the South, where migration accounted for only 6 per cent of population change in the late 1950s, the figure jumped to 51 per cent during the first half of the 1970s. On the other hand, net out-migration stood as the major reason for the slow population growth of the Northeast and North Central regions.

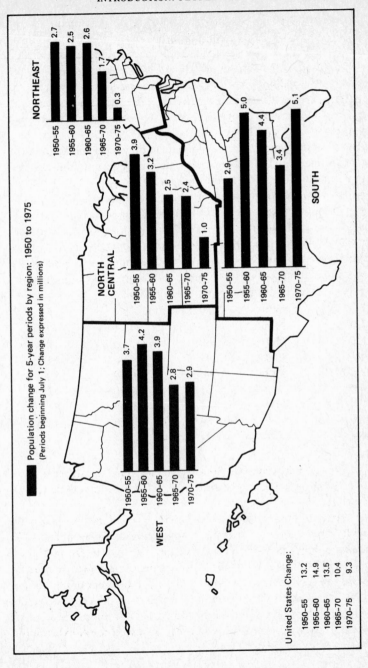

Population change for 5-year periods by region: 1950 to 1975
(Periods beginning July 1; Change expressed in millions)

NORTHEAST

1950-55	2.7
1955-60	2.5
1960-65	2.6
1965-70	1.7
1970-75	0.3

NORTH CENTRAL

1950-55	3.9
1955-60	3.2
1960-65	2.5
1965-70	2.4
1970-75	1.0

SOUTH

1950-55	2.9
1955-60	5.0
1960-65	4.4
1965-70	3.4
1970-75	5.1

WEST

1950-55	3.7
1955-60	4.2
1960-65	3.9
1965-70	2.8
1970-75	2.9

United States Change:

1950-55	13.2
1955-60	14.9
1960-65	13.5
1965-70	10.4
1970-75	9.3

MAP 2
SOURCE: US Dept. of Commerce, Bureau of the Census, *Current Population Reports*, Series P-25, No. 640 (November 1976)

Because of the Constitutional provision that seats in the lower house of Congress should be apportioned to states on the basis of population, the gradual growth of western population since 1900 and the relative increase of the South since 1965 brought steady loss of political power to the North. The 1960 census results took away three seats from Pennsylvania, two from New York, Massachusetts and Arkansas, and one each from twelve other states. California, however, gained eight seats, and Florida took four. The 1980 census led to the transfer of seventeen Congressional seats to the South and West, and shifted the majority in the House of Representatives out of the North for the first time in the twentieth century.

Whether one characterises these changes in the regional distribution of population as a 'power shift' or as the outcome of a 'regional war for jobs and dollars', they are ultimately part of a process of industrial dispersal from the older manufacturing belt of the Northeast and North Central regions that has been under way for a long time. Explanations for this phenomenon require an examination of American business during the post-1945 period.

1. Business

BOTH pundits and presidents proclaimed the central role of business in American society long before 1945. Lord Bryce thought it 'natural' that business 'should have come more and more to overshadow and dwarf all other interests, all other occupations' because of the dramatic material progress of the United States. Herbert Spencer found Americans somewhat narrow due to their 'sole interest – the interest in business'. Woodrow Wilson, urging Americans to embark upon a New Freedom, reminded them that 'Business underlies everything in our national life'. Calvin Coolidge put the matter simply during the 1920s: 'The business of America is business'.

STRUCTURE AND COMPOSITION OF BUSINESS

In 1945, 6.737 million business enterprises operated in the United States, and by 1977 the number had grown to 14.741 million. In 1968 the nation had one such business for every 40 persons in the population. The majority of these were proprietorships (owned by single persons) and partnerships, and most of them were small firms that carried out a wide variety of business from dairy farmers to dry cleaners, from cinemas to motels, from corner grocery stores to neighbourhood petrol stations. Small businesses have employed perhaps a third of the country's workforce, and about one in five married households have been directly involved in their operation.

At the opposite extreme from the individually owned petrol station with minimal assets and sales of several thousands of dollars each year, Exxon Corporation, the nation's largest industrial firm in 1980, had assets of more than $56 billion and sales of over $103 billion (throughout, references are to US billions – i.e. thousand millions). During the post-war period, American corporations, always a small proportion of the total business population, have steadily increased their share of the receipts and profits (see Table II).

TABLE II   Proprietorships, partnerships and corporations

Year	Number (1000s)	Proprietorships	Partnerships	Active corporations	All business forms
			Percentage distribution of numbers		
1945	6,737	84.4	9.3	6.2	100.0
1960	11,172	81.3	8.4	10.2	100.0
1977	14,741	77.0	8.0	15.0	100.0

Receipts (in billions of dollars)			Percentage distribution of receipts		
1945	382	20.7	12.3	66.9	100.0
1960	1,095	15.6	6.8	77.6	100.0
1977	4,699	8.0	4.0	88.0	100.0

Net profits (in billions of dollars)			Percentage distribution of net income		
1945	40	30.0	17.5	52.5	100.0
1960	73	28.8	11.0	60.2	100.0
1977	283	18.1	4.6	77.3	100.0

SOURCE: Computed from *Statistical Abstract of the United States, 1971*, p. 459, Table 710; *Statistical Abstract of the United States, 1981*, p. 534, Table 896.

By the early 1980s nine out of ten corporations did less than $1 million worth of business per year, but the 10 per cent that did an annual business of more than $1 million took 88 per cent of all corporate receipts. Corporations with assets in excess of $500,000 took in 87 per cent of all corporate receipts. Some 3,000 American corporations reported assets worth more than $250 million. Half of these 'big business' firms (mainly banks or insurance companies) were in finance, another fourth were manufacturers, and the balance came from trade, transportation, utilities and communications. In 1977 the 14 per cent of industrial corporations with assets of $1

TABLE III Gross national product: 1945–80. Origins by economic
sectors
(percentage distribution)

Year	Business	Households and institutions	Government and government enterprises	Rest of the world
1945	81.3	2.1	16.5	0.1
1950	89.9	2.2	7.3	0.5
1955	88.5	2.2	8.5	0.8
1960	87.5	2.6	9.4	0.5
1965	86.5	2.8	9.8	0.9
1970	84.5	3.1	11.6	0.5
1975	84.0	3.3	11.6	1.1
1980	84.6	3.2	10.2	2.0

SOURCE: Computed from *Statistical Abstract of the United States, 1981*,
p. 420, Table 699

TABLE IV National income by industries, 1950–79
(percentage distribution)

Industry	1950	1960	1970	1979
Agriculture, forestry, fisheries	7.3	4.2	3.1	3.2
Mining and construction	7.1	6.4	6.5	6.6
Manufacturing	31.6	29.7	26.4	25.5
Transportation	5.6	4.3	3.8	3.8
Communications and utilities	3.0	4.1	4.0	4.1
Wholesale and retail trade	17.0	15.4	15.2	14.4
Finance, insurance, real estate	9.1	11.9	11.7	12.7
Services	9.0	10.6	12.8	13.7
Government and government enterprises	9.8	12.5	15.8	13.8
Rest of world	0.5	0.9	0.9	2.2
Total	100.0	100.0	100.0	100.0

SOURCE: *Statistical Abstract of the United States, 1971*, p. 311, Table 495;
Statistical Abstract of the United States, 1981, p. 426, Table 711

million or more collected 91 per cent of all receipts and 92 per cent of the net income. About 75 per cent of the manufacturing labour force worked for the largest 500 corporations, and approximately one-third of the national workforce was employed by corporations that made up the lists compiled by the magazine *Fortune* of the top 500 industrials and the leading 50 firms in banking, insurance, finance, transportation, utilities and retailing.

The lion's share of the United States gross national product (GNP) originated in the private business sector during the post-1945 period. Tables III and IV show that while the public sector's share of the GNP and the national income (net value added to production by industry) has expanded relative to the private sector, the massive role of business has been continuous. Table IV also illustrates the relative decline of agriculture, commerce and manufacturing as a proportion of the national income, as well as the relative expansion in the contribution from finance, insurance and real estate, and services.

PRODUCTIVITY AND INFLATION

For roughly the first twenty years of the post-war era, American business prospered as part of a quarter century (1948–73) of worldwide economic growth. Compared to the twenty years before the Second World War, the post-war era experienced average economic growth rates nearly three times as high. Compared to the severe recessions of 1921 and 1937, and especially the Great Depression of 1929–33, the recessions of the 1948–73 period, though more frequent, were shorter and milder.

Like its counterparts in western Europe, American business received a staggering blow from the drastic changes in the international economic climate that date from the early 1970s and the quadrupling of oil prices at the end of 1973. In addition, American business experienced a decline in its position in the world economy. Whereas the United States led the world in economic growth during the 1950s and early 1960s, it began to lose its position in the middle 1960s. By 1980 Japanese business had displaced American business as the world leader. In steel, machine tools, automobiles, semiconductors and consumer electronics, Japan became the chief trading competitor to the United States, and it possessed a stronger manufacturing base. Japan, Germany, Italy, France and the United

TABLE V   Manufacturing output (1950–75)

Year	United States	Japan	France	Germany	Italy	United Kingdom
1950	51.7	8.6	37.6	26.9	26.4	60.9
1955	65.3	19.2	47.7	50.7	40.9	72.2
1960	67.7	42.0	64.5	73.5	60.2	83.4
1965	92.5	73.5	88.4	100.3	83.3	97.6
1967	100.0	100.0	100.0	100.0	100.0	100.0
1970	102.6	152.9	123.7	132.2	125.6	111.4
1975	106.3	168.3	136.7	137.1	139.4	112.9

Indexes: 1967 = 100
SOURCE: United States Department of Labor, Bureau of Labor Statistics

TABLE VI   Savings and investment

Year	United States	Japan	France	Germany	United Kingdom
Individual savings as a percentage of individual disposable income					
1960	4.9	17.4	9.8	8.5	7.2
1975	7.4	24.9	12.6[a]	16.9	14.1
Total government and private investment as a percentage of GNP					
1960	17.6	30.2	20.2	24.3	16.3
1975	16.2	30.8	23.3	20.8	19.7

[a] 1974
SOURCE: United States Department of Commerce

Kingdom all made superior rates of growth in manufacturing output from 1967 to 1975 (see Table V). The United States rates of savings and investment were also lower than those of its leading competitors (see Table VI).

Except for the period of the Korean War, American business operated within a context of relatively stable rates of inflation between 1950 and 1967. During the same period, moreover, produc-

TABLE VII   Inflation and productivity 1950–79

Years	Consumer price index	Productivity index
1950	72.1	61.0
1955	80.2	70.3
1960	88.7	78.7
1965	94.5	95.0
1967	100.0	100.0
1970	116.3	104.2
1975	161.2	112.4
1979	217.4	118.1

Indexes: 1967 = 100
SOURCE: Department of Labor, Bureau of Labor Statistics

tivity increases (output per person) stood at or above increases in the consumer price index. Acceleration of the rate of inflation can be traced to 1965–6, when the Johnson administration sought to finance the Vietnam War without raising taxes. Table VII shows the figures that moved a recent analyst to write: 'Beginning in 1967 inflation became a disease'. By 1981 the United States had fallen to tenth among all nations in per capita gross national product, ranking behind almost all northern European nations except the United Kingdom. The vice-president of a leading securities firm declared in a *New York Times* interview in early 1982 that: 'The United States economy is currently in the throes of a deepening and widening recession. It may turn out to be the worst slump since the Great Depression of the 1930s'.

BUSINESS AND THE STATE

The changes in the international business environment after 1945 coincided with a period during which the business community forged what historian Thomas C. Cochran described as its 'open dominance in national politics'. This development followed decades of gradual change in business-government relations. Elbert H. Gary, leader of United States Steel, expected after the Republican Party victory of 1920 that 'hereafter there will be close cooperation between the business world and those administering the affairs of government', and indeed the 1920s witnessed increased business influence in federal administration. While a period of antagonism toward Rooseveltian New Deal programmes between 1934 and 1938 cooled relations between business leaders and the administration, the boom caused by spending during the Second World War aided business considerably. Patriotism and prosperity softened the impact of the expansion of federal regulation and bureaucracy during the war, and by the late 1940s the business community had begun to accept federal, state and local government spending as a spur to the expansion of the economy.[1] Expenditures of the three branches of government have increased about nine times over the past quarter of a century, with state and local expenditures increasing 10 per cent faster than federal. Government spending made up 20 per cent of the GNP in 1978, compared to 14.9 per cent in 1949. Federal employees have increased 37 per cent since 1945, state and local employees 213 per cent, and state and local employees made up 81 per cent of the total public employment labour force.

State intervention in the American economy in the post-war era has included a variety of business-government activities marked by mutual adjustment, co-operation, conflict, compromise and accommodation. While reciprocal controls have constrained both business and government, 'a large category of major decisions is turned over to businessmen, both small and larger. Businessmen thus become a kind of public official and exercise what, on a broad view of their role, are public functions.' As Charles E. Lindblom has pointed out, conflicts between business and government, even business defeats, exist 'within a range of dispute constrained by their understanding that they together constitute the necessary leadership for the system. They do not wish to destroy or seriously undermine the function of each other.'[2]

Such political considerations both shaped and limited the scope and nature of government planning as an aspect of business operation in the post-war world. During the Roosevelt administration, liberals sought comprehensive national economic plans, but the business community desired an industry-by-industry focus. A National Resources Planning Board (NRPB) was established in the president's executive office and operated from 1933 to 1943. Criticised by the *New York Times* for opening the door to a 'cult of planning', the NRPB did little apart from calling conferences and sponsoring research. Even this limited role proved significant, however, as witnessed by the impact of a 1943 report prepared for the NRPB by Harvard economist Alvin Hansen. Like other leading proponents of Keynesian demand-stimulation theories who argued that investment opportunities in America had declined with the closing of the western frontier, Hansen called for federal government action. In his *After the War, Full Employment*, Hansen argued that:[3]

> When the war is over, the Government cannot just disband the Army, close down munition factories, stop building ships, and remove all economic controls. We want an orderly program of demobilization and reconstruction. The government cannot escape responsibility.

During the mid-nineteenth century the federal government took responsibility for promoting business by subsidising internal improvements and providing land grants to railways. Federal regulation by means of agencies such as the Interstate Commerce Commission and the anti-trust policies of the late-nineteenth century continued the process. Between 1941 and 1945, however, governmental participation in the business system assumed yet another form. President Roosevelt adopted the essentially Keynesian position that the annual federal budget could be an important vehicle of national economic policy planning, and this set the stage for expanding the federal role to encompass responsibility for economic growth and stability.

During the early part of the Truman administration, a Congress with a conservative majority passed the Employment Act of 1946. This legislation declared

> it is the continuing policy and responsibility of the Federal Government to use all practicable means . . . to coordinate and utilize all its plans, functions, and resources for the purpose of creating and maintaining, in a manner calculated to foster and promote free competitive enterprise and the general welfare, conditions under which there will be afforded useful employment opportunities . . . and to promote maximum employment, production, and purchasing power.[4]

The Act provided the president with a Council of Economic Advisers and mandated a yearly presidential report on the country's economic condition. Despite its stipulation that economic planning should serve the interest of free enterprise, the Act provoked opposition from national organisations such as the National Association of Manufacturers that espoused a competitive small business *laissez-faire* philosophy. The Council of Economic Advisers exerted little influence on presidential policy during the Truman and Eisenhower years.

The 1946 Employment Act received some of its impetus from the Committee for Economic Development (CED), a group organised in 1942 by business leaders and the United States Department of Commerce to foster maximum employment and high productivity after the war. Since its wartime inception the CED has played an important role in legitimising the theory and practice of business-government co-operation in creating fiscal, monetary and employment policies for high employment. By 1971 Republican President Richard M. Nixon could declare that 'I am now a Keynesian', and in 1977 Congress passed the Humphrey–Hawkins Act that extended the 1946 Employment Act by requiring the president to establish comprehensive annual economic goals to be reflected in each year's federal government budget. 'Whether the American people realize it or not', wrote a former president of the CED in 1981, 'national economic planning for high employment through government fiscal and monetary processes has arrived. And it has strong business and public support.'[5]

In addition to spurring the growth of government responsibility for economic stability, co-operative relationships between business and government have contributed to the shaping of other American domestic and international economic policies since 1945. During the Second World War, consultation between government departments and industry groups (a practice established during the First World War) continued, and during the Korean War some 900 'without compensation' (WOC) executives staffed important federal positions. During the mid-1950s a Congressional report indicated that between 5,000 and 6,000 industry advisory committees had facilitated exchange of information and discussed mutual interests between business and government. The prestigious Business Advisory Council contributed to the shaping of national tax legislation during the Kennedy administration. By 1968 over 2,000 retired military officers of high rank worked as executives with the hundred largest contractors for the Department of Defense. Gabriel Kolko has pointed out that these activities 'strengthened the role of businessmen as well as business values in government'.[6]

These types of consultative practices brought business leaders into the making of United States international economic policy during and after the Second World War, and the policy in turn provided benefits to business. A CED report on international trade and domestic employment, drafted in 1944 by Calvin B. Hoover, a Duke University professor serving as northern European head of the American intelligence service, helped to secure business support for three central institutions of the post-war international economy: the International Monetary Fund, the World Bank, and the General Agreement on Trade and Tariffs (GATT). After the war, Hoover and Paul Hoffman (president of the Studebaker automobile company and a trustee of the University of Chicago) became two of the chief architects of the Marshall Plan. During the 1960s the overseas operations of large corporations received indirect subsidies from the federal government. During the high point of the Vietnam War, over $25 million in exports to developing nations from Ford Motors, United States Steel, International Harvester, Caterpillar Tractor and others received financing from the Agency for International Development (AID). AID also provided insurance to American corporations engaged in investment in developing nations (nearly $7 billion worth in 1968).

During the 1970s American commercial banks lent massive sums to foreign governments plagued by balance of payments deficits, prompting one business professor to argue that 'foreign policy decisions have been made by private institutions'. David Rockefeller, the chairman of Chase Manhattan Bank, established close personal ties with Shah Mohammed Reza Pahlavi of Iran, and when Iran's oil wealth escalated, the New York headquarters of the bank received large deposits from the National Iranian Oil Company. Between 1975 and 1977, the shah borrowed in order to keep pace with the costs of his wide-ranging projects, and Chase Manhattan Bank became the head of an eleven-bank consortium that provided the shah with $500 million to help balance Iran's budget.[7]

THE MILITARY-INDUSTRIAL COMPLEX

Since the time of the Korean War, the United States has maintained what according to pre-1945 standards would be called a war readiness posture, and the annual budget for military operations has ranged from \$40 billion to over \$136 billion in fiscal 1980. President Eisenhower warned Americans of the dangers posed by 'the Military-Industrial Complex' in his 1960 farewell address, and a small army of researchers has documented the direct and indirect impact of military procurement and government stockpiling of minerals and chemicals on American business. Historian Paul A. C. Koistenen has soberly pointed out that because the military-industrial complex existed long before the Cold War, it cannot be explained as a response to anti-communism. Koistenen also concluded that 'funeral orations for the defense community are somewhat premature'.[8]

Federal government officials (particularly in the Department of Defense) and business leaders have forged co-operative relationships in the fields of aerospace, communications, information retrieval and analysis, transportation, and non-military uses of atomic energy. Much of the post-war expansion of such science-based industries has taken place in western and southern states, where this joint public-private 'post-industrial' sector has shaped the population growth and urban development of an entire regional economy.

Research and Development (R & D) has played a key role in the growth of these science-based industries in the post-war era. R & D consists of three parts: basic research, applied research, and development. The bulk of R & D has consistently gone to development, and except for the 1968–78 decade, when the 'civilian' R & D share increased from about 25 to almost 40 per cent, the US has spent higher shares on defence and space projects than other industrial countries. In 1940 R & D expenditures amounted to less than 1 per cent of the federal budget. In 1965, the peak year, R & D accounted for 12.6 per cent, and in 1976 the proportion fell to 5.6 per cent. The federal government has been the major source of R & D financing since the Second World War (53 per cent in 1976), although industry has done between two-thirds and three-fourths of the work (70 per cent in 1976). In 1959 over half of all industrial research was carried out in the aircraft, guided missile, electronic and electrical equipment industries. Machinery, chemicals, oil and gas followed close behind. During the period 1961–74 these same industries accounted for 73 per cent of R & D spending.

Aircraft and missiles absorbed 31 per cent of R & D spending from 1961 to 1974. The aircraft industry single-handedly helped the Pacific

Coast to develop its post-war population and metropolitan housing boom. Some 80 per cent of the industry's business came from the demands of military agencies during the 1950s, and when defence orders began to call for missiles in the last years of the decade, the industry suffered a decline. Many companies moved into space technology, and during the 1960s produced new lines of civilian jet planes that replaced the prop-driven models for commercial and passenger travel.

The electronics industry proves difficult to define because of its heterogeneous array of products and firms and its ties to electrical machinery, aircraft, instrument and other equipment industries. One branch encompasses components such as diodes and transistors (sometimes called semi-conductors). The other branch consists of end products: microwave communications systems, televisions. At the close of the Second World War, the nation produced less than $1 billion in the general category of electronics, but by 1967 the figure had already passed the $15 billion mark.

The various branches of the electronics industry (they sometimes overlap, as in the case of General Instruments) shared several characteristics. They matured rapidly and required a new kind of manager: highly trained engineers with PhDs or scientifically know-ledgeable holders of graduate business degrees. Being highly com-petitive, the firms were subject to swift reverses or rapid successes. Because electronics required none of the production requirements that had caused nineteenth-century firms to centralise plant opera-tions, and also given the growing presence of highways, airports, trucks and aeroplanes, electronics contributed to suburbanisation and the shift of population to the Sunbelt. Since education constituted a resource for the industry, its growth stimulated the establishment of technology-oriented graduate schools such as Florida Atlantic Uni-versity near the missile complex at Cape Kennedy.

Researchers in the Bell Laboratories, a division of American Telephone and Telegraph, invented the transistor in 1948. Smaller, more reliable, and capable of greater conductivity than the vacuum tube, its uses multiplied and by 1966 the US produced over $820 million worth. American Telephone and Telegraph did not, however, become the leader in semi-conductor technology and production, because the firm feared anti-trust prosecution for monopoly by the Justice Department. Other firms with experience in electronics – RCA, Sylvania, General Electric and Westinghouse – entered the field, but the majority of sales went to new companies such as Texas Instruments (with some 20 per cent of the market in the early 1960s).

GOVERNMENT REGULATION OF BUSINESS

Anti-trust policy in the United States, so clearly important in the shaping of the semi-conductor business, illustrates one of the ways in which Americans have called upon government to resolve conflicts arising out of competitive relationships between small and large businesses and between business and other groups in the society. Anti-trust activities, carried out by the Anti-trust Division of the Justice Department and the Federal Trade Commission, seek to prohibit unfair business practices such as price fixing and to control mergers and interlocking directorates among firms in order to promote competition. Although modifications have been introduced since, they mainly extend the authority or clarify the interpretation of the original legislation: the Sherman Act (1890), the Clayton Act (1914) and the Federal Trade Commission Act (1914). In 1911 Standard Oil of New Jersey and the American Tobacco Company had to dissolve when the supreme court supported Justice Department claims that they had acquired monopoly power in their industries. In 1945 the court ruled that Alcoa stood in violation of anti-trust laws by reason of its control of 90 per cent of the aluminium market. Because a firm's share of the market determines whether it constitutes a monopoly, and because the extent to which it uses its market share to stifle competition is a test of its legality, major firms carefully monitor their behaviour. In 1982 American Telephone and Telegraph agreed to break up its $137 billion firm, while IBM ($22 billion in sales and $3 billion in profits) had its anti-trust suit dropped by the Justice Department. The Celler–Kefauver Act of 1950 ruled that all mergers that reduced competition were illegal, and in 1968 and 1982 the Justice Department set up guidelines for mergers based on market shares. Continual debate over legal standards to be used, remedies required and enforcement procedures marked anti-trust politics, and three major presidential commissions between 1968 and 1979 recommended revisions in the laws.

The regulation of business through anti-trust occurs through the mechanism of federal government activities. Both federal regulatory agencies and state regulatory commissions possess authority to regulate businesses engaged in transportation, communications and the provision of electricity, natural gas and sanitary services. Most of the American economy in the post-war period operated free of economic regulation. In 1978 the industries listed above produced only 8 per cent of the national income and not quite 5 per cent of the total employment. All of the 50 states have commissions that regulate the prices of telephone services, all but one regulate the rates of private electric and natural gas firms, all but three regulate trucking (haulage) firms, and all but six regulate railway transportation. The chief federal regulatory agencies are the Interstate Commerce Commission (1887), the Federal Power Commission (1920), the Federal Communications Commission (1934) and the Civil Aeronautics Board (1940). The federal government (since the 1930s) has also regulated finance, insurance, security, commodity and banking industries, and (since the 1940s) newer forms of energy such as nuclear power. Economic regulation proved very controversial and critics argued that it was ineffective and weakened incentives for firms to minimise costs and to adopt new technology. In the late 1970s and early 1980s federal legislation allowed the airline, trucking, and parts of the communications industries to begin 'deregulation', and federal officials began to relax controls on banks and the railway industry.

Even greater controversy accompanied the adoption of state and federal legislation after the 1960s which aimed at regulating business practices that affect the quality of the environment, the satisfaction of consumers and the safety of employees. During the Kennedy administration, Congress passed amendments to the earlier Food and Drug Acts that required the pre-testing of drugs for safety and effectiveness, as well as labelling by generic names. The Air Pollution Control Act of 1962 established the first national statute designed to regulate air quality. The Equal Pay Act of 1963 eliminated wage differentials based on sex in industries engaged in interstate commerce. The Johnson administration 'Great Society' legislation set forth an avalanche of 'social' or 'new' regulatory measures. The 1964 Civil Rights Act created the Equal Employment Opportunity Commission to control job discrimination based on race or sex. The 1965 Water Quality Act extended federal responsibility for environmental oversight, and the 1966 Traffic Safety Act established a national safety programme. The Coal Mine Safety Amendments of 1966, and the Age Discrimination Act of 1967, which banned discrimination against workers aged 40 to 65, increased the federal role in worker protection. The 1968 Truth-In-Lending legislation forced sellers to make full disclosure to consumers of terms and conditions of finance charges in credit transactions.

Federal social regulations on business continued to proliferate during the Nixon and Ford administrations (1969–76), but their growth slowed considerably during the Carter and Reagan years. Critics charging lack of effectiveness and problems of enforcement called for revisions in such measures as the National Environmental Policy Act of 1969, the Environmental Protection Agency (1970), the Federal Water Pollution Control Act of 1970, the Occupational Safety and Health Act of 1970, and the Vocational Rehabilitation Act of 1973. By mid-1982, the Reagan administration had generated a good deal of support for the argument made by its first chairman of the Council of Economic Advisers, Murray L. Weidenbaum, that 'a reversal of the current trend of ever-increasing government intervention in business is essential'.[9]

BUSINESS AND POLITICS

Business criticism of regulatory agencies has long been a staple of American political rhetoric. Actually, both individual business firms and organisations representing business have travelled a two-way street of mutual interaction and reciprocal influence with federal, state and local governments. Conspiratorial notions that corporations have 'captured' or even dominate Washington agencies distort the real state of affairs. However, as Mark V. Nadel has demonstrated in *Corporations and Political Accountability*, 'business in general and large corporations in particular have the predominant influence over the regulatory agencies that are supposed to regulate them in the "public interest" '.[10]

During the 1960s and 1970s, partly in response to the vigorous work of Ralph Nader and other consumer-rights and environmentalist advocates, and partly because of demands for corporate 'social responsibility', the business community became more politically sophisticated. The popular *Businessman's Guide to Washington*, dedicated to the proposition that government is 'our biggest partner', went into its second edition in 1975. A *Harvard Business Review* article in 1979, while conceding that business lobbying had increased, warned against complacency and recommended careful cultivation of general public sympathy.

Despite conflicts (between, for example, large and small businesses, distributors and shippers, wholesalers and retailers), businesses have generally pulled together to create a potent political force in American society since the Second World War. Trade associations have existed since the colonial period, and by the early 1960s some 1,800 of them comprised the largest segment of the 2,000 national business organisations. About 11,000 regional, state and local business organisations, and 5,000 local chambers of commerce operated in the early 1960s. By the 1980s trade associations had assumed a much more active role in the policy-making process in Washington. With what in many cases were newly established Washington headquarters, the groups particularly worked to influence policy in the areas of health and safety regulation, environmental legislation, energy policy, consumer affairs and wage and price controls. Many of the trade associations placed their offices within a ten-block radius of the White House. Over 40,000 persons staff the 1,800 Washington headquarters of trade associations such as the American Bankers Association, the American Gas Association, the American Newspaper Publishers Association, the American Advertisers Association and the National Association of Manufacturers.

Originally founded in 1895 to stimulate trade and commerce by means of legislation and governmental promotion, the National Association of Manufacturers (NAM) has a heterogeneous membership. During the 1940s and 1950s the organisation modified its pre-war antipathy to organised labour and agreed to tolerate collective bargaining under carefully prescribed conditions. The NAM lobbied strenuously and successfully for the 1947 Taft–Hartley Act which limited labour union activity. Typically opposed to the growth of governmental regulations and federal centralisation during the 1950s and 1960s, the president of the NAM told its membership in 1955 that the United States was 'well on the way to the achievement of a Communist state as blueprinted by Marx'.[11]

The United States Chamber of Commerce, probably the nation's most conspicuous representative of business since its formation in the first years of the century, described itself as 'wholeheartedly committed to private enterprise in preference to government enterprise' during the early 1960s. The Chamber is a federation made up of state and local chambers of commerce, trade associations, professional associations and individual businesses. The organisation grew steadily from about 3,000 in 1964 to 50,000 in 1975. Then, under the presidency of Richard L. Lesher (called by some 'the John Wayne of the boardroom') membership shot up to the 250,000 mark in early 1982. The Chamber's annual budget of $60 million has allowed it to broadcast a weekly television show to 90 per cent of the nation. Its official magazine, *Nations Business*, with 7 million paid subscribers, easily ranks as the most widely circulated business periodical. The Chamber's headquarters at 1615 H Street, in an impressive building on Lafayette Park, stands directly opposite the White House. Its ability to generate thousands of letters to members of Congress on demand has made the Chamber a powerful force in national politics.

In 1973 the Chamber of Commerce and the National Association of Manufacturers successfully joined forces to convince the president of the need to end federal wage and price controls. Since then, the organisations have presented joint testimony to Congressional hearings on foreign trade and created an Energy User's Conference designed to influence federal energy policy. The National Federation of Independent Businessmen also adopted a more aggressive role in American politics during the 1970s. This group, with nearly 600,000 members who contribute from $30 to $500 each, specialises in Washington lobbying.

The Business Roundtable, formed in 1972, had become the most influential of the newer political pressure groups by the end of its first decade. With representatives from the nation's largest and most powerful corporations (their combined gross revenues amounted to roughly half of the United States GNP), the Roundtable speaks for the elite of the business community. These include the ten largest corporations in the nation, the four largest public utilities, three of the largest commercial banks, and two of the largest life insurance companies.

The Roundtable came into existence with the active co-operation of Federal Reserve Bank board chairman Arthur Burns and Treasury Department secretary John Connally during the Nixon administration. The organisation works by bringing the chief executive officers (CEOs) into direct contact with leaders in the Congress, the White House and the federal bureaucracy. A 45-member policy committee meets every other month, formulates policy goals, and appoints task force chairmen who review and monitor the work of 16 task forces. Using a strategy of 'taking negative positions in positive ways', the task forces logged impressive victories during the Ford, Carter and Reagan administrations. Working directly with Congressional sub-committees, they actively shaped the outcome of legislation concerning regulatory reform, taxation, inflation policy, consumer interests and even social security.

The Chamber of Commerce also uses sophisticated tactics to influence Congressional legislation. The Chamber has over 2,000 Congressional Action Committees, each comprised of some 30 company executives from various parts of the nation. These men make it a point personally to know and keep in touch with the senators and representatives from their part of the country. The Chamber also provides testimony during hearings on pending legislation, and its computerised mailing operation makes it possible to inform its members of the need to contact their Congressman when a bill is about to be voted upon.

In addition to working directly with Congress in the shaping of legislation, business organisations actively participate in the electoral process. During the 1950s and 1960s, because the federal criminal code prohibited corporate contributions in federal elections, com-panies either concealed all but non-partisan contributions or made them in the name of individuals. Company political education programmes for employees, voter registration drives and collections of employee contributions increased after the mid-1950s. A variety of indirect contributions (the Republican Party received substantially more from business than the Democrats) fuelled the presidential campaigns of the 1960s.

In the aftermath of the Watergate scandals, Congress in 1974 passed a comprehensive campaign-spending law. One of its pro-visions dramatically changed the role of corporations and business organisations in electoral politics. Amended in 1976, the law specifies that any organisation or association can establish a political action committee (PAC) that may spend up to $5,000 per candidate (at least five candidates must receive contributions). The number of PACs has increased rapidly since 1974, and by 1980 over 2,000 operated in the national elections. Serving as a kind of collection agency for employees, the corporate PACs increased from 89 in 1974 to 942 at the end of 1979, whereas the number of labour PACs remained almost identical (201 to 217). PACs make heavy contributions to congres-sional election campaigns. Corporate and other business PACs contributed $17.3 million to candidates for the House and Senate in

1978 (about 10 per cent of the total raised). The larger a company, the more likely it is to possess a PAC, and only Exxon, Gulf and IBM of the top ten corporations do not have PACs.

Representatives of business have also served in official governmental posts while on leave from their companies, and they have given advice to presidents as members of informal advisory groups of all kinds. During the 1950s and 1960s the federal cabinet offices of the Departments of Commerce, Defense, Health Education and Welfare, and Treasury were all headed by corporate executives on leave. President Johnson created a National Alliance of Businessmen in 1967 to stimulate business participation in efforts to create job opportunities for members of racial minorities.

Despite occasional outbreaks of antipathy – such as President Kennedy's vigorous criticism of several steel company executives – cordiality has characterised the relationship between the White House and the board room. Richard Nixon and Gerald Ford established close working relationships with business leaders during their years of Republican Party activity prior to becoming president. Jimmy Carter, for all his down-home, peanut-farmer populist image, established close communications with the leading members of the Business Roundtable during his White House years. Ronald Reagan's Business Advisory Council during the 1980 campaign, made up of 40 persons, included heavy representation (one-third) from Sunbelt computer and electronic companies and the venture-capital firms that specialised in high-technology investments in northern California's 'Silicon Valley'. The giant Bechtel Group, Inc., one of the world's largest construction and engineering firms, provided Reagan with key cabinet officers. Caspar Weinberger became Secretary of Defense in 1981, and George Shultz (former Nixon administration labour secretary, budget director and secretary of Treasury) became Secretary of State in 1982.

Individual businesses and business organisations have also participated actively in state and local politics during the post-war period. Because of the differences between the 50 states, political scientists have only recently begun to make systematic assessments of the relative strengths of 'pressure groups' representing business, labour, agriculture, consumers, environmentalists and similar organisations. Sarah McCally Morehouse recently divided the states into those where pressure groups are strong (22), moderately strong (18) and weak (10). Business groups and particular industries played a central role in the politics of all of these states. In most of the states with strong pressure groups, one major business dominates the economy and has played a determining part in politics and policy-making; agricultural producers played such a role in Alabama and Iowa; the oil industry in Alaska, Louisiana, Oklahoma and Texas; coal mine operators in Kentucky and West Virginia; copper interests in Montana; the electric power industry in Maine and Oregon. In all states, even those such as California and New York, where vigorous competition between interest groups allowed politicians to play one against the other, state chambers of commerce and trade associations along with the representatives of large corporations have played an active role in shaping state legislation.[12]

Business leaders in some states followed the example of the national Business Roundtable by establishing sophisticated political groups made up of the CEOs of the state's largest corporations. In Minnesota, pressure groups proved relatively weak because the state legislature had to reconcile the interests of many diverse groups. In the mid-1970s the CEOs of Dayton-Hudson, 3M and ten more of Minnesota's largest corporations created the Minnesota Business Partnership (MBP), an organisation designed to participate in policy-making and to clarify social and economic issues to members of the general public. Like its national counterpart, the MBP operated task forces on particular policy areas such as energy, small business and transportation. Meeting both with state legislators and with the governor of Minnesota on a regular basis, the MBP also worked to influence policy by working co-operatively with the state labour federation of the AFL-CIO.

If definitive statements about the role of business in the politics of 50 states remain elusive, generalisations about business in the nation's 80,000 local governments are even more difficult. Robert L. Lineberry and Ira Sharkansky suggest the complexities:

> Downtown merchants are interested in policies on mass transportation, urban renewal, and economic development that would infuse new life into the central city. Businessmen in the outlying areas tend to oppose such costly undertakings. Small businessmen, especially those who are downwardly mobile in the status system, are often hostile to downtown interests like department-store owners. Realtors are more concerned with zoning and subdivision regulation than with revitalizing sagging downtown areas.

Businessmen who provide services over a wide area within the community – major wholesalers and producers, for example – are more interested in community growth, regardless of the direction that it takes.[13]

Most businessmen, however, work to keep taxes low and to promote economic growth. Their political resources are impressive. Local pressure groups such as chambers of commerce provide money and publicity for favoured policy proposals. Local officials typically come from business or professional backgrounds, and city governments avoid policies that might lead corporations to leave a community.

The privileged position enjoyed by businessmen in the political systems of local communities, and the influence generated by firms and interest groups at the state and national level, faced tests during the 1970s and 1980s because of the declining position of American business in the international economy. The costs of energy skyrocketed, inflation rates steadily increased, economic growth and production lagged, and environmental problems multiplied. One of the nation's leading defenders of business admitted in 1981 that 'in comparison with its awesome productivity and profitability in the 1950s, American business today is weak and laggard. If General Motors was then a symbol of the unprecedented might of the US economy, in 1981 it seems to represent another facet of American decline.' One response of the business community took the form of a searching examination of ways to improve productivity: *Business Week*'s publication of *The Decline of U.S. Power (and what we can do about it)* offered readers a variety of policies to ponder. Another reaction consisted of recommendations that business should 'recognize labor as an important defense of free enterprise', because of its 'strong class interest in a productive, growing economy' and because organised labour stood to suffer from redistributionist social policies that favoured the poor and disadvantaged minority groups.[14]

2.   Labour

THE history of organised labour (the terms 'labour', 'labour movement', and 'organised labour', will be used interchangeably in this
chapter) in post-Second World War America began auspiciously. In
1946 union membership reached 14.4 million, 23.6 per cent of the
total civilian labour force and 34.5 per cent of non-agriculture
employment, a dramatic improvement since the 5.2 and 11.3
Depression figures of 1933. Many economists and business leaders,
regarding labour leaders as inherently irresponsible and their
organisations as incompatible with the market system, worried that
the traditional authority of business owners to control the economy
would be seriously eroded by what one called 'militant labour
monopolies'. Even a sympathetic analyst, labour economist John T.
Dunlop, who later served as secretary of labour under President
Gerald Ford, likened labour unions to diseases. In a 1948 essay that
appeared in a work that promised *Insights into Labor Issues*, Dunlop
viewed labour organisations as primarily developing among employees who held strategic market or technological positions. 'They
have bargaining power. They can make it hurt.' Likening such
employees to 'points of infection' Dunlop speculated on the consequences of spreading the disease.[1] Economist John Kenneth Galbraith, writing four years later, argued that American capitalism (the
title of his book) was increasingly marked by the strength of labour
and other powerful economic organisations whose 'countervailing
power' could check the power of business. 'In principle', Galbraith
argued, 'the American is controlled, livelihood and soul, by the large
corporation; in practice he seems not to be completely enslaved.'[2] In a
literal sense, Galbraith's judgement still holds true, but the decades
since 1945 have demonstrated the considerable success experienced
by the enemies of the labour movement in their effort to contain the
growth of labour's influence upon American capitalism.
    The story of the labour movement since 1945 is not entirely a

matter of successful business attacks resulting in gradual losses of union power. A number of factors needs to be considered in order to explain why the *New York Times* should characterise labour as 'frustrated and wary' as it prepared to celebrate the 100th anniversary of Labor Day in September 1982.[3] A complex and interrelated series of economic, social and political developments shaped organised labour. The partial nature of union membership restricted it to limited sectors of the economy, including the weaker and declining sectors. Even those unions which managed to thrive during the 1940s, 1950s and 1960s frequently differed over organisational, tactical and ideological priorities, and this disunity placed limits upon labour power. Government regulation, beginning with the Taft–Hartley Act of 1947, more often hampered the labour movement than it helped to expand its influence and power. Collective bargaining, its process and content regulated by law, benefited millions of workers, both members and non-members of unions. Management also benefited, but the relationship between labour and management has continued to be that of adversaries. Labour's attempt to organise the unorganised sectors of the economy dramatically illustrated both this adversarial relationship and the intensity with which business groups have sought to limit the extent of unionisation.

In spite of the campaigns against unions and their increasing difficulties in winning representation elections, the majority of Americans, though in declining proportions, have approved of unions. Unions themselves turned, with varying success, to the political arena in an attempt to protect their gains and widen their influence.

LABOUR UNION MEMBERSHIP TRENDS

The giants of the American labour movement in 1945 were the American Federation of Labor (AFL), a primarily trades union established in 1886, and the Congress of Industrial Organizations (CIO), which began in 1935 as an organising committee of the AFL. Dedicated to establishing industry-wide unions in basic manufacturing industries such as steel and automobiles, and in mining, the CIO separated from the AFL in 1938. Both organisations functioned as unions of unions, federations composed of national unions (e.g. the United Auto Workers of the CIO) that were themselves made up of local unions (e.g. the Detroit local of the UAW). In 1955, when the two federations merged to become the AFL-CIO, the new organisation counted 139 of the nation's 199 unions as its affiliates; only 1.7 million members belonged to independent or unaffiliated unions compared to the 16 million AFL-CIO members.

Labour unions increased their membership from 2.6 million in 1933 to 20.2 million in 1978. Most of the growth occurred when the federal government protected union organising (during the New Deal) or when the economy grew because of wartime expansion (the Second World War, the Korean War, the Vietnam War). High rates of unemployment after 1978 brought membership losses. Between 1978 and 1980 unions lost some 500,000 members, and labour's share of the workforce declined from 22.3 to 20.9 per cent. Membership losses since 1978 have come primarily in basic industries such as steel and automobiles where plant closings and layoffs have shaken entire communities in the older industrial areas. If labour's membership strength is calculated according to its share of non-agricultural employment rather than total labour force, the zenith of union strength came in 1945 with 35.5 per cent. By 1954, the proportion had declined to 34.7 per cent and it dropped still further, nearly one-third in 24 years, to 23.6 per cent in 1978. If the estimated one-fifth of the supervisory and managerial workers included in the total non-agricultural employment is subtracted, the employees eligible to join unions who actually belonged amounted to more than one-third of the non-agricultural workforce in 1980.

The overall membership trends hide significant changes that have shaped the composition of organised labour. Probably the most dramatic change is the growth of membership among service workers and the addition of over 4.5 million public employees to the labour movement between the mid-1960s and the end of the 1970s. The Communication Workers of America, with its strength in newer high-technology sectors, grew from 433,000 in 1972 to 650,000 in 1982. Half of the federal government employees, numbering 1.4 million workers, had enrolled in unions by 1978, while the number of state and local government employees who belonged to unions increased from 764,000 to 2.2 million between 1968 and 1978. As an alternative to unions, government employees also joined professional associations in record numbers. These organisations differ from unions by not always serving as a collective bargaining agent. Their members among state and local government employees increased from 1.7 to 2.4 million between 1968 and 1978. Although unionisation increased among public sector workers, labour's share of other non-manufacturing employees slipped during the post-war period. Membership has increased, but total non-manufacturing employment increased three times faster than union membership. Manufacturing industries suffered declines even in absolute numbers of labour union members. Since the peak year when 9.2 million workers belonged to manufacturing industry unions (in 1968 at the mid-point of the Vietnam War), membership fell to 8.1 million in 1978. Further losses occurred during the recession that began the following year. The manufacturing share of union membership plummeted from 51 per cent in 1956 to 41 per cent in 1970 to 34 per cent in 1980; half of the decline occurred between 1974 and 1978. Throughout the period 1945–80 the labour force grew most slowly or declined in those basic sectors of the economy where unions had established themselves by the end of the Second World War. The United Mine Workers, for example, the sixth largest union in 1951 with 600,000 members, could claim only 245,000 in 1980.

Labour's strength concentrated in the urban areas of a handful of states during the entire post-1945 period. New York was still the leading labour union state in 1980 with 2.7 million members; this constituted 38.7 per cent of the non-agricultural employment, a slip of 1.5 per cent since 1970. California, with 2.6 million union members, and Pennsylvania, Illinois, Ohio and Michigan, with over 1 million members each, contributed over half of all the members to the nation's labour movement. Labour has been weakest in absolute members in rural states such as South Dakota, Wyoming, Vermont, North Dakota, Alaska and Idaho. Union membership has made its poorest showing as a proportion of the labour force in North and South Carolina, Florida and Texas.

DISUNITED LABOUR

In November 1979, George Meany, 85 years old and confined to a wheelchair, turned over the presidency of the AFL-CIO he had held since 1952 to his successor Lane Kirkland. Meany died a few weeks later. The election of conservative Republican Ronald Reagan to the Presidency of the United States in November 1980, the centenary of National Labor Day in 1982, and the massive unemployment and loss of union membership in the depressed mining, steel and automobile industries all stimulated considerable reflection upon the state of the labour movement. The divisiveness within organised labour stood out as a central concern. Critics from the left, such as Sidney Lens, · castigated the AFL-CIO for its collusion with capitalist management and condemned its complicity with the Cold War and the arms race. The head of Democratic Socialists of America, writer and activist Michael Harrington, regarded the new AFL-CIO president as an improvement, because Kirkland seemed willing to co-operate with left political groups outside the labour movement and beyond the Federation's control.[4] Indeed, Kirkland's willingness to make common cause with other interest groups paralleled his desire to unify labour itself. In 1981, the United Auto Workers (UAW) voted to rejoin the AFL-CIO after an absence of 13 years. Kirkland saw this as a successful step towards a programme of unity that included bringing other independent unions into the AFL-CIO.

The return of the 1.3 million autoworkers to the AFL-CIO represented a considerable boost to the Federation's claim to speak for American labour, as well as to its treasury. As the nation's third largest union, the UAW's importance was undeniable. But the UAW had been losing members for over a decade, as the automobile industry sought relief from the impact of foreign competition through retrenchment and automation. The independent teamsters and the NEA, on the other hand, increased their membership during the decade of the 1970s, and their positions as the largest unions meant that their inclusion in the AFL-CIO would have practical as well as symbolic importance.

The Teamsters Union and the members of the NEA were the largest of the 68 independent national unions which in 1978 made up 28.5 per cent of total union membership with a strength of 6.2 million members. The NEA, with 1.7 million teachers enrolled in 1978, embraced collective bargaining during the 1970s, but it never affiliated with the AFL-CIO because of its reservations about being considered part of the labour movement. The Teamsters Union, on the other hand, belonged to the AFL until 1957. In that year, the McClellan Senate committee hearings on racketeering and crime in labour-management relations put the spotlight on the Teamsters Union, even then the largest in the nation. Its president, Dave Beck, was convicted of embezzlement and expelled from his post as the AFL-CIO vice-president. Beck's successor as teamster president,

James Hoffa, was also convicted in 1964. Stating that 'We would never lower our standards to match the standards of the business community or the marketplace', George Meany convinced the Federation of the need to expel the Teamsters and two other unions even before Beck's conviction.[5] Meany also presided over the AFL when it expelled the International Longshoremen's Association in 1954 for harbouring criminal elements.

In 1950 the CIO expelled eleven national unions, some one-fifth of its membership, for alleged communist control, and by 1968 only four of the eleven still existed as separate organisations. The episode pointed to the importance of the bitter controversies over anti-communism and loyalty to the US that contributed to labour's disunity. The United Mine Workers voluntarily withdrew from the AFL in 1947 when John L. Lewis, the UMW's volatile president, refused to file an affidavit declaring opposition to communism. Walter Reuther, like John L. Lewis one of the moving forces in the establishment of the CIO and its president from 1952 until the merger with the AFL in 1955, presided over the United Auto Workers' disaffiliation from the Federation in 1968. Although Reuther was disappointed that the Federation had become complacent and satisfied with the status quo, he especially disliked what he considered to be the rigid and unrealistic anti-communism of the AFL-CIO under George Meany's direction.

GOVERNMENT REGULATION OF LABOUR

The issues of anti-communism, racketerring and crime that played so important a role in the fragmentation of organised labour during the 1940s and 1950s also contributed to the shaping of legislation that imposed regulations on how union activities were conducted. At the same time, legislators responded to the desires of organised business to limit the membership growth of unions that followed the 1935 National Labor Relations Act (Wagner Act).

The Wagner Act was explicitly biased in favour of labour, for it protected the worker's right to join unions and placed the federal government in the position of 'encouraging the practice and procedure of collective bargaining'. The Act also provided for secret ballot elections as the means by which workers would decide whether to be represented by a union, and it established a federal National

Labor Relations Board to enforce the law. The supreme court declared the Wagner Act to be constitutional in 1937, and labour historians credit the law for much of the increase in union membership from 3.6 million in 1935 to 14 million in 1947.

When the war drew to a close in 1945, so did the shaky wartime truce between business and labour. *New York Times* columnist James Reston wrote in September that in the automobile industry 'both sides seem to take the view that they have taken a lot of guff from the other side during the war and are now free to fight it out'.[6] The labour movement was generally critical of President Truman's policies for the reconversion from war to peace, and it launched a wave of strikes during the latter part of 1945 and 1946. Disputes rocked the maritime, trucking, railway, coal, oil, auto, electrical equipment, telephone, meat-packing and steel industries. More members participated in more strikes during these months than in any similar period before or since. Four and a half million workers walked the picket lines in 1946.

The National Association of Manufacturers took the lead in welding together a coalition of trade associations and corporations determined to enforce industrial peace by means of federal legislation to amend the Wagner Act. Their Declaration of Principles intended to create regulations that would decentralise the collective bargaining process and 'balance' it in favour of management rather than labour. Both the official NAM position, and the more hardline proposals of dissidents within the group who wanted the Wagner Act abolished altogether, became the basis for the Taft–Hartley Act passed in June 1947. The NAM did not single-handedly succeed in persuading Congress to enact the law; anti-labour Republicans and conservative Southern Democrats eagerly supported it, and moderate Congressmen who believed the public demanded a check on 'labor monopolies' added their votes. Congress passed the law over President Truman's veto, and the National Association of Manufacturers promptly took credit for the new measure and assumed the role of its defender.[7]

Although Taft–Hartley did not repeal the Wagner Act, it made a fundamental change in the character of government regulation contained in federal law. For the first time, controls were placed upon the actual substance of the collective bargaining agreement as well as on the procedural matters. The closed shop, a provision that prohibited the hiring of non-union employees, became illegal. Other measures likewise limited union activities. Management could bring suit against unions for breaking contracts or damaging company property during strikes. A new federal agency, the Federal Mediation and Conciliation Service, came into being, and the government could obtain injunctions requiring a 'cooling-off period' of 80 days during a strike considered dangerous to health or safety. Several measures placed the government in the position of supervising the internal operations of unions: leaders had to swear that they did not belong to the Communist Party, unions had to make their financial statements public, and they could not make financial contributions to political campaigns. In 1951 Congress amended the Act to allow contracts establishing a union-shop (a provision stating that employees must join the union within 30 days after being hired) without a majority vote of the employees.

Because Taft–Hartley included a clause that allowed state laws regarding the union-shop provision to supersede federal law when a conflict occurred, anti-labour coalitions in numerous states successfully lobbied for such 'Right-to-Work' (anti union-shop) laws during the early 1950s. By 1954, 15 states had placed such laws on the books and the number today stands at 20. The 1947 measure directly contributed to keeping labour restricted to its areas and sectors of strength developed by the end of the Second World War. The 'Right-to-Work' states coincide with the regions of the US that have demonstrated the greatest economic growth since 1945. In addition to Taft–Hartley's influence in slowing the expansion of union membership and bargaining rights, the measure pressured unions to create the bureaucratic procedures necessary for fulfilling the demands by the government for public scrutiny of internal union decision-making and financial accountability. One historian concludes that 'Taft–Hartley showed that, after years of uncertainty, the practical conservatism of American business was once again triumphant in national politics'.[8]

The merger that created the AFL-CIO in 1955 occurred partly because the new presidents of the two federations, George Meany and Walter P. Reuther, sensed that the Eisenhower administration would bring more punitive labour legislation, similar to Taft–Hartley. The merger put an end to the expensive and fruitless practice of 'raiding', in which a union from one federation tried to increase its membership by stealing workers from a union in the other federation. However, the merger did not protect organised labour from further regulatory legislation such as the Labor-Management Reporting and Disclosure Act (Landrum–Griffin Act) passed by Congress in 1959.

The background to Landrum–Griffin was a series of investigations, including those by New York State in 1952–3 and the McClellan committee in 1957, into corruption and racketeering in the unions. The AFL, as mentioned above, expelled the International Long-shoremen's Association in 1954 following the New York State investigations. During the McClellan hearings, in 1957, the AFL-CIO adopted a Code of Ethics and expelled the Teamsters and two other unions. The investigations helped to propel Jimmy Hoffa (as well as Robert and John F. Kennedy) into the public eye. More importantly, they demonstrated that the leaders of several unions, including the nation's largest, had enriched themselves by racketeering, had used union funds for personal aggrandisement, had abused the democratic process by intimidating members who dissented from the official policies, and had severely violated the civil rights of members. Congress intended the Landrum–Griffin Act to remedy these abuses by union leaders, as well as to increase federal government regulation of internal union activity.

The Landrum–Griffin Act imposed four major responsibilities on unions. They had to comply with a 'Bill of Rights' that protected individual union members; they needed to make financial disclosures and demonstrate their freedom from transactions where a conflict of interest existed between the parties; they were prohibited from improper trusteeships; they were subject to federal safeguards against the manipulation of union elections in favour of incumbents. A recent study of the impact of the Landrum–Griffin Act concludes that while unions have improved democratic decision-making, most changes have been undramatic. Passage of the law did establish a favourable climate of opinion for members who had the courage to assert themselves and seek redress for civil rights violations.[9] One episode, involving the United Mine Workers Union, demonstrates the potential of the law. Complaints of violations of election laws caused federal court rulings that set aside the 1969 re-election of incumbent president Tony Boyle. In the court-ordered election to decide the presidency in 1972, Boyle was defeated by a reform slate headed by Arnold Miller. Subsequent to the 1972 election, Boyle was tried, convicted and sentenced to life imprisonment for the murder of his opponent in the 1969 election, Jacob Yablonski (who was killed along with his wife and daughter).

The Landrum–Griffin Act of 1959, like the Taft–Hartley Act of 1947, was imposed upon organised labour rather than being the consequence of union wishes for government regulation. In 1974, unions benefited when the Taft–Hartley Act was extended to employees in private, non-profit hospitals. For the first time, government required these institutions to recognise and bargain with employee organisations. In 1977 the AFL-CIO tried to make the regulatory process more palatable when it sought to convince Congress of the need to reform the National Labor Relations Board. The proposal was designed to make it harder for employers to defy or delay compliance with the rulings of a more efficient NLRB. Had the 1977 legislation been passed, it would have represented the first amendment to the Wagner Act intended to strengthen union organising. George Meany called the battle over the Labor Law Reform Act of 1978 'the toughest legislative fight I have seen since I came to Washington'. Lined up against the AFL-CIO stood the Business Roundtable, the National Association of Manufacturers, the United States Chamber of Commerce and the National Right to Work Committee. Passed by the House of Representatives by a decisive margin in late 1977, the measure died in the Senate in 1978 when its supporters could not get enough votes to end the five-week-long filibuster against it.[10]

COLLECTIVE BARGAINING

Since the passage of the Wagner Act in 1935, the federal government has protected the right of workers to form unions and to bargain with employers over terms of employment. The federal National Labor Relations Board or a similar state agency establishes the unit to which the employees represented by the union belong. Bargaining takes place over wages, salaries and other forms of compensation, work rules, employee job rights, the respective power of union and management in the bargaining process, and the enforcement of the contract as well as the settlement of grievances. The law stipulates that agreements worked out by collective bargaining apply to all employees in the bargaining unit, not merely the members of the union involved. Some 25 million US employees laboured under agreements arrived at through collective bargaining in 1976.

Collective bargaining varies by industry and region. By the end of the 1970s about two-thirds of manufacturing workers were covered by collective bargaining agreements, but the proportion fell below 25 per cent in retail trade, restaurant work and clerical work. Such agreements covered 75 per cent of workers in transportation, contract construction and longshoring, but in textiles, lumber and leather product manufacturing the percentage came to less than 50. Manufacturing workers were more likely to work under collective bargaining agreements in the North Central states (over 75 per cent) than in the southern states (less than 50 per cent). Service workers such as barbers, cab drivers and hotel employees were more likely to be covered by a collective bargaining agreement in large cities than in small towns. Some 190,000 separate collective bargaining agreements stood in force at the end of the 1970s, negotiated by 70,000 local unions affiliated with 175 national unions with over 5,000 employer associations and a vast number of individual employers.

Government control of collective bargaining has shaped the process and the content of agreements since the Second World War. Federal laws have allowed unions to bargain for contracts covering entire industries, as well as to place benefits such as pensions and health insurance on the bargaining table for inclusion in a contract. State laws, and federal legislation such as the 1978 Civil Service Reform Law, have made it possible for government workers to join unions or employee associations and to bargain for contracts. Arizona, Idaho, Kansas and California have passed laws regulating collective bargaining in agriculture since 1970. The federal laws, beginning with the Wagner Act, had excluded agricultural workers; the California law demonstrated how legal provisions could favour labour. Some legislation aided unions by establishing federal regulations that forced businesses to improve conditions of work, thereby establishing minimum standards later used as the basis for bargaining. This is the case with laws specifying minimum wages, pension guidelines and health and safety codes. Government regulation also benefited the management side. Prohibition of the closed shop, restrictions on boycotts and picketing and federal imposition of anti-inflationary wage codes all tended to strengthen the hand of business.

The presence of the government at the bargaining table did not end the adversarial relationship that has characterised labour-management relations since the Second World War. Since union wages average around 15 per cent higher than payment for comparable work by non-union workers, employers usually attempt to block organisation. In addition, the existence of collective bargaining agreements provides workers with contractual rights that limit the prerogatives of employers over discipline and discharge and permit workers to decide jointly on terms of employment, thereby challenging the employer's prerogatives. A handful of unions, notably in steel, the needle trades, and to some degree automobiles, have moved towards a policy of collaborating with management. But these are special cases of declining industries where concessions have been sought for the sake of mutual advantage. Rank and file scepticism of such accommodation has limited its use, in spite of periodic calls by journalists, academics and government officials for more co-operation.[11]

By the end of the 1970s, 94 per cent of all workers covered by a collective bargaining agreement were subject to a clause that prohibited them from striking during the life of their contract. Despite such prohibitions, unauthorised strikes have regularly taken place during the post-war period. In 1976, 2,787 occurred; two-thirds were in the mining and construction industries. In addition to such 'wildcat' strikes, strikes for a new contract have continued to constitute labour's weapon of last resort since the record numbers of 1945–6. The media have characteristically exaggerated their impact, at least since 1960 when the time lost by workers on strike has averaged less than two-tenths of 1 per cent of time worked. Federal intervention such as that in strikes by coal and steel workers during the early post-war period under the Taft–Hartley Act emergency provisions has not occurred in more recent years. Public employees, teachers most frequently and in the largest numbers, adopted the strike as a bargaining chip, and on rare occasions even police and fire fighters have illegally withdrawn their labour. Business has not been uniformly opposed to strikes; employers in steel, coal and electrical equipment have begun to see a long strike as a way to weaken their unionised workers.

LABOUR MILITANCY, EMPLOYER RESISTANCE

The struggle of workers to form unions, strengthen their numbers and improve terms of employment has generated counter-attacks by employers throughout American history. The period since 1945 differs from earlier periods because the role of the state has expanded so dramatically. In several other respects, however, American labour history demonstrates long-term continuity. First, long and bitter conflict has been the price paid by workers to establish unions in unorganised sectors of the economy or non-union areas of the US. Second, organised business groups have actively fought to limit union expansion. Both labour and capital have used techniques of industrial warfare appropriate to the task, and both sometimes allowed the end to justify the means. Both sides, and in this respect the enhanced role of both government and mass media affected the post-1945 story, have used imaginative lobbying programmes, election campaigns and advertising to gain public support. Labour militancy can be dramatically illustrated by the history of attempts to organise California farm workers. Employer militancy has been especially noticeable in the attempts to extend state 'Right-to-Work' laws that prohibit union shop contracts and in the growing use of consultants to discredit established unions in the workplace.

Agricultural workers first attempted to organise unions in the 1880s. For a variety of reasons, including the seasonal nature of the work, the migratory and often temporary character of the labour force, and intense employer resistance, these efforts came to little until the 1940s. In Hawaii, Jack Hall of the International Longshoremen's and Warehousemen's Union (ILWU) led a successful campaign to have the legislature pass a Hawaiian Labor Relations Act in 1945. Unlike the Wagner Act, the Hawaiian measure included farm workers, and by the end of the 1940s the ILWU had organised a majority of the territory's farm workers.

Success in Hawaii contributed to the revival of attempts to organise farm workers in California. California growers and union organisers struggled bitterly during the 1930s, but the unions made little headway against the combined forces of the state Chamber of Commerce, the Associated Farmers of California, and occasional anti-union vigilante groups. California was an important organising test for the unions because it had led the nation in large-scale farms for decades, with 60 per cent of large truck farms (market gardens), 60 per cent of fruit farms, 53 per cent of poultry farms, 40 per cent of dairies, and 30 per cent of the cotton farms. Large-scale 'factories in the field' of the California variety were also important in pre-war Texas, which had the second highest number, but even at that only 0.09 were in the Lone Star State compared to 36 per cent in the Golden State.[12] California maintained its position as the 'agribusiness' capital of the US and by the late 1970s it led the 50 states in agricultural productivity as well as in numbers of hired agricultural workers. In 1978 California had as many farm workers as the four other leading agribusiness states (Texas, North Carolina, Florida, Washington) combined.

During the Depression years of the 1930s, over 300,000 poverty-striken refugees from Oklahoma, Texas, Arkansas, Missouri and other drought-ridden areas migrated to California. John Steinbeck painted a dramatic portrait of this 'Dust Bowl Migration' in his novel *The Grapes of Wrath* (1939). By the mid-1930s, these migrants, pejoratively called 'Okies' and 'Arkies', had displaced the Mexican workers who previously dominated the farm labour force in California. But the wartime demand for military personnel, shipyard and aircraft workers attracted these white, US citizens from agriculture and growers once again relied upon Mexican workers. Between 1942 and 1964, some 4.5 million braceros (men who work with their arms) crossed the border under the auspices of a labour-contracting system supervised by the federal government. Originally designed to supplement the American labour force, the braceros quickly became the mainstay for California and Texas agribusiness. Their transportation, housing, living conditions and wages were controlled, they were separated by their special status from American workers, and they were almost impervious to unionisation. Some 50,000 braceros worked in California and Texas in 1945. During the peak year of 1957, 192,400 were imported, and in 1964, the year the programme expired, there were 128,000 in California alone where they made up 25 per cent of seasonal farm workers.

Growers resented the loss of the bracero programme, particularly since it controlled wages and provided relatively docile workers. They complained even more during the years between 1965 and 1980, as a series of farm-worker unions, aided by civil rights organisations and a governor of California, gradually achieved unionisation in key sectors of California agribusiness. In September 1965, the Agricultural Workers Organizing Committee (AWOC) a mainly Filipino American union affiliated with the AFL-CIO, called a strike against 33 grape-growers in the San Joaquin Valley. Two weeks later AWOC was joined by a largely Mexican American independent union called the National Farm Workers Association (NFWA) headed by a charismatic community organiser named Cesar Chavez. The strike came at the height of militant civil rights campaigns for black equality. Labour unions and church groups throughout California donated food and money to the strikers and enthusiastically walked the picket lines. Chavez proclaimed the strike to be *La Causa*, and launched his crusade with a nationwide boycott against products made by Schenley Industries, the largest corporate owner among the struck vineyards. The boycott proved successful, partly through the publicity and support provided by Senator Robert Kennedy and Catholic bishops and partly through the favourable media coverage given to the UFW's heroic 300-mile march to the state capitol in Sacramento. Schenley and several wine grape-growers agreed to hold elections for a collective bargaining agent for their workers.

AWOC and the NFWA merged to become the United Farm Workers Organizing Committee (UFW), which eventually affiliated with the AFL-CIO in 1972. Between 1966 and 1973, the UFW extended its organising campaign to table grape workers and then to lettuce workers; these were California's leading crops in value of product except for cotton, which was almost completely mechanised. During 1967 and 1968, Governor Ronald Reagan, California Senator George Murphy and Richard Nixon, Republican candidate for president, condemned the UFW boycott. But widespread support by organised labour and a number of big city mayors made the boycott effective, and in 1970 all but about 15 per cent of the table grape-growers signed contracts with the UFW. The lettuce boycott was less successful. Chavez's union, disliked by many growers who regarded it as more a part of the civil rights movement than of the labour movement, found itself competing with the Teamsters' Union which also tried to organise lettuce workers. Several grape-growers signed contracts with the Western Conference of Teamsters (WCT) rather than renew those with the UFW that were expiring in 1973; Chavez's group challenged the Teamsters and found itself plagued with court cases and confronted with violence. But the UFW and its supporters defeated a state ballot proposition that would have limited union activities and won an important state supreme court case.

The UFW prospects improved substantially when the newly elected California governor, Edmund G. (Jerry) Brown, Jr., took personal responsibility for pushing a state law through the legislature that set up a state agricultural relations board with the authority to supervise election for a union among California's 250,000 farm workers. Strikes during harvest time were declared legal, much to the chagrin of most growers, and the union gained the right to publicise its boycotts and picket employers who sold boycotted products. The

UFW won 229 representation elections to the 116 won by the Teamsters in the first year of the board's operation. By the end of 1977, Chavez's union had some 30,000 members who represented a wide cross-section of farm workers with the heaviest concentration of members in lettuce, grapes and tomatoes. In 1977 the UFW and the WCT signed an agreement giving the Teamsters jurisdiction over workers in the packing sheds and truck drivers and the UFW jurisdiction over the field workers. The establishment of the agricultural labour board and the success of the UFW marked the beginning of a new era in agricultural unionism in the US, but some older traditions continued into the new era. When the UFW tried to renew contracts and increase wages in 1979, growers hired armed guards to discourage militant pickets, violence broke out, and one UFW member was killed.

The militant response of California growers to the UFW, while it included the use of armed guards to keep union organisers off company property, also included lobbying the legislature and governor's office, challenging union activity through the judicial system, and advertising to sway public opinion to the side of the employers. Employers throughout the US who are anxious to resist unions have used the same tactics as the farm growers in California during the post-war period.

Since 1945, American business ideology has gradually accepted labour unions as legitimate organisations that allow employees to protect themselves against undesirable personnel practices. Most executives, however, have not been willing to surrender the right of management to exercise ultimate power over company policy, and they have also found unions guilty of a number of undesirable practices. They have claimed that unions reduce efficiency by demanding restrictive work rules, and they have criticised the increase of worker control of the work process as an infringement of managerial rights. Unions, according to such critics, have minimised the market constraints that require management to cut production costs, and they have demanded unreasonable wage settlements. Another undesirable result of unions, according to critics, is their tendency to magnify misunderstandings between employer and employee, thus creating unnecessary friction and suspicion that likewise has lowered efficiency. Arguing that unions achieved their strength because of government favouritism rather than through real service to workers, businessmen have criticised the rights of unions to tactical weapons such as the boycott, the picket line, the union shop contract and industry-wide collective bargaining.

Given the hostility of businessmen to the union-shop contract, few were surprised when eleven states immediately established state right-to-work laws in 1947 after Congress passed the Taft–Hartley Act. All these states were in the Sunbelt or midwest regions, where unionism had made little headway. Six more states, in the same regions, passed similar laws during the 1950s, but the campaign was stopped in 1958 when all but one of six right-to-work proposals on state ballots were quashed by the electorate. Voters repealed the Indiana law in 1965, and it was not until 1976 that change occurred when Louisiana enacted a right-to-work law. In 1977 and 1978, the National Right to Work Committee and its Legal Defense Foundation, lobbying and judicial activist groups founded in 1958 and 1968 respectively, spent $100,000 on advertisements calling for a national right-to-work law. The Foundation contributed over $2 million to help stop the Labour Law Reform Bill supported by the AFL-CIO in 1977–8.

Employers in the states that allow union shop contracts have been alert to possible opportunities to avoid unionisation, and they have increasingly supported the development of a cadre of professional anti-labour attorneys who specialise in 'union busting'. The rationale of such consultants was stated by the authors of a 1973 volume on how to 'avert, beat, out-negotiate, unload', or if necessary 'live with' unions. Management consultants I. Herbert Rothenberg and Steven B. Silverman counselled employers to 'search out and explore the frailties and weaknesses of their adversary, exploit them . . ., and do every proper thing and take every reasonable action that will lead to victory'.[13] By 1979, some 1,500 lawyers, psychologists and management consultants were conducting an estimated multi-million dollar business in the US. One Chicago firm employed a nationwide staff of 60 consultants, and in 1977 the National Association of Manufacturers established the Council for a Union Free Environment which advises its 450 member firms on non-union management techniques. The AFL-CIO and academic analysts have argued that these business consultants have been directly responsible for lowering the success rate of unions in representation elections from 55 per cent in 1970 to 45 per cent in 1978.

LABOUR AND POLITICS

Attacks on the labour movement by employer groups, while they may have slowed the growth of unionisation and weakened the ability of unions to win bargaining elections, did not lead the American public to disapprove of unions in general. Since the Gallup Poll began measuring opinion about unions in 1936, a majority of the public has defended their right to exist, although the proportion in favour has declined significantly from a high of 76 per cent in 1957 to a low of 55 per cent in 1981. But when asked whether they supported overt political activity such as campaigning for particular candidates or raising financial contributions for candidates, majorities of 60 and 80 per cent of the public have disapproved. During the 1950s and 1960s, union members themselves consistently told pollsters that they wanted their unions to lobby for specific legislation and did not mind being reminded by their unions to vote. Less than one-third, however, approved of rank and file financial contributions to candidates, campaigns to turn anti-union politicians out of office, or the formation of a labour political party based on explicit working-class suppor-ters.[14]

Labour politics in the United States has generally been the pressure group rather than the independent political party familiar to Great Britain and the Continent. By the Second World War, the AFL had established a regular, if modest, presence in Washington as a lobbying group. Stubbornly non-partisan since the time of its founder Samuel Gompers, the AFL during the early post-war years followed the lead of the less cautious CIO and gradually aligned itself with the Democratic Party. The AFL and the CIO both created political action committees in the 1940s. After the merger, the AFL-CIO established its Committee on Political Education which has operated on all government levels. COPE, which by the late 1970s was the biggest non-corporate Political Action Committee, adopted aggres-sive lobbying tactics, began endorsing candidates, and launched advertising programmes aimed both at union members and the general public.

George Meany, president of the AFL-CIO, boasted that the Federation was 'the single most effective political organization in the country', but the historical record suggests a much more modest evaluation of labour effectiveness in politics.[15] The issue is compli-cated by the sheer size and diversity of the US, as well as by the federal system of government. The judicious conclusion made by seasoned labour analysts and policy-makers Derek Bok and John T. Dunlop for the period from 1945 to 1970 still applies in 1983. 'All in all', they wrote, 'labor may well have less affirmative political influence than other interest groups, because so many of its major goals encounter opposition from other powerful groups.'[16] During the 1960s and 1970s businessmen more often agreed with Meany's assessment of the power of the labour movement than did left-of-centre academic and intellectual critics of the AFL-CIO. Using the spectre of 'Big Labor' as a scare tactic, businessmen attempted to rally support for union-busting activities. Critics on the left pointed to the evidence of labour movement stalemate as a sign that both rank and file members and the general public regarded union leadership as out of step with the times. They also pointed to the increasing support given by union members to Republican Party and Independent presidential candidates in 1972, 1976 and 1980 as evidence of rank and file disillusionment and the need for a revitalised labour movement.

Since late 1979, when Lane Kirkland assumed the presidency of the AFL-CIO, the Federation has taken a number of steps to increase its national political influence. In early 1983, Kirkland declared that the Federation would announce its choice for president in the 1984 election before the primaries and caucuses. This bid for increasing union influence during the nominating process clearly conveyed the importance placed by the AFL-CIO upon the outcome of presidential elections. The ambiguity of labour's political situation was also made clear when in mid-1983 the Gallup Poll found that even among union membership families, 47 per cent said a labour endorsement would make no difference in their vote and 18 per cent claimed it would make them *less* likely to vote for the candidate of labour.[17]

3. The Changing Nature of Work

JOHN Gunther, preparing for his 1947 book *Inside U.S.A.*, asked a United Steelworkers of America official to define the word 'steel'. Steel, said the union leader, is America. In 1947, 85 per cent of the nation's products contained some form of steel made in the US and 40 per cent of America's workers depended either directly or indirectly on the steel industry for their livelihood. 'What makes this a great nation above all', Gunther wrote, was its ability to turn out more steel than Great Britain, pre-war Germany, Japan, France and the Soviet Union combined. In 1950 American steel production amounted to 46 per cent of the world's total. But between 1950 and 1978 steel production grew by 41 per cent compared to the 377 per cent expansion of world production, and the American share of world production dropped to only 17 per cent. By 1979 nearly 14 per cent of American steel was imported, compared to only 5 per cent in 1960. Between 1977 and early 1981 the industry's plant-closing programme pruned back steelmaking capacity by 11 per cent. In mid-1981 *Business Week* identified steel as the foremost of the 'creaky industries that once constituted the sturdy base on which the United States economy was built'. In mid-1983, with unemployment in some steelmaking communities hovering near 45 per cent, the United Steelworkers of America took out full page advertisements in newspapers in major cities declaring that 'The Administration Must Act Now to Save America's Basic Steel Industry'.[1]

The crisis of American steel reflects several profound changes in the US economy that affected the nature of work during the post-Second World War period. At the root of these changes lies a tangle of complex issues: the growth of multinational corporations seeking cheap labour outside the US; the flight of capital from older industries requiring expensive modernisation (like steel) to newer sectors (such as communications) that utilise up-to-date technology; tax and tariff policies of the federal government; concentration of control over the economy by large conglomerates; and increasing competition from overseas.

The post-1945 workforce, shaped by such forces, experienced a shift from goods-producing to service-producing industries. Whether applauded as the harbinger of a more humanistic post-industrial society or condemned as a symptom of the degradation of work under monopoly capitalism, this set of changes has sorted workers into categories more complex than traditional blue- and white-collar distinctions. The situation became even more complex due to the steady rise of women in absolute numbers and as a proportion of the paid labour force. Also important during this period were the mechanisation of the work process itself and the impact of technology upon workers and their attitudes toward work.

THE RISE OF SERVICE EMPLOYMENT

The United States in the post-war period stood foremost among those industrialised nations of the world where agricultural occupations seemed more and more a relic of the past. By the end of the 1970s the low-income nations of India, Indonesia, Burma, Bangladesh, Pakistan and Vietnam, with a total labour force of about 298 million, had 71 per cent of their combined workforce in agriculture, compared to 10 per cent in industry and 19 per cent in services. The combined workforce of the United States, West Germany, Italy, Britain and France, about 250 million, consisted of a service sector employment of 58 per cent, an industrial workforce of 31 per cent, and only some 7 per cent in agriculture. In the United States itself, the agricultural workforce after the Second World War dropped dramatically from 17 per cent in 1940 to 6.2 per cent in 1960. From 1970 to 1980, the employment in agriculture, forestry and fisheries combined fell from 4 to 3.5 per cent.

The decline of agricultural employment occurred as part of the overall migration of workers from goods-producing to service-producing industries. In 1940 the US employed 42 per cent of its labour force in goods-producing industries, but in 1980 only 33 per cent of the American working population made their living in that sector. Service-sector employment consequently increased from 58 to

67 per cent of the labour force. About two-thirds of the decline in goods-production employment occurred in manufacturing, which in 1948 accounted for one of every three American workers. Less than one in four workers were in manufacturing in 1977. In 1948, 20.9 million Americans produced goods, and 27.2 million worked in the service sector, out of the total labour force of 48.1 million. In 1977, the workforce had grown to 79.5 million, and 54.4 (more than the entire 1948 labour force) were in services compared to 25.1 million in the goods-producing industries. During that period, while both goods and service workers increased in numbers, the service sector added about 7.5 people for every one added by manufacturing.

As the size of the workforce and the proportion in services has increased, there has been a change in the educational backgrounds and occupational activities of workers. In 1948 the median for years of school completed by the labour force was 10.6; by 1978 it had risen to 12.6 per cent. Only half of the workforce had finished high school in 1957; 9 per cent were college graduates. In 1978 three out of four workers had finished high school, and one-third had finished college, or attended graduate school or college.

The proportion of the labour force in white-collar jobs increased from 31 per cent in 1940 to 52 per cent in 1980. In the mid-1970s the Department of Labor found that a substantial difference existed between white-collar jobs in services and in manufacturing.[2] In services, 42 per cent of the white-collar workers occupied professional, technical, managerial or administrative, and sales positions, whereas in manufacturing, these high-level jobs accounted for only 25 per cent of white-collar workers. White-collar workers also increased their share of federal government jobs, making up 74 per cent in 1960 and 83 per cent in 1980. Government service employment also expanded considerably in the post-war workforce. Civilian workers receiving government paycheques increased from 6.4 million in 1950 to 16.2 million in 1980. Nearly all of the increase came from new jobs created by state and local governments, whose share of government employees grew from 60 per cent in 1950 to 74 per cent in 1980.

A detailed examination of the 1960s underscores the chief characteristics of the changing post-war workforce. As in the 1950s the fastest growing occupations were professional and technical workers. This group increased by 55 per cent, almost three times the rate of growth in total employment, and the proportion rose from 10.8 to 14 per cent. Among these workers, jobs for programmers, systems analysts and other computer specialists grew the fastest. Professional workers in government, especially college teachers and secondary school teachers (serving the post-war baby boom children) grew 150 and 80 per cent respectively. In addition, jobs for recreation workers grew 80 per cent and for social workers by over 100 per cent. Clerical jobs also increased greatly and clericals became the largest single occupational group, displacing blue-collar operatives by 1970. Jobs for secretaries and typists, concentrated in service industries such as finance and trade, increased over 80 per cent and were relatively unaffected by office automation. Numbers of shipping and stock clerks, and telephone operators, by contrast, increased slowly as machines replaced human labour. Employment in sales occupations grew, but slowly, at 14 per cent for the decade, with real estate and insurance sales workers growing faster than the others at 36 per cent. Managerial and administrative jobs grew 9 per cent. Service workers, at 40 per cent, were the third fastest growing group during the 1960s, and the largest increases were in health and cleaning occupations. Craftworkers and operatives, both blue-collar categories, were among the slower growing occupations, increasing at 12 and 11 per cent respectively. The number of operatives grew less than 2 per cent, and machinists declined by 25 per cent. The number of farm workers declined from 4 million to under 2.3 million, just below 3 per cent of total employment.[3]

The increase of professional and technical occupations, and those in clerical, service and government jobs during the 1950s and 1960s appeared to some analysts in the early 1970s to herald the arrival of an economy where the majority of the workforce would escape from repetitive manual labour. White-collar workers increased from 31 per cent in 1940 to 52.7 per cent in 1981, whereas blue-collar workers (craftsmen, operatives and labourers) declined from 39.8 to 31.1 per cent. Furthermore, the blue-collar occupations that experienced the highest relative decline were those that required the fewest skills, such as labourers. At the same time, it was equally true that millions of workers who took up clerical, service and sales jobs in what the US government described as white-collar sectors (letter carriers and elevator operators, for example) remained in jobs better described as 'manual' than 'mental'.

By the end of the 1970s it was increasingly clear that the steady decline of labouring and agricultural jobs and the growth of professional, clerical and service positions did not imply 'a generalized upgrading of work'. It was a mistake, as Thomas M. Stanback, Jr. and his colleagues pointed out in *Services: The New Economy* (1981) 'to speak, uncritically, of the rise of services . . . the important observation is that there tends to be heavy concentration of employment in better-than-average and in poorer-than-average jobs'.[4]

WOMEN AND THE WORKFORCE

One set of developments within the workforce during the post-war period that qualified the benefits of service employment concerned the changed role of women in the labour force. Andrew Levison suggested the link between women's work and general changes in the workforce in his 1974 book *The Working-Class Majority*. 'The euphoric concept of a middle class majority, the end of manual labor, and the new age in human history were all', he cautioned, 'based on including the wives of steelworkers who went to work as cashiers and salesgirls as middle class.'[5]

While single American women have traditionally worked outside the home in substantial numbers during the twentieth century (37 per cent did so even in 1890), the presence of large numbers and a significant proportion of married women in the labour force has been a phenomenon of the period since 1945. In 1940, 14 per cent of all married women were working, but by 1980 the rate had increased to 50.2 per cent. A number of factors contributed to this development: women found themselves pushed out of the household and pulled into the workforce. 'Pull' factors included the increase in the number of jobs in the clerical and service sectors of the economy, the increased wages available during the prosperous years of the Korean and Vietnam wars, the invention and distribution of time and labour-saving devices in the home, and the shortage of single women in the 1950s due to low birth rates in the 1920s and 1930s. Women also found it increasingly necessary to work in order to secure newly defined individual and family material necessities.

Between 1940 and 1960 the number of women working doubled, as did the proportion of the workforce who were married (from 15 to 30 per cent). The number of working mothers increased even faster, by an astounding 400 per cent, from 1.5 million to 6.6 million. Nearly 40 per cent of mothers with children between 6 and 17 were in the labour force by 1960, and the typical female worker was over 41 years of age. During the thirty years after the war, the age group that grew the fastest among women workers was that between 45 and 54, though during the Vietnam War years, wives under 35 began to join the labour force faster than the older group. By 1974 just over one-third of mothers with pre-school children (under 6) were working. During the same period, three of every five of the workers who added 38.6 millions to the labour force were women. By 1978, 51 per cent of all American families claimed a wife or a mother who worked in the paid labour force, and a quarter of the nation's children were supported solely by a woman. By 1982, 53 per cent of all adult women were part of the workforce.

Prior to the Second World War, the typical employed married woman came from a lower income family, but in the early post-war years wives of white-collar husbands were more likely to join the labour force than those whose spouses worked in factories. During the 1950s and 1960s the wages of a working wife added an average of 15 to 25 per cent to a family's income. One survey found that two-earner households had 45 per cent more to spend on recreation and gifts, 23 per cent more for household appliances, and 95 per cent more for eating in restaurants. Women's wages did not correspond to the wages of men doing comparable work, and women's mean income declined relative to that of men between 1940 and 1960. Furthermore, the proportion of women in better paying professional jobs declined from 45 to 38 per cent between 1930 and 1966. While professional jobs for women decreased, the proportion of women in lower paying clerical jobs increased from 53 to 73 per cent. By 1960 about two-thirds of women workers had jobs in settings where the majority of employees were women, and 48 per cent were in jobs where 80 per cent of their coworkers were women. A 'pink-collar ghetto', as some called it, was particularly noticeable in sales and clerical work, as well as among elementary school teachers (85 per cent women in 1960).[6]

During the 1960s different rates of growth for women in the professions compared to those in clerical or service occupations continued. In 1960 women held about half of all service occupations, not including private household jobs, and over two-thirds of all clerical jobs. The proportion of women in most occupational groups increased some 2 per cent between 1960 and 1970, but those in clerical positions grew to 5.5 per cent and in service jobs 3.4 per cent. In professional and technical jobs, however (the fastest growing occupations in the decade), the proportion of women increased less tnan 2 per cent. The greatest advances for women took place in those occupations where women had already become a major presence. Women's share of service workers rose from 51 to 55 per cent, and in personal services (such as school monitors or recreation attendants) their proportion increased from 53 to 66 per cent. Although the number of service workers in private households fell over one-third during the 1960s, women still held over 96 per cent of the jobs in 1970. In a few occupations, significant numbers of women moved into jobs traditionally reserved for men. Women bank officers and managers increased from 8.7 to 17.6 per cent, female bus drivers rose from 10 to 28 per cent, women accountants were 1 in 4 instead of 1 in 6, and women increased their employment in the skilled trades slightly from 3.1 to 5 per cent.

Between 1972 and 1980, 10.2 million women joined the American labour force, and 83 per cent of the jobs they occupied were in four industrial groups: professional services; wholesale and retail trade; finance, insurance and real estate; and manufacturing. The 1970s saw the proportion of married women in the workforce with children under 6 rise to 44.9 per cent in 1980 and those with children from 6 to 17 increase to 62 per cent. The proportion of males in the labour force, on the other hand, continued to decline, from 83 per cent in 1960 to 77 per cent in 1980.

Women increased their white-collar employment at a faster rate than men during the 1970s, but by the end of the decade, however, they still clustered in relatively sex-segregated parts of the economy at the bottom of the wage scale. Over a third of all women workers were in clerical jobs, and the wages of women workers still averaged 59 per cent of men's wages, the same as at the beginning of the decade. Only 10 per cent of women workers earned $15,000 or more in 1977 compared to 48 per cent of males, and 12 per cent of the women earned less than $5,000 compared to 5 per cent of the men. In the same year, women college graduates earned a median income that was actually below the median income of male high-school dropouts. By 1980 two-thirds of all workers earning the minimum wage established by the federal government were women. In services, which comprised seven of the nation's ten lowest paying industries in 1980, women made up between 41 and 82 per cent of the production workers, but in the five industries that paid the highest wages, only 5 to 15 per cent of the labour force were female.

RACE AND THE WORKFORCE

The shifting character of the economy has brought no more vast improvements to racial minority groups than it has to women. Black and other non-white workers (the blacks were about 90 per cent) numbered 6.8 million, or 10.7 per cent of the labour force, in 1954. By 1981 non-white workers had grown to 13.6 million, or 12.7 per cent of the workforce, with black workers amounting to 93 per cent of all non-white workers. During the post-war period, non-white males have gradually come to participate in the labour force in lower proportions than white males. This has become especially true of black teenagers. Non-white females, however, tended to work in larger numbers than their white counterparts, although the differences have been narrowing. Between 1948 and 1981, the proportion of non-white women workers over 16 rose from 45.6 to 53.6, whereas the proportion of white women increased from 31.3 to 51.9 per cent.

The higher proportion of black women in the workforce during the post-war period reflects the displacement of black males from rural agricultural jobs into metropolitan areas where work has been difficult to find, the growth in black female-headed households, and the apparent greater acceptability of black women than black men. By 1980, 40 per cent of black families were headed by females, as compared to 15 per cent of all US families. Lower levels of education and discrimination played a role in restricting non-whites to low-paying jobs. By 1980 these accounted for 62 per cent of all black occupations compared to 45 per cent of the workforce as a whole. The median income of black families in 1979 was only 59 per cent as large as the median for all races, and only 39 per cent of black families had incomes of $15,000 or more compared to 64 per cent of all US families. Black unemployment, higher than for whites throughout the post-war period, was double that of whites in 1980 (14 per cent compared to 7 per cent). By 1980, 39 per cent of black teenagers were unemployed compared to 18 per cent of teenagers in general, and the unemployment rate for blacks between 20 and 24 was double that of the overall US population for that age group (at 24 per cent).

TECHNOLOGY AND MECHANISATION

Few occupations have been entirely immune to the impact of

technology, and some work settings have been completely trans-formed by the introduction of new machines. The years of high productivity between 1947 and the beginning of the 1970s coincided with rapid growth rates in research and development expenditures. Employment of engineers and scientists, and applications for patents, plus output per worker in an hour rose 100 per cent, and the amount of goods and services produced per hour doubled as a result of technological advances.[7]

The decline of the agricultural workforce, like the growth in large farms, was a direct consequence of technological changes. Manual workers became expendable as farm machinery assumed many of the tasks traditionally assigned to animals and human power. Encour-aged by inventions and experiments at state universities and the federal Department of Agriculture, farmers used technology to modernise sugar beet harvesting, tomato picking and cotton harvest-ing, made vast improvements in irrigation, more effectively control-led insects and diseases, and even mechanised dairy farming and cattle feeding. The scope of agricultural mechanisation is apparent in three types of agriculture. In 1944, 7 per cent of the sugar beet crop was mechanically harvested, but by 1958 machines picked the entire crop. In 1979 California growers introduced a new machine for picking tomatoes, and by 1983 virtually all tomatoes in the state were harvested by machines. In 1963 only 1.5 per cent were mechanically picked. Mechanical harvesting of cotton grew from less than 10 per cent of the crop in 1949 to all but 4 per cent twenty years later. The output per person in agriculture between 1950 and 1982 increased almost 6 per cent per year, nearly three times faster than all other US industries. As the number of workers in agriculture fell from 10 million in 1945 to 3.3 million in 1981, their labour increasingly took the form of tending machines. The California tomato-picking machines, with 20 workers aboard, took the place of 150 hand workers and harvested two-thirds more per day.

Productivity within coal mining increased by four times between 1930 and 1969. Coinciding with a precipitous decline in demand for coal in the early post-war years, this productivity increase displaced two of every three workers employed in 1948. Mechanisation in coal mining steadily progressed even before the Second World War ended, and between 1945 and 1969 productivity increased from 5 tons per person day to 15.6 tons. Labour conflict, the inaccessibility of coal in older mines and machine breakdowns led to falling productivity rates in underground mines during the 1970s. At the same time, the output of surface mines increased dramatically. In 1941, surface mining accounted for only 9.2 per cent of total coal production, but increased to 19 per cent by 1945 and 62 per cent in 1982. The use of large efficient earth-moving and ore-loading machines made surface mining more mechanised and increased its productivity. Even at its nadir in 1978, surface mining was three times more productive than underground mining. In 1945, some 383,000 workers mined 577 million tons of bituminous coal, nearly all of it underground. In 1981, butiminous coal production increased to 774 million tons, the workforce declined to 208,000 and 34 per cent of that workforce engaged in surface mining produced 62 per cent of the total output.

Like the farmworkers displaced by tomato- and cotton-picking machines and the coal miners made redundant by the continuous mining machines, stevedores lost their jobs to sophisticated hoisting machinery and containerised vessels, and office clerks were replaced by automated billing and office machines. Mechanisation in the automobile and steel manufacturing industries displaced some 400,000 members of the United Auto Workers and the Steelworkers union between 1955 and 1962, and about 60,000 workers lost their jobs on the railways when the supreme court ruled in 1963 that the companies could rightfully introduce labour-saving machinery. During this period Congress became involved in an accelerating national debate over the consequences of 'automation', a term for the mechanical and electronic techniques and equipment used to control the production process. President Kennedy established a Labor Management Policy Committee in 1962 which argued that automation was necessary. The committee therefore called for business and government co-operation to forestall unemployment resulting from job displacement.

Congress passed several measures designed to offset technological unemployment during the mid-1960s. The National Commission on Technology, Automation, and Economic Progress, established by Congress in 1964, accurately predicted in 1966 that during the following decade growth would occur in service-producing occupations. By the late 1960s only 1.5 per cent of the workforce were in advanced automated industries, while around 4.5 per cent worked in settings where automated production was just beginning. As the shift to service employment continued during the 1960s and 1970s, so did the demand for labour; typically, those workers on the unemployment rolls lacked the experience to fill the jobs listed in the advertisements. In the latter years of the 1960s the shortage of workers for highly skilled occupations was more of a problem than high rates of unemployment among surplus workers. During the 1970s, also, the demand for labour continued to rise despite the general slowdown of productivity. Demand for labour expanded, both in absolute numbers and in the ratio of employees to the working age population. So did the imbalance between labour demand and supply. This was dramatically clear after 1979, when the unemployment rate due to recession edged up to 10 per cent, while at the same time industries requiring highly skilled personnel could not find workers to fill jobs.

In the fastest growing occupations during the post-war period – professionals, technical specialists, medical specialists, engineers and clerical employees – new machines changed the nature of work and created entirely new occupations. Attorneys and physicians have by necessity become more specialised as their knowledge has expanded with the use of electronic information retrieval systems. Both professions also came to depend upon such machinery and the technicians who operate it. The field of medicine has been transformed in two decades as technical workers have become indispensable in administering and interpreting the results of patient tests carried out by sophisticated machinery. The number of engineers in the workforce doubled between 1950 and 1970, while the machines produced by these engineers spawned a vast array of technical jobs filled by computer programmers, as well as machine operators. Computer specialists, whose numbers more than doubled between 1972 and 1981, were not even listed as an occupation by the Department of Labor in 1949.

The advent of punched-card data processing after the Second World War revolutionised the work of clerical employees, and in 1951 the first large-scale electronic computer, UNIVAC, was installed in the US Bureau of the Census. Up to 1955 scarcely two dozen computers were operating in the US but there were 11,000 by 1960, and double that number in 1965. Larger businesses adopted computers to keep track of payroll records, issue cheques, control inventories, and oversee the paying of bills. During the 1970s, micro-electronics and solid-state circuitry led to smaller and cheaper computers, inexpensive copying machines, word processors and micro-computers for office work. Between 1972 and 1980 the number of telephone operators, stenographers and keypunch operators declined, and the number of typists increased less than 5 per cent. Jobs for secretaries increased by about 30 per cent, but the real growth in office work took place among computer and other machine operators whose numbers increased by over 170 per cent.

THE QUALITY OF WORKING LIFE AND THE MEANING OF WORK

As the workforce changed in response to the rise of service industries, and as workplace conditions were increasingly affected by mechan-isation, both corporate management and labour leaders, in co-operation with the federal government, sought to maintain and enhance workers' satisfaction. The impact of mechanisation on the actual conditions of work has varied enormously, and the testimony of workers in public opinion polls offered a similar diversity. Empirical research designed to test whether the evolution of the labour force and changes in the work process have destroyed worker's skills and reduced their autonomy and control over their work has yielded ambiguous results.[8] Nonetheless the presumption that a satisfied worker is one who participates in workplace decisions has received impressive confirmation during the post-war years, and some attempts have been made to democratise and humanise the work-place. Employees themselves, especially since the 1960s, have demonstrated their own concern for the quality of their working lives through the techniques they have adopted to increase leisure time, add variety to their working careers, and limit the significance of their jobs as an indicator of success and well-being.

During the 1950s, as white-collar and service occupations grew steadily, the number of manufacturing workers increased slowly. Machine operators in manufacturing grew by less than 1 per cent, and machinists and unskilled workers in auto plants declined in number. The numbers of foremen in manufacturing, however, increased by over 40 per cent. The combined experience of closer supervision, greater attention to productivity and automation of the work process stimulated dissatisfaction among factory workers. Workers in service jobs, like blue-collar employees generally, watched professional and managerial incomes rise 68 per cent, while their own wages increased only 39 per cent. Ely Chinoy, interviewing automobile workers during the early 1950s, found the great majority so dissatisfied with the unrelenting pace and numbing monotony of their jobs that they talked about leaving the factory even though they had no alternative employment. But the longer they worked in the auto plant, the less they fantasised about entering business or starting a farm. Small increments in wages and security took the place of independence in their aspirations. Chinoy found that some workers blamed themselves for their failure to move beyond factory work, like the unskilled 38 year old man who had worked in the plant since graduating from high school. 'I bought a car and that was my downfall. I couldn't afford to leave if I was going to have the car. Then I got married – and I certainly couldn't afford to quit.' Most of the workers, however, rationalised their behaviour and defined achievement 'to include the search for security, the pursuit of small goals in the factory, and the constant accumulation of personal possessions'.[9]

Sociologist C. Wright Mills, in his 1951 study of white-collar workers, found similar evidence of self-depreciation, rationalisation and redefinition of success among the growing numbers of professional and service employees. These were 'the new little Machiavellians, practicing their personable crafts for hire and for the profit of others, according to rules laid down by those above them'. Mills described 'the new little people, the unwilling vanguard of modern society', as 'hollow people' who accepted their working roles like 'cheerful robots', and he also pointed to a feature of working life which became increasingly significant during the 1960s and 1970s.

All four aspects of occupation – skill, power, income, and status – must be taken into account to understand the meaning of work and the sources of its gratification. Any one of them may become the foremost aspect of the job, and in various combinations each is usually in the consciousness of the employee. To achieve and to exercise the power and status that higher income entails may be the very definition of satisfaction in work.[10]

Five national surveys of American attitudes made between 1957 and 1978 reinforced the important distinctions between skill, income, status and power that Mills stressed in *White Collar*. People with high incomes have consistently been more likely to describe themselves as very happy, and those with low incomes more often complain of hard lives, poor health and inadequate housing. High status has uniformly been assigned to professional workers such as physicians and scientists; service workers without skills have been at the bottom of the occupational ladder. Americans in the prestigous professions believed that they had more happiness than they expected, whereas blue-collar workers have reconciled themselves to receiving less personal satisfaction than they anticipated. Clerical and sales workers have typically responded with mixed feelings; poorly paid and unable to claim the status associated with professional work, about half of them reported satisfaction, the other half dissatisfaction.

Whether a job is considered interesting or challenging is the criterion which has consistently determined whether workers find their work satisfying, according to the five national surveys. Here again, the professional workers have been most satisfied and the operatives and service workers less satisfied. On the other hand, impressive majorities of both men and women have claimed in all five surveys that they were satisfied with their jobs. Although often discontented with particular aspects of working conditions, wages or personnel policies, about one-third have reported being completely satisfied and most of the others have been more satisfied than dissatisfied. Simply being able to hold a job proved an important criterion for personal satisfaction, as witnessed by the emotional distress reported by the unemployed. Like Ely Chinoy in his autoworker study of 1951, an analyst at the University of Michigan in 1981 stressed that job satisfaction has been consistently higher among older workers. Such a worker, having accepted the limits imposed by his occupation, brings 'aspirations into close relation with his achievements. The satisfaction he expresses results from this accommodation.'[11]

It was mainly the younger members of the workforce, with no personal memory of the Great Depression and with higher expectations than their parents, who brought quality of work life issues to public attention during the late 1960s and early 1970s. Using absenteeism and tardiness as ways of expressing their rebellion against management discipline, factory workers in the automobile industry provoked the UAW vice-president, Douglas Fraser, into admitting that 'the young workers won't accept the same kind of discipline their fathers did'. The issue assumed front page importance in March 1972, when workers at the Chevrolet Vega plant in Lordstown, Ohio, called a strike to protest about recently instituted procedures designed to increase productivity by speeding up the assembly line.

In the flurry of public discussion that followed the Lordstown strike (over 140 books and articles sought to measure its implications), business, labour and the federal government addressed themselves to the complaints dramatised by the young strikers (whose average age was 29) at the Vega plant. Following the lead of earlier sociological studies by Elton Mayo and Fritz Roethlisberger that demonstrated how worker participation in decisions increased their sense of well-being, some corporations instituted 'job enrichment' programmes; over 2,000 such innovations were under way in 1974. The Federal Department of Health, Education, and Welfare endorsed proposals to redesign jobs, making them more 'humanistic', in its 1972 report on *Work in America*, and Congress established the Center for Productivity and the Quality of Working Life in 1975. The concern for productivity (and corporate earnings) symbolised in the title of the Congressional centre illustrated the adversarial approach of business and labour that was expressed in Congressional hearings and reports on the nature of working life. The AFL-CIO itself adopted a defensive position on the matter, for it was generally reluctant to give issues of 'humanizing the workplace' equal weight with wages and benefits in the collective bargaining process. Lagging productivity and rising unemployment after 1974, in the end, rendered the issues increasingly academic. By 1977, one sociologist concluded that 'the problems *of* work in America seem to have given way to the problems of *getting* work in America'.[12]

4. Regional Metamorphosis

THE driving forces of business investment and federal government activism fostered a metamorphosis in the regional distribution of population, jobs and income during the post-war period. Combined with the cultural predispositions of most Americans, regardless of class or ethnicity, to seek urban amenities with low population density, the dynamics of American capitalism since 1945 propelled the West and the South into the front ranks of metropolitan America. The older metropolitan areas of the Northeastern and North Central states likewise experienced dramatic change as they either took advantage of the new economic and social realities or suffered their consequences.

Journalists during the 1960s and 1970s popularised the phrases 'westward tilt' and 'the rise of the Sunbelt' to evoke the drama of the regional metamorphosis, but business leaders and government bureaucrats started the process in motion, and its genesis came during the Second World War. Shipyards and staging areas for the Pacific theatre, aircraft plants and ordnance factories, like the military bases and research centres that grew up overnight in southwestern deserts, all absorbed thousands of temporary residents between 1942 and 1945. While the war may have triggered the new regional growth machine, the migration of the new residents to southern and western metropolitan areas kept it humming along at high speed after 1945. The military personnel, war workers and their families who had migrated to San Diego or Portland, Houston or Miami, or returned to the US through San Francisco, stayed to make a living.

By the end of the decade, Houston's population of 596,000 surpassed its 1940 figure of 385,000. By 1970, the metropolitan populations of the 'Southern Rim' and Pacific Coast had increased to

13.4 million in California, 5.8 million in Texas, 3.8 million in Florida and 2 million in Virginia. Between 1940 and 1970, the West and South went from 42 to 48 per cent of the total US population, and to 50 per cent by 1976. Their share of total US personal income increased likewise, from 33 to 43 per cent between 1940 and 1970.

A REGIONAL PROFILE AT MID-CENTURY

The economic power bloc among the US regions at mid-century was unquestionably the southern New England, Middle Atlantic and Great Lakes states that made up the manufacturing belt of the nation. This area – sometimes termed the 'American Ruhr' – still contained 46 per cent of total US population in 1957, only 3 per cent less than at the turn of the century. With 64 per cent of the total manufacturing employment and 53 per cent of total personal income, this great industrial heartland justifiably advertised itself to the world as the foundation of America's vast productive capacity.[1]

At the same time, four states within this regional powerhouse were experiencing relative decline: New York, Pennsylvania, Massachusetts and Rhode Island. Two of the five regions showing high relative growth rates in population, to be sure, fell within the manufacturing belt: the eastern Great Lakes states and the Atlantic Seaboard states. The other three most rapidly growing regions were in the Sunbelt: the Far West, the Southwest and Florida.

Population growth during the 1940s pointed to the increasing importance of the South and the West. Until the 1930s the manufacturing-belt states had surpassed the national average in their rates of population growth alongside the West. During the 1940s only the Southwest, the Rocky Mountain states, and the Far West populations grew faster than the national average, and the southeastern states for the first time (except for the Depression decade) added population at higher rates than the Middle Atlantic states. The Far West's population was nearly two-thirds urbanised, about the same proportion as the Great Lakes states, and the southwestern states, with 55 per cent urban population, were more urbanised than the Great Plains or southeastern states. By mid-century all of the Southern Rim and Mountain states were becoming urban faster than the manufacturing-belt states. Michigan's urban growth around Detroit due to the automobile industry allowed it to grow by almost

10 percentage points since 1910. All of the other leaders in urbanisation stood outside the manufacturing belt, with California, Texas, Florida and North Carolina at the top of the list.

Changes in economic productivity and employment rates likewise demonstrated the rise of the West and the South during the 1940s and early 1950s. In agriculture and mining, industries where employment nationwide declined, the West and the South showed smaller declines or healthy increases. Eleven states experienced significant shifts in mining employment; two-thirds of the increases came in Texas and Louisiana, and three-fourths of the declines occurred in Pennsylvania, West Virginia and Kentucky. These latter three had been the leading coal-mining states. The four states that produced most of the nation's oil and natural gas, however (California, Texas, Oklahoma and Louisiana), added thousands of workers. Employment in oil and natural gas in those states increased over 90 per cent between 1939 and 1954. Along with Kansas, these states produced 85 per cent of total oil and natural gas and employed 78 per cent of workers in these industries. The states that made the greatest increases in their workforce in the production of salt, gypsum, potash, phosphates, sand, gravel, stone, clay and other non-metal mining were also Sunbelt states, whereas New York, New Jersey, Pennsylvania and Ohio all experienced declines.

From 1939 to mid-century the US agricultural workforce declined about 15 per cent, with the largest numerical losses taking place in the deep South and Texas, followed by the New England states (except Maine), New York, Ohio, West Virginia and Virginia. Missouri and Oklahoma also experienced absolute declines in agricultural workers. California, however, increased its farm worker population by nearly 25 per cent, and Florida, Arizona, New Mexico and the Mountain states also added agricultural workers. Because of mechanisation and other factors, fifteen of the fifty states made absolute increases in the value of their farm produce. Seven of these fifteen were Sunbelt states. California and Florida, along with Arizona and the southeastern states all substantially increased the value of their field crops, livestock, poultry, fruit and nut crops and vegetables by the mid-1950s. Agricultural productivity in the Northeast, on the other hand, either declined or grew very modestly.

The westward and southern shift also appeared in manufacturing, which in 1954 absorbed 28 per cent of the total US labour force. The two leaders in employment increases in manufacturing were California and Texas, although all of the Sunbelt states except North and South Carolina added factory workers. On the other hand, all of the northeastern states except Ohio and Indiana experienced relative or absolute declines in manufacturing employment. In food-processing industries, such as meat-packing and dairy products, the Sunbelt, spurred by population and income increases as well as by technology, increased its ability to supply its own needs. Food-processing employees declined, however, in all of the northeastern states except for Wisconsin. The textile industry, which lost almost half its workforce during the 1940s and early 1950s, was dominated by five southeastern states: North and South Carolina, Georgia, Alabama and Virginia. New York City employed nearly 35 per cent of all workers in the garment industry, which like textiles experienced slow growth in the early post-war years. New York state, however, like New Jersey, Michigan and Wisconsin lost jobs in the garment industry relative to their earlier share of the total, and Connecticut, Ohio, Indiana and Illinois suffered declines in absolute numbers. All of the Sunbelt states, except New Mexico, increased their workforce in the garment industry, California by 13 per cent. The record of furniture, paper products and chemical industries was much the same. For manufacturing in general, the 1940s witnessed a shift from the traditional factory belt of the older regions to the Southwest and the West.

The Sunbelt as a whole, from Virginia to Texas, and from New Mexico to the state of Washington, led in the growth of service industries at mid-century. Employment growth in wholesale and retail trade, transportation and public utilities, finance and real estate, plus government and miscellaneous services, soared between 11 and 30 per cent in Florida, Texas and California. Elsewhere, with only a few exceptions, the growth rate in service employment ranged from a low of 0.1 per cent in Mississippi to 4.9 per cent in Michigan.

Of all the regions that grew quickly during the 1940s and early 1950s, the Far West made the greatest gains, and California provided most of the impetus. Its population increase of nearly 6 million, about three times higher than any other state, included substantial numbers of retired persons with incomes who sought out the southern California sun and the sands of Pacific beaches. California's share of the US population increased even faster than its share of US employment, and its urbanisation rate put it among the leaders in the nation. Manufacturing gave the Golden State much of its strength by mid-century, and almost half of its manufacturing capacity was devoted to transportation equipment. The aircraft factories of southern California fostered much of this development, but the decentralisation of the automobile assembly process also played a part. Following manufacturing, government employment, state and local as well as federal, was central to California's growth, with agriculture close behind. The state's cotton, vegetables, fruits, nuts and horticulture had made impressive showings in the national market by mid-century. Los Angeles's location gave the state access to regional markets, and the growth of California's population and income allowed its home market to boom in the decade after 1945.

Florida's growth in the early post-war years was second only to California's, but the two states differed in several respects. Florida's economy was considerably less diverse than California's; it had no regional metropolis comparable in function to Los Angeles (Atlanta occupied that position in the South); and it lacked the educational institutions that attracted the growing high-technology industries to California. Like the Golden State, though, Florida's share of US population had grown faster than its share of employment, while construction, trades and services provided much of its employment growth.

The single most important ingredient in the growth of Texas, the nation's third most rapidly developing state, was oil. In the space of a decade the Lone Star state had come to produce half of all US petroleum and a good deal of its sulphur and salt. Texas had also become a growing power in oil refining (27 per cent of the national total), chemical, rubber, glass, aluminium, and even steel production by the mid-1950s. Like California, government employment in Texas also increased rapidly, much of it (as in California) related to military contracts.

The Sunbelt states of California, Texas and Florida showed the greatest rates of growth during the early post-war years, but Michigan, Indiana and Ohio, along with Connecticut, New Jersey, Delaware and Maryland continued to expand their economies as well. By mid-century, the Great Lakes states had become so specialised that their strength depended upon the manufacturing of metal products, rubber and chemicals. The Atlantic coast states became prosperous for different reasons. Maryland and the District of Columbia housed the growing numbers of federal government employees; Delaware and New Jersey expanded their production of market gardening for the surrounding metropolitan populations, New Jersey and Connecticut attracted wholesale trade and financial services.

All of these healthy areas in older regions, however, had begun to show unmistakable evidence that their former dominant role in the nation's manufacturing was threatened by the movement of automobile, furniture, paper, tobacco, textiles, apparel and leather production into the regions of rapid growth. This phenomenon affected the core of the manufacturing-belt region to the extent that Massachusetts, Rhode Island and Pennsylvania, as well as Illinois and New York, were actually part of a declining region by mid-century. New York and Illinois, furthermore, demonstrated even faster relative decline in their traditional activities (centred in New York City and Chicago) as leaders of the nation's wholesaling, finance and insurance, transportation and public utility sectors. After a decade of post-war prosperity, the regional distribution of population, jobs and income demonstrated the vitality of the West and the South, as well as the signs of decrepitude appearing in the older industrial heartland. The nation was poised on the brink of a regional metamorphosis.

GOVERNMENT AS AN ENGINE OF REGIONAL GROWTH

We have seen in Chapters 1 and 2 how business and labour used government to further their economic goals. Western and southern business and labour leaders, and their organisations, used government as a tool for inducing regional growth during the post-war years. At the same time, their counterparts in the Northeast and North Central regions asked government to ease the effects of competition and unemployment. During the 1950s, southern and western business organisations successfully campaigned for right-to-work laws that helped keep unions out, wage rates low and the 'business climate' salubrious. During the 1960s and 1970s, southern and western state and local governments, typically more responsive to business lobbyists than to labour activists, established a pro-growth policy of low tax rates and financial incentives designed to attract new manufacturing firms as well as fast-growing service industries. Jacksonville, Florida, for example, tempted a Westinghouse Corporation subsidiary with an industrial site of 850 acres. The city agreed to build an access bridge costing $137 million and pledged to maintain it free of charge. In addition, Jacksonville agreed to buy two of the company's generating systems for its municipal power plant ($2.2 billion), to market bonds worth $180 million to provide the company with working capital, and to build a vocational training centre ($11 million) for company employees.[2] Incentives such as these, it should be stressed, succeeded more in attracting new industry to the West and the South than in drawing old industries from the Northeast and North Central states.[3] During the late 1970s and the first years of the 1980s, faster growing parts of the Sunbelt, particularly Texas, successfully used such techniques to convince new industries that location in slower growing California would be a liability rather than an asset.

Federal government support also provided a boost to southern and western development. From Franklin D. Roosevelt's administration through to the presidency of Jimmy Carter federal government spending to stimulate economic demand served the Sunbelt region well. The public investments in roads, water, electric power, sewerage and other municipal facilities encouraged private investment in manufacturing and service industries. A Texas case illustrates a typical process. Co-operation between Humble Oil Company (later Exxon Corporation), Rice University, Texas representatives in Congress, and Vice-President Lyndon B. Johnson resulted in choosing a site near Houston for the manned spacecraft centre of the National Aeronautics and Space Administration (NASA) in 1963. The land, given to the university by Humble, was then donated to the federal government for NASA's use. Once the NASA project was under way, a real estate development firm that was a subsidiary of Humble began constructing a 15,000-acre industrial, commercial and residential community adjacent to the space centre. By the mid-1970s, about 4,000 scientists, engineers, technicians and administrators worked at the renamed Johnson Space Center, and another 7,000 employees worked in adjacent companies on NASA contract jobs. The total payroll brought some $150 million to the local economy.[4]

Defence-related projects such as the manned space flight centre aided the economies of Massachusetts, New York, Illinois and Maryland during the 1960s, as well as the economy of Texas. The greatest beneficiaries, however, were the far western states. With less than one-sixth of the US population, these thirteen states by the time of the Vietnam War had developed research and industrial firms sufficient to attract one-fourth of all Department of Defense (DOD) civilian and military personnel, one-third of major military contracts, one-half of all research and development awards, and two-thirds of the work on missile research. NASA spent nearly half of its budget in the western states during the 1960s. By 1980, the West plus the South housed 83 per cent of all DOD personnel and 71 per cent of its major installations.

The fastest growing state in this region during the 1950s and 1960s was California, and defence spending was the single most important factor in California's spectacular growth in the two decades after 1945. Defence spending stimulated subsequent development of the California economy during the 1970s, allowing it to become an international leader in high-technology research and production.

CALIFORNIA: THE PRIME CASE OF REGIONAL METAMORPHOSIS

The Second World War set in motion a massive migration to California and made it the US leader in aircraft and ship products. The war also propelled the state into the front ranks of defence-oriented scientific research and development. Dr. E. O. Lawrence, a physicist who had built his first cyclotron in 1930, presided over the rise of the Radiation Laboratory at the University of California, Berkeley, to one of the nation's leading centres for research in theoretical physics. Enrico Fermi, J. Robert Oppenheimer, and a distinguished staff worked under Lawrence's direction doing research on elements 93 and 94, later used in constructing the atomic bomb. Charles L. Lauritsen headed a research team at Cal Tech in Pasadena that worked on weapons research, particularly on rockets. Lauritsen consulted with Oppenheimer, then director of the Los Alamos laboratory that built the atomic bomb, and the Cal Tech team created some of the components necessary for the A-bomb's explosive system. With $83 million from the Office of Scientific Research and Development, the main federal agency supervising wartime scientific research, Cal Tech received the second highest number of contracts (MIT was first). The University of California at Berkeley was number five, with $15 million worth of contracts.

With the onset of the Cold War in 1946, California's scientific and research facilities, military bases, weapons testing ranges, aircraft industry and skilled workforce made it a logical destination for federal defence dollars. The Department of Defense poured more money into California between 1946 and 1965 than into any other state. At the beginning of the 1960s, California had more active-duty military and civilian DOD personnel than any other state, and military payrolls added over $1 million per day to the burgeoning economy of San Diego. By 1957, industries that designed and produced aircraft, missiles and electronic products employed some 400,000 workers. These firms alone produced 20 per cent of the employment increase in California between 1947 and 1957, and if the multiplier effects of the defence-oriented industries are considered, fully half of the state's employment growth during that decade can be attributed to defence spending.

Beginning in 1953, California surpassed New York as the Defense Department's major source of supplies, services and construction. From 1951 to 1965, $67.2 billion (20 per cent of the total) of DOD contracts came to California, and between 1961 and 1965, another $5.3 billion in NASA contracts came to the state (41 per cent of NASA's spending). During the period 1946–65, $28.9 billion worth of wages and salaries were generated by direct defence spending in the state. Although some portion of these monies did not remain in California because of subcontracting, most research and development awards were retained. A very high percentage of its initial grants likewise stayed in the state. In addition, California received numerous contracts initially made to other states. When all the defence money expended in California from 1946 to 1965 is tallied, it amounts to more than two-thirds of all business expenditures on new plants and equipment for durable goods in the nation during those years, and nearly as much as the US spent on economic and military aid to Europe and the Far East.

California attracted defence spending after the war because of the stimulus provided by the federal government's wartime aircraft manufacturing programme. Thomas C. Werbe, Jr., Deputy Assistant Secretary of Defense in charge of supply and logistics, explained this phenomenon shortly before President Eisenhower in 1960 warned the nation about the dangers of the 'military-industrial complex'. California's success, said Werbe, is 'primarily a product of the upward trend in military procurement of aircraft, missiles, associated electronics, and related research and development work, and the existence in California of substantial research, development and production facilities that are able to compete successfully for this work.' During the 1950s, the state continued to finance the development of scientific and technological education at the University of California, Berkeley, Stanford University and Cal Tech, and graduates of these schools characteristically remained in the state. In 1959, over one-fifth of the National Academy of Science lived in California, including eleven Nobel Prize winners. In addition to the three world-famous institutions at Berkeley, Stanford and Pasadena, the state also had more than two dozen highly respected scientific facilities. The state also benefited from the DOD's practice of awarding a contract for an entire weapons system (e.g. the B-70 bomber) to a single firm. Because this policy tended to favour large aircraft firms, half of which were in California, the state's firms were able to expand their operations by doing the work themselves rather than subcontracting to more specialised companies. California firms also tried to secure and maintain their high level of success in winning contracts by hiring recently retired military personnel with Pentagon connections as company officers. This 'revolving door' policy, though regulated by Congressional legislation passed in 1960, became a standard feature of national life during the 1960s and 1970s.[5]

By the time of the Kennedy administration (1961–3), defence-related production was California's most significant manufacturing industry. Of the 661,000 new manufacturing jobs created between 1950 and 1963, more than 60 per cent were in aerospace industries alone (ordnance, electrical equipment, aircraft and instruments). The infusion of federal contracts into the state allowed it to weather the recession of 1954 with lower unemployment than the national average and cushioned California during the 1958 recession as well. When the DOD shifted its priorities from aircraft to missiles, over 120,000 workers lost jobs in the aircraft industry, but while individual workers suffered, the California economy maintained its momentum. In the Los Angeles–Long Beach area, some 80,000 workers were laid off between 1957 and 1963. At the same time 90,000 new jobs opened in electrical machinery and ordnance industries. Defence employment in 1963 stood at 27 per cent of all manufacturing jobs in the state and 8 per cent of its total civilian labour force. Probably, and this is a conservative estimate, one-third of all non-agricultural workers in California during the early 1960s were dependent upon defence expenditures. One study in 1966 concluded that defence spending between 1957 and 1962 accounted for 17.2 per cent of California personal income and between 20 and 27 per cent of the growth in income from outside the state.

In 1967 employment in aerospace industries peaked at one-third of all California manufacturing jobs, with 596,999 workers. From 1967 to 1971, however, the DOD and NASA made sharp cuts in spending. DOD contracts dropped from $6,689 million to $5,293 million (a cut of 20.9 per cent), and NASA contracts fell from $1,563 million to $523 million (a 66.5 per cent cut). The workforce, especially those in ordnance who produced space and military missiles, was cut by 26.2 per cent down to 440,300 workers.

By 1977 aerospace employment was almost back at its 1967 peak with 560,600 workers, and California's share of the total defence funds for the 1972–80 years averaged 17.2 per cent. Throughout the 1970s military expenditures were more important to California's economy than to the US economy as a whole. In 1980, 17.5 per cent of all direct military expenditures were in California. The greatest share were contracts for RDTE (research, development, testing and evaluation), construction and services. California captured 19.3 per cent of total US contracts and 14.8 per cent of total US payroll. Between 1972 and 1980 California maintained a fairly constant share of military expenditures. The proportion of total military expenditures fluctuated around 17.2 per cent.[6]

The geographic dispersal of defence spending helped to shape the pattern of California's growth during the Cold War period. During 1946 to 1965 virtually all defence spending for production and research, along with NASA funds, went to Los Angeles, San Diego, Santa Clara and Orange counties. Most military and civilian DOD personnel were stationed at marine and navy bases in San Diego, Ford Ord (Monterey) and around the San Francisco Bay Area.

Los Angeles County, however, took the bulk of defence production monies, some $50 billion worth of value. Between 1950 and 1962 alone, despite cutbacks in aircraft production after 1957, the number of manufacturing employees soared by 92 per cent. Employment in electrical machinery and parts production increased an incredible 568 per cent, and one analyst put the proportion of the county's workforce in defence industries during the mid-1960s at over 50 per cent.

Orange, San Diego and Santa Clara counties likewise increased their manufacturing employment during the 1950s and 1960s because of defence spending. Orange County's tenfold increase in manufacturing was almost completely accounted for by the electrical industry. San Diego increased its manufacturing by 276 per cent from 1950 to 1963. During the same years 70 per cent of its manufacturing workforce was directly involved in defence work. Santa Clara County's manufacturing workers increased 444 per cent during the same period, with electrical machinery employment rising a phenomenal 600 per cent.

During the 1950s, the three California cities that grew fastest in manufacturing employment – Los Angeles, San Diego and San Jose – were also the leading cities in the state's population growth. Most of the increase occurred in Los Angeles County, with Orange, San Diego, Santa Clara and Sacramento counties following. Los Angeles County grew more than any other US county during the 1950s, adding 1,171,000 persons. The majority of the fastest growing parts of these counties were directly dependent on defence industries. Anaheim and Fullerton, with increases of 616 per cent and 303 per cent, were the most important defence contract areas of Orange County. Sunnyvale, with a 438 per cent population increase, was the home of Lockheed Aircraft's Missile System Division, which in 1959 alone received a contract worth $400 million. Mountain View, another Santa Clara County growth area during the 1950s, contained a major jet airbase and numerous aerospace and electronics laboratories and had a 307 per cent rate of population increase. James L. Clayton, author of the most comprehensive study of the impact of the Cold War on California economic growth between 1946 and 1965, concluded that it is 'inescapable that defense spending has been the primary reason for California's rapid population growth since World War II. Other factors, such as an attractive climate and a substantial number of persons seeking retirement in California, have been important as an attractive force, but not of the same magnitude as defense jobs.'[7]

The leverage provided by military-industrial development after the Second World War placed Los Angeles County among the world leaders of economic productivity. The Los Angeles area is now the world's fourth largest urban area in population. Its gross product amounted to about $125 billion in 1982, making it number 20 among the world's nations. The gross domestic products of Belgium, Czechoslovakia and Switzerland, as well as Indonesia and Korea, were lower. As the major contributor to California's economy, Los Angeles County produced more than a third of the state's gross state product; half a million jobs were created there between 1972 and 1982, and some 45,000 new jobs were added in 1982. With its almost 7.6 million residents and more than 3.3 million labour force, Los Angeles stood as the second largest centre of population and employment in the United States. Of the 100 largest industrial and merchandising firms in California, 63 have headquarters in LA County; its large and highly diversified economy stands firmly upon a base of manufacturing, trade and service sectors. Manufacturing accounted for about one-quarter of the county's total employment in 1982, and 30 per cent of those jobs were in the defence and aerospace industries. Los Angeles also accounts for about 30 per cent of all tourist spending in California, and it is the North American continent's leading trade gateway to the Pacific Basin. The Los Angeles–Long Beach harbours and airport facilities constitute the third largest port system in the US in dollar volume of trade.

In 1982 the county with the largest share of military contracts after Los Angeles was Santa Clara. Located just south of San Francisco, Santa Clara is one of the nine counties that make up the greater San Francisco Bay Area, and as of mid-1983, Santa Clara County is the centre of high technology in the United States. Approximately one-third of all semi-conductors, one-fifth of all guided missiles and space vehicles, and one-eighth of all computers made in the United States come from Santa Clara. During 1982 its firms shipped some $10 billion in high-technology products.

During the 1970s Santa Clara County's economic growth was stimulated most by high-technology industries. Of the 125,000 manufacturing jobs added since 1971, 101,600 were in four categories: computing equipment, electronic computers and accessories, communications equipment and technical instruments. The proportion of the workforce employed in electronics manufacturing has also been rising faster than that of the state as a whole. In 1982, 33.9 per cent of electronics employment in California was in Santa Clara County: in 1973, the proportion had been only 25.3 per cent.

Electronics first developed as an adjunct to the aerospace industry during the Second World War, but it has since become a separate and identifiable sector. The industry's critical invention, the vacuum tube, took place in Palo Alto (Santa Clara County) in 1913. Although the industry developed in New England, with important research at

MIT, Harvard and the Bell Telephone Laboratories, federal grants encouraged applications to aerospace technology in California during the Second World War. Federal government grants provided further stimulus to westward migration after they were used to establish the Stanford Research Institute and the National Advisory Committee of Aeronautics. The transistor was invented in 1946, and by 1949 California employed an average of 32,400 workers in electronics compared to 79,300 in traditional aerospace. Over the years, the industry evolved from a supplier for the government sector to a non-defence capital goods industry. The ratio between the two sectors evened out in the early 1960s when the integrated circuit came on the scene, leading directly to the development of the memory chip in 1970. In 1982 over 368,000 workers were employed in the electronic sector, compared to 250,000 in the aerospace sector.

Currently, about 85 per cent of California's electronics industry employees produce components, communications equipment and computers. About two-thirds of these employees are located in Los Angeles and Santa Clara counties, but a growing number are finding work in San Diego and Orange counties. In addition to the shift from aerospace to industrial and commercial uses, there has been a shift in activity from Los Angeles to Santa Clara County where components and office computing and accounting equipment dominate the industry.

Two of the nation's ten fastest growing publicly owned firms were located in Santa Clara by the early 1980s. Apple Computer, with headquarters in Cupertino, was the fastest growing firm in the nation with sales that grew 356 per cent between 1977 and 1981. ASK Computer Systems, with Los Altos headquarters, experienced a 156 per cent annual increase in sales revenues during the same period. Both of these firms maintained their momentum during 1982; Apple's sales went up 74 per cent to more than $500 million, and ASK's sales reached $23 million after a 75 per cent increase.

By 1980 one out of every ten Americans lived in California, the most populous state since the 1970 census. Los Angeles County had the largest population of all USA counties, and the Los Angeles metropolitan area stood in second rank following New York. The nation's largest numbers of Mexican-Americans, Chinese and Filipinos lived in California, and more Japanese lived in California than in any other state but Hawaii. California had more motor vehicles than any other state, and only Texas outranked it in interstate highway mileage. With the largest labour force the state led all others in economic output and total personal income. If it were actually a nation, California would be among the economic leaders and would surpass Canada, Italy and Brazil. California was the nation's number one agricultural and industrial state. It produced 10 per cent of the nation's cash farm receipts with only 3 per cent of the farms and farm acreage. California stood in first place in 1978 in the manufacture of food products, machinery, electric and electronic equipment, aerospace, dairy products and beef cattle, as well as ranking first in retail sales, foreign trade and corporate profits. The California government's general budget ranked number one in both revenue and expenditure, and a greater number of Californians received public assistance than residents of any other state. California also led the nation in its number of public and private schools, public school students, college students, graduates of high schools and colleges, and total educational funding.

Not surprisingly, California's reputation during the 1960s and 1970s attracted migrants from all over the world who wanted to share in what its boosters called 'the California spirit'. Governor Edmund G. (Jerry) Brown, Jr. (1975–82) did nothing to dispel such self-congratulation by describing the state as 'The Pacific Republic of California'. Actually, by the time Brown began his campaign for a new humanistic-technological era, California's growth had begun to lag relative to other parts of the Sunbelt and Mountain states, and its critics, some of them with undisguised pleasure, argued that its time in the sun had come and gone. Other critics, expressing what one federal grants official described as 'California envy', argued that the Golden State had been unfairly advantaged by government largesse. Equity, according to this argument, required federal government regional aid programmes that would allow slow-growing, and declining, regions to adjust to their subordinate status relative to California and the West and South generally.

SUNBELT VERSUS FROSTBELT

California and Texas dramatically demonstrated the growing importance of the South and West, but states such as Virginia, Georgia, Colorado and Oregon, more representative of these regions, also developed their economic independence of the older regions and increased their national importance. As the West and South as a whole continued the growth trajectory that California, Texas and Florida had demonstrated at mid-century, the Northeast and North Central states lost more and more of their economic power. Between 1960 and 1975, jobs in the South and West increased by 70 per cent (compared to the national increase of 46.6 per cent), but the Northeast and North Central regions showed increases of only 21.7 and 36.2 per cent. During the economic downturn of 1970–5, the Northeast lost over 35,000 jobs, while the South gained so many (3.3 million) that it accounted for over half of all US new economic growth during the five-year period. The picture in manufacturing was similar. While US manufacturing employment grew slowly between 1960 and 1975, the South added nearly 1.5 million jobs in manufacturing, the North Central region grew slightly, and the Northeast lost 781,000 manufacturing jobs. Between 1975 and 1981, the Northeast created one new job for every ten, and the North Central region made one for every eight. The South, however, boomed ahead with one new job for every four in 1975, and the West created one for every three. The West and the South also showed the greatest growth in construction, income and, of course, population. During the 1970s, the South and West added 21 million new residents compared to the 76,000 of the Northeast and the 2.3 million of the North Central region.

The growth differentials between the South and West and the older manufacturing belt continued to increase during the latter part of the 1970s. Congressional delegations and governors from states burdened with declining 'sunset' industries plunged headlong into political lobbying aimed at redirecting federal economic aid to their benefit. Their southern and western counterparts did likewise, their hand strengthened by the steady shift of Congressional seats from the Frostbelt states to the Sunbelt (17, for example, in 1982 alone). In 1976, *Business Week* predicted a 'new war between the states' over federal aid, and certainly the stakes were high enough to warrant political combat: over $90 billion in federal grants-in-aid during 1981, as well as income from conventions, urban development and new jobs. By 1983, the Reagan administration (heavily stacked with western and southern Republicans) argued that regional differences were fading to the point that the federal government could reduce its counter-cyclical economic aid to distressed regions, states and local governments. The Northeast-Midwest Congressional Coalition, on the other hand (strongly Democratic), argued that regional disparities, particularly in ability to raise revenue through taxation, were actually increasing. In the politics of regional development it was increasingly clear, as one scholar noted, that 'socioeconomic data are weapons rivaling pens and swords.'[8]

5.   Suburban America

AMERICANS have been moving from cities to suburbs since the nineteenth century, but America became a suburban nation only in the years after 1945. (The term 'city' refers to central city governmental units, and 'metropolitan' or 'urban' area means the central city plus the total built-up area surrounding it. The suburbs are those parts of the metropolitan area located between the city limits and the metropolitan boundaries.[1]) Between 1940 and 1980 the number of official metropolitan areas increased from 168 to 318 and urban territory occupied 16 per cent of the total land area of the US instead of 7 per cent. The metropolitan population, which grew from 69.5 million to 169.4 million, made up 74.8 per cent of the total US population instead of the 1940 figure of 52.8 per cent. The suburbs became the home of a majority of the urban population during the 1960s, and between 1940 and 1980 suburbanites grew from 32 per cent of the urban population to 60 per cent. In 1940, the suburbs housed only 15.3 per cent of the total US population; by 1980 43.4 per cent of Americans lived in suburban communities. The suburbs grew almost three times faster than the cities during the 1940s, more than four times faster during the 1950s, and more than five times faster during the 1960s. During the 1970s, when US central cities actually experienced an average annual rate of population decline of 0.1 per 1,000, the suburbs grew by 16.7 per 1,000. Suburban population increased at much higher rates than the US population as a whole for every decade since 1940.

The 1950s and 1960s witnessed the high point of post-war suburbanisation. The suburban population growth rate was 48.5 per cent compared to the 10.7 per cent growth rate of central cities, and during the 1950s the suburbs added 19 million people compared to the 6 million added by central cities. Fully 76.2 per cent of the population growth in metropolitan areas during the 1950s resulted from the suburban population boom. By 1960, nine of the nation's fifteen largest urban areas had suburban majorities compared to only three in 1950. Central cities in the West and the South were still growing during the 1950s, but elsewhere (and especially in the manufacturing belt), the suburbs grew as the cities declined. Buffalo, New York, for example, lost 8 per cent of its population while its suburbs added some 52 per cent more residents. Boston's population declined by 13 per cent, whereas its suburbs increased by 18 per cent. Six of the fifteen largest suburban areas experienced growth rates of over 100 per cent, and six others increased between 50 and 100 per cent during the 1950s. During the 1960s, however, only Houston's suburbs had more than a 100 per cent rate of increase and only four grew at rates between 50 and 100 per cent. Nonetheless, over 95 per cent of the total population growth of metropolitan areas in the 1960s was accounted for by the increase in suburban residents, and by 1970 all but two of the country's fifteen largest metropolitan areas had suburban majorities. By 1983, the multi-centred settlements of the outer metropolitan areas were overtaking the older core cities and inner suburbs as the locus of American community life.

The explosive growth of suburban populations in America's metropolitan areas occurred because of business investments, family choices and federal government policies. Federal policies facilitated business and residential migration to suburban settings, and the suburban economy grew to impressive proportions after 1945, shaping both occupations and income distribution in the suburbs. Social class and ethnic diversity have been continuous since the 1950s, but 'It would certainly not be an overstatement to claim that blacks have largely been denied entrance to the suburbs'.[2]

THE FEDERAL GOVERNMENT, BUSINESS AND THE SUBURBS

When military personnel and war industry workers resumed their civilian lives in 1946 and began to form new families, they found themselves in the midst of a housing shortage. According to 1947 estimates, between 2.7 and 4.4 million families lived in shared accommodation, and half a million resided in temporary quarters. The building industry responded to the housing demand by increasing the size and scale of its operations, and the larger firms dominated the business by the end of the 1950s. The larger firms (engaged in mass production, with over 100 employees and more than 100 houses built per year) increased their share of the market from 24 to 64 per cent between 1949 and 1959. The large firms favoured the large, inexpensive tracts of land outside city limits, where their mass production techniques could be most effective. They increased their profits by keeping land and labour costs low through buying cheaper land and adapting the assembly line to the construction business. Between 1950 and 1956 the demand for housing and the activities of the large house-building firms combined to create a monumental suburbanisation process. During those years, two-thirds of the increase in US housing units occurred in metropolitan areas, and 80 per cent of this increase took place in suburbs.

Several Congressional laws encouraged the suburban housing explosion of the early post-war period. The 1934 National Housing Act, intended to put unemployed builders to work, also established a Federal Housing Administration (FHA). This agency exercised its powers to participate in the business of house building by insuring mortgage loans made by banks and building and loan associations for the construction and sale of homes. In 1944, Congress voted to help returning GIs by passing the Servicemen's Readjustment Act. These two measures put the federal government firmly in the housing business and led to reduced loan payments, fully amortised loans, lower interest rates and lower mortgage foreclosure rates. By 1972 some 11 million families owned their own houses because of FHA assistance, 22 million had improved their properties with FHA help, and (due to FHA and Veteran's Administration aid) families living in owner-occupied units increased from 44 per cent in 1934 to 63 per cent in 1972. The federal legislation so effectively stimulated afford-able new housing during the early 1950s that families frequently could buy suburban housing for less than they would have paid for rented quarters in the city.[3]

The predominantly white families that moved to the suburbs during the 1950s and 1960s believed, like most Americans, in racial discrimination. FHA policy reinforced the existing patterns of racial segregation, since the housing agency systematically refused to assist racially mixed cities to construct new houses or improve older homes. At the same time, the FHA provided massive aid in the form of guaranteed loans to the builders and buyers of suburban properties, thus contributing to the creation of a 'white noose' around the increasingly non-white cities. The FHA and VA financed about half of all suburban housing construction during the 1950s and 1960s, and the FHA carried out what one of its administrators called 'a conservative business operation' rather than a programme of providing housing for all social groups on an equal basis. As a consequence, according to one US Senator, the federal government during the post-war period 'legitimized' the creation of 'lily-white suburbs'.

If FHA and VA housing policies helped to attract white middle-class families to suburban houses during the 1950s and 1960s, the federal public housing programme helped to push them out of the central cities. Originally passed in 1937 with support from President Roosevelt, the United States Housing Act was hailed by reformers as the first step in eradicating urban slums. Like the FHA, the Housing Act also intended to help eradicate unemployment, and while it allowed the federal government to subsidise housing projects, local governments with the approval of state legislatures had to initiate their construction. In 1962, over 2 million Americans found public housing enough of an improvement over their previous quarters to live in the nation's half million units. Compared to Britain, however, few Americans paid their rent to government landlords (in 1979, less than 2 per cent compared to over 25 per cent). For most of the first thirty years of the public housing programme, the federal administrators allowed local government housing agencies to establish racially segregated projects if they so desired. In addition, the fact that the programme emphasised slum clearance meant that most of the low-rent units were constructed in the older sections of cities. Typically, these were poor areas with high concentrations of black families. As more and more blacks moved into the high-rise 'projects' that went up in deteriorating inner city neighbourhoods during the 1950s and 1960s, the suburban alternative looked better and better to white families living nearby. Like most Americans, they tended to blame the city's social problems on the increasing numbers of black residents.

The public housing programme did not foster suburbanisation as clearly as the FHA and VA programmes. The supreme court's 1954 ruling (*Brown* v. *Board of Education, Topeka*) that segregated public schools violated the Constitution was not at all designed to contribute to the exodus of white families from the cities. But the court steadfastly refused to consider the issue of residential segregation as it affected schools. As city after city adopted school integration policies during the 1960s and 1970s, white parents, who equated increases in black school enrolment with declining educational quality, often moved to the suburbs in order to enrol their children in white schools. Court-ordered busing of children, racial antagonism between students, and disciplinary problems between teachers and students seemed antithetical to effective learning. A homogeneous white suburban school seemed much better suited to educational achievement. In 1970 twenty cities had school populations of more than 45,000 pupils. Only four of the cities had black majorities, but sixteen had school populations where blacks were in the majority. The white families which headed for surburbia hoped to leave behind urban traffic congestion and air pollution, and they looked forward to lower property tax rates and more spacious living conditions. They also wanted to leave behind urban crime and poverty, 'problems' which most Americans equated with black and other non-white city dwellers.

The federal housing programmes that were so important in developing the suburban option during the post-war years favoured the suburbs over the cities partly because legislation was shaped more by the house-building business than by the public welfare profession. Business lobbyists also shaped the federal highway legislation that led to expressway and freeway construction which, in turn, stimulated the suburban option. The housing lobby brought together trade associations representing the construction industry and the speculative sectors of the finance business. The National Association of Real Estate Boards and the National Association of Home Builders therefore played active roles in housing legislation. The highway lobby, on the other hand, drew its membership from automobile manufacturers, road contractors, oil companies, producers and distributors of construction materials and equipment, as well as from automobile clubs, trucking associations, investment bankers and state highway officials. The American Road Builders Association, with over 5,000 members drawn from all phases of the road construction industry, made itself well known in Washington and worked to convince Congress of the need to subsidise highways rather than railways or urban transit systems.

During the early 1950s leading groups within the highway lobby launched their 'Project Adequate Roads', designed to persuade the new Republican administration to support highway building. President Eisenhower, in tune with the general preference for private automobile transportation, responded with a breathtaking proposal:

the federal government would commit itself to a massive programme to build over 41,000 miles of interstate highways over a thirteen-year period. Eisenhower established an advisory committee that included top representatives from highway lobby firms, and the committee prepared a report which Eisenhower then sent to Congress. In June 1956 Congress passed (with only one opposing vote) a Highway Act which authorised the $32 billion project. The Act came at a time when the highway lobby's interests coincided with the high point of America's post-war love affair with the automobile. By the 1960s, three-fourths of urban commuters travelled to work in their own automobiles, and between 1956 and 1969 urban highway mileage increased from 36,000 to 56,000 miles. High-speed metropolitan expressways increased from 8.2 per cent of the total urban highway mileage to 34.6 per cent. The Highway Act paid fully 90 per cent of the cost of the interstate highways and 50 per cent of other federally aided road construction. The dramatic increases in highway mileage gave commuters the ability to cover larger areas in the same, or sometimes less, travelling time.

By creating the interstate highway programme, the federal government facilitated the suburbanisation of commerce, industry and services, as well as the suburbanisation of residential housing. Once the lower priced land outside city limits became accessible companies could also consider other suburban advantages, such as room for up-to-date one-storey factories, spacious parking lots, lower property taxes and easier recruitment of management and professional staff intent upon raising children in a suburban environment. Real estate developers, alert to the potential new property market, took the attitude that 'every company in a multi-storey factory in an urban location became a prospect for a new building overnight'. Manufacturers and distributors, aware that the new highways allowed high-speed connections between major metropolitan areas, chose locations at highway intersections and made the limited-access beltways around cities into 'the accidental main streets of the outer cities'.[4] Completion of the Capital Beltway surrounding Washington DC in 1962 brought about 800,000 new residents to its bordering communities during the following decade, as well as a dozen regional shopping centres catering to their needs. The desirability of such suburban locations was enhanced in 1977 by another federal action. The Interstate Commerce Commission allowed the trucking industry to operate without expensive licences in a deregulated zone up to

SUBURBAN AMERICA 93

twenty miles beyond city limits. This ruling stimulated increased competition that led to lower shipping rates for the outer metropolis.

Real estate developers hurried to establish industrial parks in outlying areas, thereby benefiting from the demand for suburban locations and stimulating further deconcentration of manufacturing. Scarcely 100 such sites existed prior to the 1950s, but by 1980 there were about 3,000, and over half went into operation after 1965. Medium-sized and small firms found industrial parks especially desirable. They are close to interstate highways and therefore firms have easy access to suppliers and customers. The developers usually assumed all responsibilities for preparing and maintaining the site and buildings, thereby relieving tenants of management responsibilities. Sharing the costs of services such as rubbish removal also kept fees to a minimum. Amenities such as planned recreational facilities and landscaping were installed as an incentive for high employee productivity. Tam O'Shanter industrial park near Chicago was placed on what had been a championship golf course. Volkswagen Corporation located its factor for the Rabbit model amid the green rolling hills of Allegheny County near Pittsburgh. Some 800 small silicon chip and semi-conductor plants sprang up during the 1970s in the industrial parks in California's Santa Clara County.

Like the manufacturers, insurance companies, real estate and service industries increasingly placed their offices in suburban locations. As the metropolitan fringe came to house a majority of the nation's well-to-do white population, suburban sites provided corporations with ready access to a pool of educated and skilled workers. The publishers of *Reader's Digest* created a 'business campus' in prestigious Westchester County, New York, by the 1950s, but the suburbanisation of office activities really came of age after the mid-1960s. Office parks (purpose-built, like industrial parks) also became a feature of the outer city during the 1970s. Major US corporations established their regional offices in office parks near major metropolitan airports, and smaller and medium-sized firms followed their example.

The Research Triangle Park in the suburbs of Durham and Raleigh, North Carolina, and the Forrestal Center outside Princeton, New Jersey, cater to high-technology firms connected to the nearby Duke and Princeton universities. The Oak Brook office park near Chicago's O'Hare Airport houses the headquarters of McDonald's Corporation. Altogether, among the leading 500 US corporations the numbers with suburban headquarters increased from 47 in 1965 to 170 in 1978. During the 1970s suburban Westchester County and adjacent Fairfield County, Connecticut, became the site of the largest number of corporate headquarters outside New York City. IBM and *Reader's Digest* were among the first in this New York City suburb, but General Telephone and Electronics, Continental Oil, Xerox, and Kennecott Copper have followed. Suburbanisation of office activities has not been restricted to the northeast. The Atlanta suburbs contained only one office park in 1964, but ten years later there were 40 parks housing almost 25,000 employees. In the Dallas metropolitan area, the suburban share of total office space increased from 26 per cent in 1970 to 46 per cent in 1976.

Office parks and corporate headquarters dramatised the increased economic advantage and the growing prestige of a suburban address. The shopping centres and super malls of the outer cities, similar by-products of the interstate highway programme, shifted retail business to the peripheral areas and further contributed to metropolitan decentralisation. The outward migration of families in the first post-war decade supported small and medium-sized retailers who offered convenient locations along highways and plenty of free parking. Large downtown department stores started establishing suburban branches in the late 1950s. Early post-war regional shopping centres such as Shopper's World in Boston, Northgate in Seattle, and Southdale near Minneapolis, served as models for the later, more extensive, 'super regional' shopping plazas of the 1970s and 1980s. By 1978 some 18,000 shopping centres were strung out at choice locations on the suburban highway network. From the Cherry Hill Mall of southern New Jersey, to Houston's Galleria, to San Jose's Eastridge Mall, to the Woodfield Mall in suburban Chicago, these commercial agglomerations offered their customers all kinds of retail merchandise as well as personal services and recreation. The Woodfield Mall was the world's largest, with four major department stores, some 230 other shops, parking spaces for over 10,000 automobiles, and yearly sales of about $200 million. 'If you had to pick one thing that would typify civilization in the United States,' remarked the business editor of the *Atlanta Journal* in 1978, 'a front-running candidate would be the suburban shopping mall'.[5]

OCCUPATIONS AND INCOME IN THE SUBURBS

As business firms and white families moved to the suburbs, they took with them jobs and income that otherwise would have contributed to city tax revenue and employment opportunities for residents of the urban core. Consequently, with few exceptions, the rise of the suburban economy meant a corresponding decline in the economy of central cities. In the US as a whole, the manufacturing-belt cities, and the oldest cities especially, lost population while western and southern cities continued to attract new residents. Northeastern and north central cities also experienced out-migrations of middle- and upper-middle-income white residents at the same time that they attracted low-income non-white migrants. In New York City alone, some half million whites departed and about the same number of blacks arrived during 1960 and 1970.

Manufacturing jobs have gradually provided a smaller and smaller proportion of American workers with their livelihood in the years since 1945. The suburbs, however, did not experience the staggering losses of manufacturing jobs that plagued the older cities in the North East and North Central states. On the contrary, between 75 and 90 per cent of all new US manufacturing jobs have been created in suburbs since the late 1950s. In the manufacturing belt, the older cities lost 1.3 million such jobs while the suburbs gained 2.3 million. Even in the West and South, where cities made impressive additions to their manufacturing labour force, the suburban factories did far better. Southern and western suburbs added about four times more manufacturing jobs than central cities between 1947 and 1972. The story was much the same in retail and wholesale jobs. The greatest losses also occurred in the older and larger cities of the manufacturing belt in these employment areas. Cities in these states lost 2.6 million manufacturing, wholesale and retail jobs, while the suburbs gained 4.7 million. These trends continued through the 1970s. During the 1970s many central cities added jobs in the white-collar service sector, but here again the suburban employment growth was much faster. In Baltimore and St Louis, business service jobs declined, while in the suburbs of these cities they grew by more than 200 per cent. Consumer services of all kinds, and construction, likewise experienced substantial growth due to the fast growing suburban population and the demand for new buildings.

As the suburbs became the leading growth centres for manufacturing, wholesale and retail trade, and (to a lesser extent) services, they naturally increased their share of metropolitan blue-collar and white-collar workers. Cities, on the other hand, except in the professional, clerical and service sectors, experienced employment declines. During the 1960s, white-collar jobs in the suburbs increased twice as fast as blue-collar jobs, and white-collar jobs accounted for more than two-thirds of the female employment in suburbia. The growth of both white-collar and blue-collar jobs in the urban fringe meant a corresponding shift in commuting patterns. During the 1960s, commuters to cities increased 13 per cent, but those commuting between suburbs increased 40 per cent, and by 1970 the city to suburban commuters had risen from 4 per cent of all metropolitan employees to 7 per cent. These trends continued during the 1970s, as the blue-collar workforce became as large a part of the suburbs as of the cities. By the end of the 1970s, with industrial jobs moving even further beyond central city limits, the non-metropolitan areas housed the largest percentages of blue-collar workers. White-collar jobs, even in many of the Sunbelt metropolitan regions, continued their migration to the outer city. Glendale, California – the 'bedroom of Los Angeles' in the early post-war years – experienced an office building boom in 1980. As downtown LA office space and housing became more scarce and expensive, the suburbs became 'the hottest thing in commercial real estate', and Glendale began the construction of half a dozen high-rise office buildings.[6]

When manufacturers and trade and service firms established new jobs outside the central city, they precipitated a migration of income to the suburbs that contributed to an ever-widening dollar gap between families in the core and on the periphery of urban America. Well-to-do families did not entirely abandon downtown USA as a residential option, but only about one-third of them made their homes in cities by the late 1970s. As skilled, well-off white families left the cities and poor, unskilled non-whites moved cityward, the median income of city families dropped from 89 per cent of the suburban median to 79 per cent between 1960 and 1978. In the mid-1970s, the median income of both white and black suburban families was higher than their centre city counterparts, and the suburbs housed the lowest percentages of America's poor families.

SUBURBAN SOCIETY

Well-to-do urban families sought out semi-rural home sites near forests and lakes in suburban territory long before Abraham Levitt and his sons began their mass production of houses on Long Island farmland near New York City in 1948. During the 1950s and 1960s suburban communities came to house a more diverse population, one that was more representative of the metropolitan core cities. Real estate developers and building contractors attracted middle-income families by selling them smaller, more modest versions of those houses standing in the older wealthy enclaves. Families of moderate means bought houses in the factory-built tracts constructed by firms such as Levitt in New York and Pennsylvania, or Doelger in the San Francisco Bay Area. They also found their suburban housing in aging, but structurally sound, homes that had been left behind by an older middle-class population in the better neighbourhoods of suburban towns like Plainfield, New Jersey. Poor and low-income families, including small numbers of blacks in the decaying centre of Plainfield and those in Yeadon, a small suburb just outside Philadelphia, also began moving into fringe territory during the 1950s and 1960s.

Despite the social diversity that could be found outside city limits in the early post-war years, journalists and academics became obsessed with the metaphor of mass production suggested by the dramatic appearance of row upon row of interchangeable houses adjacent to metropolitan highways. Consequently, the suburban society of the 'new middle class', those white-collar workers that C. Wright Mills caricatured as 'the cheerful robots', captured the American imagination during the 1950s and early 1960s. Novelist Sloan Wilson saw the purpose-built bedroom communities of the period as soul-deadening places where *The Man in the Gray Flannel Suit* (1955) lived a hectic life of mediocrity with a frustrated wife and conformist children. John Keats, the cover page of his *The Crack in the Picture Window* (1956) decorated with whimsical drawings of malevolent property developers, put his John Drone character in a tract of 'identical boxes . . . spreading like gangrene' that created the 'fresh air slums we're building around the edges of America's cities'.[7]

William H. Whyte's study of Park Forest, Illinois, a suburb of Chicago, appeared in his best selling *The Organization Man* (1956). To Whyte, suburbia offered a rational solution to rootless, upwardly mobile families seeking the best housing for their money. Once installed in their new homes, however, these middle-class suburbanites submerged their individuality beneath a collective ethic of classless conviviality. Sociability, so intense it 'transcended mere neighborliness', and the chance to 'plunge into a hotbed of Participation', offered a sense of belonging to residents. Whyte was sceptical. Even though the 'web of friendship' was of high value to the families of Park Forest, Whyte worried that they would become 'imprisoned in brotherhood'. Like his fellow critic of the new middle class, C. Wright Mills, Whyte preferred the image of the bureaucrat fighting the organisation to the image of *gemutlichkeit* at the *kaffe klatsch*.[8]

While critics differed in the intensity of their attack on the suburbs, Whyte studied life in Park Forest and several other communities. By the beginning of the 1960s a number of scholars had emulated Whyte's participant observation research technique and published books describing the daily life of particular suburban communities. This second generation of suburb watchers was more interested in whether the class and ethnic realities of cities persisted in suburbs than in 'the dehumanized collective that so haunts our thoughts'.[9] Sociologist Bennett M. Berger was puzzled by the willingness of pundits to generalise about US suburbs on the basis of evidence about the middle-class white-collar variety. The Ford Motor Company auto workers who lived in Berger's San Francisco *Working Class Suburb* (1960) did not trade in their old values and behaviour patterns when they made down payments on their new tract homes. Most of Berger's auto workers thought of themselves as members of the working class despite their suburban location, and even the minority who felt comfortable with a middle-class label did so because they equated the term with owning a home and having a 'decent standard of living'.[10]

Berger interviewed his auto workers in 1957, and in 1958, a continent away in a New Jersey suburb of Philadelphia, sociologist Herbert J. Gans moved into the newest Levittown to study suburban life from the inside. The residents of Levittown also brought their ethnic and class perspectives with them when they moved from the city. But on the whole, *The Levittowners* (1967) lived 'fuller' and 'richer' lives than their parents had in the central cities. The working-class families were less suspicious; the Protestants were more tolerant. 'These and other changes', according to Gans, came about 'not because people are now better or more tolerant human beings, but because they are affluent.'[11]

By the 1970s careful scholars like Berger and Gans had done enough empirical research to demonstrate that socio-economic differences between groups both in suburbs and in cities were more significant than socio-economic differences between suburban and city communities. Far from being the homogeneous hothouses of conformity feared by critics of the 1950s, the suburbs by the 1970s had come to recapitulate the class and ethnic divisions that ordered society in the cities as well. When Scott Donaldson tried to bury *The Suburban Myth* once and for all in 1969, he summarised the findings of a decade of research. He was hopeful about the future of suburban America. Suburban communities, by inviting industrial and commercial development, were building stronger, more balanced, economic foundations. The realisation that unregulated growth could create future headaches moved suburban governments to introduce controls on development. Suburbanites, furthermore, *liked* living in the suburbs, and the outer city environments were unequivocally better places for raising children. Donaldson also defended the practice of building houses that looked like 'little boxes' that many had criticised as a source of instant blight. They might be ugly, he argued, but they were also relatively cheap and could provide low-cost housing for lower income families displaced by slum clearance in the cities; the problem, however, was that suburbanites throughout the US had carefully segregated their communities in order to create societies open only to whites.[12]

Social exclusivity extended beyond the racial discrimination that kept all but a small percentage of black families from the suburbs. Indeed, since the nineteenth century well-to-do Americans had insulated themselves from city nuisances, both physical pollution and socially objectionable groups, by migrating beyond the city limits. By the 1960s the desire to control which groups could qualify as one's neighbours was a well-established function of local government. Suburban residents, although typically unwilling to grant large power to their local governments, were anxious 'to channel it to a few limited functions'. Among these, said Herbert J. Gans, one goal was 'primary . . . the protection of the home against diversity'.[13]

Excluding blacks from the suburbs has a long history in the US. Most of the comparatively few who have found their way to suburbia have for decades been restricted to a handful of very small segregated enclaves. These widely scattered settlements – black residential islands in a lily-white suburban area – have accounted for approximately 3 per cent of suburban populations outside the South since the First World War. Between 1960 and 1977 blacks increased their share of the suburban population from 4.7 to 6 per cent, a rise of from 2.7 million to 4.6 million (18.8 per cent of the total US black population). In 1977 almost 3 of every 5 blacks lived in central cities, compared to only 1 of every 4 whites. Small increases in black suburban populations occurred in the 1960s, but between 1970 and 1977 black suburbanites increased by more than a third, with the West showing almost twice the national increase and the northeast only one-third the national increase. This dramatic reversal of a half-century's increasing concentration of blacks in cities was a product of rising income levels for relatively small numbers of the black population. The percentage of suburban blacks living in poverty declined significantly from 44 per cent in 1960 to 20 per cent in 1977. Increased black suburbanisation did not, however, signify a weakening of racial exclusivity in the outer cities. The new black suburbanites of the 1970s moved into areas already housing blacks, areas being abandoned by whites. Instead of opening up the suburbs for racial diversity, black suburbanisation meant 'a strong trend toward resegregation and the perpetuation of a dual housing market for blacks and whites'.[14]

The dual housing market, with its connotation of separate and unequal listings of houses for sale (with whites offered the preferred suburban choices, and blacks restricted to central city and less desirable suburban properties) persisted throughout the post-war period because of business practices, local government co-operation and federal government complicity. The builders of suburban tract housing supervised initial sales with the intention of keeping black families out. Both in the new post-war tracts and in older suburban areas, sales agents, often merely catering to the racist preferences of their white customers, discouraged blacks from obtaining information about housing for sale in 'white' areas. Banks and savings institutions played a role in perpetuating suburban segregation by favouring white borrowers. Individual house owners, sometimes members of 'civic clubs' (Houston) or principals of 'gentlemen's agreements' (Atlanta) maintained racial exclusion by pledging to resell their houses to whites only; this practice has not been restricted to the South. As discussed previously, the federal government housing policy until the early 1960s fostered white suburbanisation, and its record since then has fluctuated from toleration of residential segregation to lackadaisical enforcement of fair housing legislation. Local governments, typically vehicles of community preference, usually mirrored the racist attitudes of their suburban constituents by zealously enacting zoning laws designed to enforce exclusivity.[15]

Some local governments, sometimes reflecting a particularly liberal-minded community, but most often infused by a desire to maintain racial balance (i.e. to stop white home owners from selling *en masse* to affluent black families anxious to escape an adjacent central city ghetto), enacted suburban 'open housing' ordinances during the early 1970s. In the Chicago area, a multi-racial group called the Leadership Council for Metropolitan Open Communities championed this approach. A private group, the Council provided legal assistance to families with complaints stemming from housing discrimination in suburban areas. By the late 1970s the Council was attacked by two groups, the local branch of the black Southern Christian Leadership Council and the powerful National Association of Realtors. The black critics complained that suburban open housing laws limited black suburban residents to specific quotas. Seeing nothing objectionable about predominantly black suburbs, the SCLC local president fumed that 'integration-maintenance plans really put a quota on the number of blacks a suburb will take. Where do they get off doing that?' At the same time, the real estate group (a nationwide trade association with some 600,000 member firms) criticised the programme for interfering with a family's freedom of housing choice as well as a property broker's ability to sell homes without govern- ment interference.[16]

By the beginning of the 1980s the courts had in numerous instances upheld the counter-attacks against suburban integration laws, and there was little prospect for disintegration of the suburban 'white noose'. Given the obstacles facing black families whose incomes made a suburban option available, it is not surprising that the rates of black suburbanisation have been so far below those of whites. Moving out of the black ghetto promised an escape from some of the worst features of city life: crowded schools, street crime, deteriorated housing, drugs. Moving into the suburban (often 'resegregated') world also meant 'leaving family, friends and churches and embarking on a scary odyssey into unknown, often hostile territory'.[17] That such fears were realistic was dramatised with brutal clarity in the Contra Costa County suburbs of the San Francisco Bay Area during 1981 when local hoodlums with Ku Klux Klan sympathies welcomed black families with burning crosses and beatings. One middle-class black executive living in Chicago's Arlington Heights suburb believed that: 'Most black families in the suburbs think of getting out by the time their daughters are teenagers and start dating.'[18] The rising numbers of affluent blacks heading for those suburbs open to them, on the other hand, demonstrated that all those Americans who could afford to do so preferred to get out of the city.

6.   The Cities

In 1945 the delegates of 50 nations assembled at San Francisco's Civic Center to draft a charter for the United Nations; by 1952 the Organisation had moved into its permanent New York City head-quarters. The two events dramatically illustrated the world-wide recognition these port cities had earned during the preceding century. Throughout the post-war years, San Francisco and New York City, along with Chicago and Los Angeles, strengthened their leadership as national centres of international trade and banking, overseas manu-facturing operations, advertising and other business services. They therefore continued to attract the headquarters of the nation's largest corporations. Another dozen and a half cities, led by Philadelphia and Boston, Cleveland, Atlanta and Houston, either maintained or expanded their importance as base cities for the industrial and commercial activities of their regions. Detroit, Pittsburgh, Rochester and San Jose, on the other hand, continued to serve as centres of research, administration and production for the automobile, steel, scientific equipment and electronic industries respectively. Another group of cities specialised in the production of goods and services, whether civilian (Buffalo, New York, and Youngstown, Ohio) or military (Norfolk, Virginia, and San Diego, California). Certain cities depended upon government employment, notably Washington DC, and others housed large educational enterprises, such as New Haven, Connecticut. Some cities, like Austin, Texas, did both. While many of these cities earned their livelihoods by maintaining pre-Second World War activities, some – Las Vegas, Nevada, is the most dramatic example – grew by attracting a new post-war source of income: the pensions of retired employees and the paid vacation benefits of leisure-seeking Americans.[1]

American cities have all been subject to economic and social stress caused by the gradual shift of economic activities, income and population to the Sunbelt states and to the suburbs. By the early

1980s the Sunbelt cities that had benefited from these trends during the 1960s and 1970s began to experience the consequences of rapid growth: pollution, overtaxed city services and high crime rates. The older manufacturing-belt cities suffered from high unemployment rates as plant closures multiplied, from increased social service costs as low-income minority residents became a larger percentage of the population, from a declining tax base as affluent homeowners and businesses fled to the outer cities, and from aging bridges and streets crumbled through neglect. 'World Cities' such as New York and San Francisco displayed a complex mixture of sickness and health as they struggled to combine both the international economic activities that provided their livelihood and the increasingly redundant low-income minority populations that drained their treasuries. 'Industry and citizens', wrote city planner J. E. Gibson in 1977, 'moved out of the city to save money.' Planners George Sternlieb and James W. Hughes agreed that 'obsolescence' plagued cities all over the nation, but argued that it reflected social preferences as well as economics: 'We are not dealing with an acute attack of disease but rather a long term chronic problem in which the central city in the classic mold simply does not relate to the life style either enjoyed or desired by the bulk of Americans.'[2]

DIMENSIONS OF CITY CHANGE

Throughout US history the primary source of change in American cities has been the business system. During the 1950s and 1960s, as we have seen in Chapter 4, the Northeast and North Central states reversed their traditional role in the American economy. The West and the South became the source of most of the new manufacturing jobs, as well as the site of research and development crucial to the growing defence-oriented economy. After 1969, what had been a relative decline turned into an absolute decline, and the manufacturing belt lost more than 1.3 million manufacturing jobs by 1977. The regional shifts of income that accompanied the loss of manufacturing jobs were not balanced by the in-migration of service jobs into the older cities. In addition, the suburbanisation of manufacturing jobs represented a further loss of income.

Cities in the Northeast and North Central states, their powers like their boundaries circumscribed by state legislatures, possessed no veto over the suburbanisation of jobs and income in their metropolitan areas. They had neither the legal authority nor the moral influence to counter successfully business's search for cheaper labour, land and transportation, and a 'better business climate'. Western and southern cities, already beneficiaries of economic decisions that brought them new jobs, were able to capture revenue from taxes upon new businesses and residents; state laws in these regions made the annexation of outlying areas relatively easy. Older cities in the manufacturing belt, however, could not resort to annexation as a technique for capturing additional income; state laws passed in the late nineteenth and early twentieth century designed to insulate suburbs from financial responsibility and social problems in the cities made annexation nearly impossible. At the same time, the manufacturing-belt cities had established a political tradition that placed a high priority upon expenditures for schools, welfare and health care. Although revenue for such services declined, the demand for them did not. The newer cities of the South and the West, by and large, lacked the urban ethnic and working-class political organisations which had made the provision of social services the major source of their staying power. Instead, like the earlier opponents of 'political machines' in the Northeast and North Central states, the newer western and southern cities emphasised a brand of fiscal conservatism keyed to the interests of business rather than working-class constituents and looked upon expansive social service budgets with a jaundiced eye.[3]

The inability of the North Central and Northeast cities to grow by means of annexation made them vulnerable to the economic consequences of suburbanisation. Their traditional commitment to relatively high social service expenditures made them vulnerable to the costs of caring for the people displaced by national and international economic transformation. Migrants and immigrants alike, hoping to find their future in New York or Chicago, flocked to the older manufacturing regions, bringing with them high expectations and hope for success. Southern and western cities also attracted poor families displaced by economic changes and refugees from international political crises between the 1950s and 1980s, but the Sunbelt cities could absorb the impact better than the manufacturing-belt cities. Even so, the grim evidence of grinding poverty in Los Angeles, San Antonio, Houston and Miami revealed the fact that while the consequences of displacement varied by region, the problem as it affected urban areas was primarily one of the cities, not the suburbs.

BLACK MIGRATION

The suburbs continued to whiten with the addition of families who could financially take advantage of post-war jobs and housing; the cities filled up with poor families of every complexion. The majority of the poor were white, but in the central cities the rapid darkening of the population gave the impression that poverty was a characteristic of black people; this fitted the prejudices of most Americans and facilitated the propensity of popular wisdom to blame urban problems on the victims of economic transformation.

Like the other 16 million Americans who gave up rural life for an urban existence, the 4 million blacks who flocked to cities were redundant in the increasingly mechanised farms of the post-war South. Mechanisation took place with remarkable speed, so that between 1940 and 1965 the proportion of blacks living on the land declined from one-half to one-fifth. Between 1958 and 1964 alone, the use of mechanical cotton pickers in the Mississippi River Delta area increased from 27 to 81 per cent; the story was much the same in the upper South. Sometimes the black tenant farmers and share croppers moved to a southern city, but most of them headed for six states outside the South: California, Illinois, Michigan, New York, Ohio and Pennsylvania. Their destination was the cities in the largest metropolitan areas. These were precisely the cities beginning to experience the highest rates of decline in manufacturing jobs. The black newcomers faced an unemployment rate double that of whites, for they were moving into an urban economy on the decline. By the last years of the 1950s persistent unemployment among the growing concentrations of blacks contributed to political scientist Morton Grodzins' argument that 'the nation's most pressing social problem tomorrow . . . [is that] many central cities of the great metropolitan areas of the United States are fast becoming lower class, largely Negro slums.'[4]

Black migration from the South declined a mere 6 per cent during the 1960s, and while the numbers settling in the North Central states declined by 30 per cent, the West and the Northeast attracted even larger numbers than they had in the 1950s. The black population grew fastest in the larger central cities, and the twelve largest (New York, Chicago, Los Angeles, Philadelphia, Detroit, Baltimore, Houston, Cleveland, Washington DC, St Louis, Milwaukee and San Francisco) held more than two-thirds of the black population outside the South by 1968. The black populations of New York and Los Angeles doubled between 1950 and 1968.

POOR WHITES

As the movement of blacks into these central cities accelerated, so did the migration of whites into the suburbs. In the largest cities, the ratio of white flight to black settlement was approximately 2 to 1. Some whites, however, joined the blacks in their cityward movement. Most of the whites came from impoverished areas that had either never recovered from the Great Depression or had never participated in the industrial growth of the metropolitan Northeast and North Central states. While not segregated by race like the black newcomers, these poor whites could usually afford to live in only the most deteriorated parts of the cities. During the late 1960s Todd Gitlin and Nanci Hollander described such an area in their tribute to the people of Chicago's 'Uptown': 'hillbillies, crackers, stump-jumpers, ridge-runners, white trash' with '20 percent on welfare, on a summer night some playing guitars, twanging songs of Hank Williams and Johnny Cash'. Nearby: 'the stripped-down, burned-out shells of the American dream, and their dusty license plates of origin: West Virginia, Virginia, Kentucky, Tennessee, Alabama.'[5] During the 1970s the continuing decline of the agricultural labour force and the persistent erosion of the metropolitan economies in the manufacturing belt produced a steady stream of young white migrants headed for the larger central cities. Sometimes influenced by the 'hippie' movement of the late 1960s, with its stress on inner peace and communal co-operation, more often motivated by a desire to escape from troubled low-income families, these transient young adults became increasingly visible in rundown districts such as San Francisco's Tenderloin and New York's Lower East Side during the 1970s.

FOOTLOOSE INDUSTRY

The cities of the largest metropolitan areas in the Northeast and North Central states found themselves enmeshed in massive social changes as their populations shifted increasingly from white to non-white and as the proportion of low-income people increased.

Smaller and medium-sized cities changed as well, especially those directly dependent upon basic industries such as steel and auto-mobiles during the 1970s. The exceptional cases, such as Columbus, Ohio, and Indianapolis, Indiana, depended less on declining indus-tries and had lower population densities than most. Buffalo, Louis-ville and Detroit were more typical. Buffalo's decline had been apparent since the opening of the St Lawrence Seaway in 1959 reduced its regional importance, and it suffered in the 1970s when Bethlehem Steel, General Motors, National Gypsum Company and Ashland Oil laid off large numbers of workers. When the Chevrolet division installed computerised machinery to operate the engine assembly production process, it cut the workforce from 10,000 to 3,600. Louisville, Kentucky, another old and established manu-facturing centre, lost some 19,000 manufacturing jobs during the 1970s, as General Electric, International Harvester and Brown and Williamson Tobacco Company (Kools, Raleighs, Viceroys) either closed their Louisville facilities or made severe contractions in their operations. While the city added 73,000 jobs in services, the new jobs generally paid lower wages and tended to go to workers – frequently females – other than those displaced from manufacturing. Ham-tramck, Michigan, its population dropping from 55,000 just after the Second World War to 24,000 in 1979, braced itself for a period of more precipitous decline when the Chrysler Corporation closed its 'Dodge Main' assembly plant early in 1980. Loss of the plant meant the disappearance of the $1.3 million per year in tax revenue (out of a total of $8 million) that Hamtramck had come to expect from Chrysler Corporation. Like Hamtramck, Detroit was vulnerable to footloose industry. Both cities watched their traditional source of income disappear: when the Cadillac Division closed its Detroit plant in 1980, 'Motown' lost the last of its General Motors operation.[6]

GENTRIFICATION

As businesses and residents left the older cities, they abandoned factories and warehouses as well as nineteenth- and early twentieth-century houses. This development occurred just as service jobs were increasing in the central business districts of US cities. It also coincided with the coming of age of the 'baby boom' generation and its high proportion of college graduates. The 25- to 34-year-old age group increased by 49 per cent during the 1970s, much faster than the US population as a whole, and this group increased in all but one of the twenty largest cities at the same time that all but nine of them showed absolute population declines. While this young city population grew the most in the newer cities and especially those of the South and West (85 per cent in Houston, 88 per cent in Phoenix, 84 per cent in San Diego), New York City, Chicago, Boston and Philadelphia also added younger residents. This age group provided many of the customers for the real estate developers and contractors who restored Victorian and Edwardian housing (sometimes displacing several low-income minority families in favour of a well-to-do couple interested in architectural preservation). This age group also flocked to the restaurants and boutiques built into the recycled factories and warehouses of San Francisco's Cannery and Ghirardelli Square and Boston's Faneuil Hall and Haymarket.

The recycling of older city areas by the new affluent employees of the emerging service economy attracted considerable publicity during the 1970s, and pundits hailed the beginning of a 'Back to the City' movement that would restore the lagging economies of the older cities. The US Census Bureau dampened such optimism when it announced the sober reality behind the dramatic headlines: for every male with an income of $15,000 per year or more moving into American cities, nearly three were moving out. While 'gentrifying trends probably expanded the size and number of middle-to-upper income enclaves' in some large cities, the change occurred 'without raising city incomes enough to establish a new trend toward convergence of city and suburban income levels'.[7]

Gentrification, while it provided profitable investments for developers and islands of amenity for affluent preservationists, seemed insignificant compared to the steady stream of non-white migrants and immigrants into the cities during the 1970s. The rate of black cityward migration slowed during the 1970s, and millions of blacks either moved from the rural South or returned from the North to southern cities. The increases of blacks in southern cities therefore tended to be more dramatic than the increases elsewhere. The continued outmigration of the white population, however, when combined with higher birth rates of blacks and other non-whites, meant that cities everywhere continued the trends under way during the 1950s and 1960s. Middle- and upper-income populations, mostly white but with small numbers of blacks, kept searching for suburban alternatives; where cities did increase their white populations (San Jose and San Diego, California, and Phoenix and San Antonio for example), they did so by using the annexation process. Besides the gains in black populations, US cities also gained large numbers of American Indians, Asians and people of Hispanic descent. By 1980, Newark and Gary, along with Detroit, Baltimore, New Orleans, Washington, DC, and Atlanta had black majorities, and in Memphis and St Louis, blacks were nearly the majority. Blacks and other non-whites made up the majority of Chicago's population. Hispanics outnumbered blacks in New York, Los Angeles, San Diego, San Francisco, Denver and Phoenix, and they constituted the majority in San Antonio.

IMMIGRANTS IN THE CITIES

The increases in the numbers of Hispanics and other non-whites in the cities followed upon the liberalisation of federal immigration laws in 1965. Immigration to the US, following a long decline after 1920, picked up again during the late 1960s, and between 1970 and 1980, the percentage of residents born outside the US increased from 4.7 per cent of 203 million to 6.2 per cent of 226 million. Although almost half of these new immigrants settled in the suburbs of the nation, another 6.6 million established themselves in the cities and in the large metropolitan centres along the coasts (New York, Miami, Los Angeles and San Francisco). San Francisco's Asian population increased 55 per cent during the 1970s, from 13 to 22 per cent of the city's population. Its traditional Chinatown expanded into the North Beach Italian-American neighbourhood, and a new Chinatown emerged two miles to the west along Clement Street. Large parts of downtown Los Angeles devoted themselves to the retail shopping needs of that city's Mexican immigrants, and dozens of shops and restaurants catering to the approximately 100,000 Koreans sprang up along LA's Olympic Boulevard. San Jose's Hispanics nearly tripled in number, while its Asian population skyrocketed from 17,400 to 137,400. In 1978, black Lieutenant Governor Mervyn M. Dymally declared that California would soon become the nation's first 'third-world state' with racial minority groups in the majority. The comment caused some raised eyebrows, but few denied the possibility.[8]

The changes wrought by immigration in US cities during the 1970s appeared wherever newcomers arrived in substantial numbers. Older neighbourhoods containing cheap housing became overcrowded. Public schools struggled to meet the demand for instruction in the English language and basic skills needed for employment. Health and welfare departments reeled from increased case loads necessitated by the sudden arrival of thousands of disoriented refugees. Anxious to secure steady employment, immigrants eagerly sought work in the low-paying occupations available to unskilled applicants. They often found themselves competing with blacks, and even where competition did not occur its possibility created resentment among unemployed native residents. Tensions between the various non-white minority groups, similar to those that sparked confrontation among European immigrants in nineteenth-century American cities, worsened during the 1970s as the lagging economy declined into full-scale recession after 1979. Cities in the South and the West, though better able to cope with the financial impact of large-scale immigration than those of the Northeast and North Central areas, found themselves likewise buffeted by social change.

SUNBELT CITIES

The city of Miami, Florida, owed much of its prosperity during the 1960s to investments made by members of the Cuban business and professional class who preferred America's capitalism to Castro's revolution. The federal government provided generous resettlement aid to the Cubans, and they invested heavily in projects that rejuvenated the city's declining central business district. By 1970, Miami's immigrants outnumbered its blacks by 2 to 1, and two-thirds of the immigrants were Cubans. The revitalisation of downtown Miami helped to stimulate the creation of a new economy tendering services to the growing Cuban population and goods to the metropolitan area. Retail sales increased 44 per cent between 1967 and 1972 and the value of the city's manufactured goods increased 86 per cent. By the end of the 1970s, Miami was developing a reputation as the 'Gateway to the Latin Dollar'. American and European banks established branches; import and export business (as well as illegal drug traffic) to Latin and Central America boomed; and affluent families from Venezuela, Colombia, Ecuador and Argentina made

Miami into a cosmopolitan cultural, recreational and financial centre. The port became the world's leader in cruise ships, and over 100 of the leading American corporations established headquarters for their Latin American and Caribbean operations in Miami.[9]

Miami's black population did not share in the city's progress during the 1960s and 1970s, and the persistence of high rates of black unemployment and poverty contributed to growing black resentment and frustration that exploded into violence against symbols of public authority in 1980 and 1982. The Liberty City ghetto riots in May 1980 caused eighteen deaths and the destruction of $100 million worth of property; the Overtown ghetto riots of 1982 led to two deaths and started after a Hispanic police officer killed a black man. Although one black man achieved a seat on the five-member City Commission by the 1980s, two of the remaining four (including the Mayor) were Hispanic. The city traditionally lacked a substantial black business and professional class which, in cities like Atlanta, usually provided black candidates for public office. When the Cubans arrived in the early 1960s, the local job market still operated along segregated lines, and blacks filled the jobs associated with the tourist industry. Cubans and other Hispanics, willing to work for lower wages, displaced the blacks and by the 1980s Miami's Hispanic population included the presidents of three dozen banks and the owners of newspapers, radio and television stations, hospitals and cemeteries. Nearly 30 per cent of the black population lived in poverty throughout the 1970s and the black unemployment rate was twice that of the city as a whole.

The disparities that separated Miami's black ghetto from its glittering downtown existed in other cities in the South and the West. The Miami riots were similar to the 1965 Los Angeles riots in Watts, in that they expressed the frustrations of growing numbers of blacks and other non-white central city residents whose lack of skills and education made them redundant even in the relatively healthy cities of the fastest growing regions of the US. By the late 1970s the largest Sunbelt cities had higher percentages of their ethnic minority populations living in poverty than was the case in the largest cities of the Northeast. In Houston, Texas, the gap between rich and poor widened during the 1970s even as the state's per capita income increased from 90 per cent of the national average to 97 per cent. The benefits of the Lone Star State's energy boom did not trickle down to the 'quiescent, relatively meek, disorganized and historically under-paid group of people' who made up Houston's working poor. The city's 4 per cent unemployment rate, low by Northeast and North Central region standards, existed alongside the fact that 'while it is probably easier to get a job in Texas than just about anywhere else, it is not necessarily easy to get one that pays a living wage if you are unskilled, black or Mexican-American'.[10]

Sunbelt cities such as Houston frequently expanded their taxable territory by means of annexation during the post-war period (Houston grew by 50 per cent in fifteen years). This helped them avoid the economic problems of Frostbelt cities such as New York and Cleveland. By the end of the 1970s, however, the costs of city services were increasing, the problems of poverty and crime were multiplying, and the more affluent residents were becoming restless about paying the price. Like the migrants to the suburbs in the Northeast and North Central states eighty years earlier, well-to-do white residents in one of Houston's wealthiest communities tried to separate themselves from their city in 1978. Similar outbreaks of suburban independence emerged in other parts of the South and West. Sunbelt cities feared that loss of the ability to grow through annexation would eventually bring 'the same problems of obsolescence that haunt New York and Chicago'.[11]

THE FEDERAL GOVERNMENT AND THE CITIES

An excellent indicator of the changing relationship between cities and the federal government is the increased responsibility that Congress assumed for federal aid programmes after 1960. In 1959 John F. Kennedy pointed the way when he voiced his concern for 'the 22 million Americans who live in our cities in sub-standard housing . . . without hope of tomorrow.' Kennedy considered the question of 'what we should do about the cities' to be 'the great unspoken issue in the 1960 election'. Kennedy was also quick to admit that he thought 'the overall outcome of the 1960 campaign is going to be decided in the cities'. After the 1965 Watts riots and the 164 ghetto 'disorders' during the first nine months of 1967, political calculation and perception of crisis moved legislators to pass an avalanche of federal grants-in-aid programmes for the cities.[12]

Arguing that 'the national purpose' required unprecedented action, Congress enacted 136 new programmes of federal aid to cities between 1963 and 1967. The Model Cities programme of 1966, designed to establish prototypes for economic and racial progress, declared that 'improving the quality of urban life is the most critical domestic problem facing the United States'. Similar sentiments accompanied the passage of legislation establishing food stamps for the hungry, regional and community health centres, medical insurance, anti-poverty programmes and aid for elementary and secondary education. In 1960, 44 grant programmes for state and local governments existed. The number increased to 530 by 1970 with the total amount of grants increasing from $7 billion in 1960 to $70 billion in 1977. When the Democratic Party captured the White House in 1960, it moved to widen its urban constituency by making urban issues a high priority. The riots during the 'long hot summers' of 1965 to 1968 were powerful reinforcements. Between 1961 and 1972 federal aid to non-urban areas increased by 182 per cent, total federal aid spending increased by 405 per cent, and aid to urban areas increased by 590 per cent; most of the increases came during the Democratic administrations of Kennedy and Johnson.

Besides massively increasing direct federal aid to cities, the Johnson administration and Congress established a cabinet-level agency for urban affairs. This Department of Housing and Urban Development (1965) was followed one year later by a Department of Transportation charged with improving mass transit in the cities. Existing executive branch agencies such as the Department of Health, Education, and Welfare also extended their work in cities and made solving urban problems a high priority.

The speed with which the Johnson administration established new programmes for solving urban problems and allocated federal dollars directly to cities created new political conditions that ultimately undercut the new federal urban activism. The members of poor and ethnic minority groups who participated in federally established activities such as the anti-poverty Community Action Programs sometimes adopted aggressive attitudes towards mayors, city councils and governors. Refusing to accept less than they had come to expect given the high priority and national purpose announced by Johnson and the Congress, militant poverty warriors mounted demonstrations at city halls and angrily confronted elected public officials. The fact that these often militant groups received their paycheques directly from Washington and were thus independent of local control galled members of city governments who had sometimes worked in vain for years to increase federal aid. In Oakland,

California, for example, the mayor in 1968 charged that the federal government was contributing to social revolution by providing militant groups with five times the $1 million that the city itself received in federal aid. Liberal supporters of the initial legislation, impatient for results, regarded the cumbersome operation of the programmes as intolerable and the predictable waste and inefficiency of the bureaucracies involved as unacceptable. Philosophical conservatives, opposed on principle to the centralisation of authority over social welfare, housing and education implied by the legislation, used the problems of implementation to validate their scepticism. By the presidential election of 1968, growing sentiment to reassert the authority of local and state governments over city problems had helped to create a political coalition favouring a 'New Federalism' for the cities.

Direct federal urban aid did not disappear during the Nixon and Ford administrations (1968–76). However, a new era began, ending the most controversial aspects of the Great Society programmes and establishing revenue-sharing programmes that transferred government financial assistance directly to local governments rather than to the personnel of federal agencies in cities. In 1971, President Nixon asked Congress to enact legislation for 'a new partnership' that would 'provide both the flexibility and resources for State and local government officials to exercise leadership in solving their own problems'. Whereas the Great Society legislation carried the implicit assumption that economically disadvantaged and minority groups, traditionally ignored by local governments, needed federal help to achieve equity, the New Federalism proceeded from the belief that whatever the nature of city politics, the federal government should not interfere. Federal aid would be welcome according to the New Federalism, but it should have no strings attached.

The AFL-CIO, speaking as a friend of the urban poor and defending the Democratic party's policy of direct aid to particular city programmes, attacked the New Federalism. So did civil rights organisations, which correctly perceived that social programmes beneficial to minorities would not survive the scrutiny of hostile local governments. Interest groups representing state and local public officials predictably provided the revenue-sharing legislation with its strongest lobbying support. The United States Conference of Mayors, the National League of Cities, and similar organisations saw the Nixon proposal as an answer to long-standing financial problems stemming from the growing gap between revenue and expenditure in the cities. In 1971, the National Urban Coalition announced that US cities would be $94 billion in the red even if they received the federal aid promised in revenue-sharing legislation. Eventually, but only after a classic Congressional compromise, Nixon signed the New Federalism into law in 1972. The controversy over who should decide how federal aid to cities should be spent and on what kinds of programmes was settled in favour of the state and local governments. At the beginning of his term in office, President Nixon soberly informed the American people that 'we face an urban crisis'. By the beginning of his second term, he believed that 'City governments are no longer on the verge of financial catastrophe' because 'The hour of crisis has passed'.[13]

Nixon was badly mistaken, for the major causes of fiscal crisis in American cities had more to do with long-term economic and social changes than with who set the priorities for spending federal dollars. Nonetheless, because of the large sums involved (some $4.5 billion in 1974) revenue-sharing became a political prize, and debates over how the revenue should be shared ('allocated') made the question of federal aid to cities a perennial issue during the 1970s and early 1980s. It was increasingly clear that if a 'Second War Between the States' actually existed, it was in large part the outcome of attempts by growing cities and declining cities in competitive regions to shape federal aid policy according to their respective needs.

Besides federal aid to resolve social problems in the cities, the federal government also committed itself during the post-war period to co-operating with private enterprise in the growth and development of central business districts (CBD). While CBD development came primarily from decisions made in the economic and social market, government policies also played a role. Typically more responsive to organised Washington lobbies representing business and to business leaders in their home states and districts, than to organised labour or unorganised city dwellers themselves, members of Congress assumed what was good for business would be good for the cities. City governments and downtown businesses in the older cities, sometimes co-operating with other interest groups, tried to use federal assistance to cushion against the adverse effects of market decisions. They aimed to achieve central city growth in the midst of regional decline. Business leaders in the newer cities, generally operating more freely than their counterparts in the Northeast and

North Central states, also made common cause in the name of growth. They also had few scruples about using federal assistance whenever it was available. The political coalitions of growth-oriented organisations in cities all over the nation, like the entrepreneurs who had built the transcontinental railways after the US Civil War, saw no harm in accepting government aid provided they were not required to accept government direction and control over their projects.

Renewal of the cities by means of public-private co-operation (see Chapter 7) came earlier than federal aid for the solution of urban social problems. Congress established the basic legislation for slum clearance and urban redevelopment when it passed the Housing Act of 1949, and amendments were made in 1951, 1961 and 1968. In 1974 the federal urban redevelopment operation was absorbed, along with other direct federal programmes for cities, into a special revenue-sharing system. Most urban scholars agree that the urban renewal process was more successful in aiding the selective rejuvenation of downtown business than in housing the poor and minority families who lived in ghettoes demolished by the programmes. During debates on the original legislation, the Senate committee drafting the measure stressed the importance of building new homes for disadvantaged families: 'the primary purpose . . . is to help remove the impact of slums on human life rather than simply to assist in the redevelopment of cities'. However, local redevelopment agencies routinely violated the requirements for residential housing, and by 1961 only 28,000 new units had been constructed in place of the 126,000 demolished. Some 113,000 families and 36,000 individuals were displaced; two-thirds were black and Puerto Rican. Although Congress insisted in 1968 that a majority of all replacement housing be sold at low or moderate prices, the high rates of displacement of the poor continued into the 1970s. Urban renewal was justly described as 'Negro removal' during the post-war years.

The purposes of non-governmentally-assisted commercial CBD revitalisation since 1945 have been frankly defended on a profit and loss basis, but groups such as the International Downtown Executive's Association lobbied for indirect federal subsidies, friendly state government tax abatements and co-operative local government assistance. Perhaps architect John C. Portman's formula for success typified the philosophy of commercial CBD rejuvenation. Creator of Atlanta's Peachtree Plaza Hotel, the Hyatt-Regency Hotel in San

Francisco and the Los Angeles Bonaventure Hotel, Portman became famous for his high-rise megaliths surrounding multi-storey atriums topped by revolving restaurants. 'You've got to take space', said Portman, 'and merchandise it for human use and human activity. We try to see what man likes in his environment and then crank that in – that's cranking in success.'[14] Portman was right about what constituted success; Americans flocked to his hotels to enjoy the ambiance, to see and be seen. They were the affluent ones – visitors to the big cities. The vast majority of Americans, however, told the poll takers what they had told them in 1946; they would rather live almost anywhere else but in cities.

7. Metropolitan Politics

THE history of metropolitan America since the Second World War has been shaped more by business and the federal government than by local governments. The changes within the economy, the rising power of the West and the South, the decline of the central cities and the growth of the suburbs all profoundly affected local governments. In some cases, mayors, city managers, city councils, or county commissioners helped to guide and to monitor metropolitan changes. But even where strong local leaders – Robert Moses in New York or Richard J. Daley in Chicago – personally influenced the built environment, they did so in spite of, not because of, their power as local officials. Cities and suburbs have always been legal creatures of state governments in the United States, and the degree of control they could exercise over their own affairs was always carefully specified in city charters or general provisions embedded in state constitutions.

The fragmentation of metropolitan government into overlapping legal entities, such as counties, cities, townships or special districts, likewise contributed to the limited scope of local governance. In other ways, local governments have become dependent upon decisions beyond community control. The relative importance of property taxes as a source of local government revenue declined from about three-fourths in the 1930s to just over one-third in 1977. By the late 1970s state and federal aid provided nearly 10 per cent more revenue than property taxes for local governments. While dependence upon local property taxes made communities vulnerable to the vicissitudes of the real estate market, dependence upon state and federal aid required local officials to cultivate state legislators and Washington politicians. As communities became more dependent upon influences originating outside their borders, participation in community politics and policy-making declined. The proliferation of 'grass-roots' community organisations during the 1960s and 1970s did not result in a revival of the high rates of mass participation in local governance (especially elections) typical of the late nineteenth century. 'The most obvious characteristic of participation in local politics', wrote two political analysts in 1974, 'is how little there is of it.'[1]

The fact that local governments possess limited powers has not dampened debate about the nature of politics and policy-making in American communities during the post-war period. Fascinated by the intensity of politics within this limited arena, a generation of scholars has probed the roles of various actors in community policy-making.

DEBATES OVER COMMUNITY POWER

The debate about community power during the post-war period slowly settled into a contest between pluralists, elitists and Marxists. Pluralists drew upon a research tradition begun by Robert A. Dahl's study of New Haven, Connecticut (1961). Power – the ability to achieve goals even when opposed – was seen by the pluralists as fragmented among a variety of competing groups. No one faction, according to this view, could dominate a majority of decision-making areas in the local community. The pluralists denied that economic and political power inhered in the same individuals, and they rejected the notion that a national ruling class existed which included those who made crucial decisions about public policy at the local government level. Pluralists argued that a flourishing competition among groups of many kinds ensured equitable representation to the mosaic of occupational, ethnic and other pressure groups who mobilised themselves to participate in local policy-making. For pluralists, community policy emerged rather logically from the politics of interest group bargaining and accommodation.[2]

The elitist alternative to the pluralist point of view began with Floyd Hunter's analysis of Atlanta, Georgia (1953). Elitists argued that policy-making was the outcome of decisions made by a well-defined group of representatives of economic institutions. While the pluralists saw governmental office-holders playing the central role of orchestrating local growth or decline, elitist writers claimed that private economic interests actually pulled the strings. Political institutions, though important, played an entirely secondary role to the activities and initiatives of business leaders according to the elitist thesis. The most thorough analyses from an elitist point of view linked local economic power to nationwide manufacturing, commerce, banking and professional groups. Pluralists reassured their readers that democracy of a kind persevered by means of the interplay of group competition. Elitists denied the existence of democracy except as a satisfying symbol with which elites lured the masses into acceptance of widespread inequalities of income, wealth and opportunities. In some cases, questions of resource distribution were simply non-issues, because elites carefully drew up the agenda of local government to avoid these controversial questions. In communities, as well as nationwide, political office-holders, whether elected officials or appointed bureaucrats, represented a cohesive upper economic class.[3]

Elements of the elitist interpretation appeared in the Marxist approach, but Marxists rooted their argument in class analysis. For Marxists, community power resulted from decisions made by a ruling class which controlled the major income-producing property of the nation in relation to a working class whose labour provided the profits that sustained American capitalism. From a Marxist point of view, 'if there is an upper class it must be a ruling class, because staying "upper" is what "ruling" is all about'.[4] Because Marxism was frequently confused with economic determinism in the United States, Marxist scholars of community power took pains to point out the ways in which their theories directed attention to complexity.

Pluralists and elitists tended to exaggerate the extent to which local communities controlled their own policies. Marxists tended to see a much too mechanical relationship between the capitalist state, the ruling class and the local government. In most cases, allowing for particular histories, local governments more often acted out of desire to secure the economic interests of their entire community (as defined by business leaders and city fathers) than they did to satisfy the interests of specific social groups outside the business community. Criticism of such a business-oriented system of community politics and policy-making remained relatively weak because potential dissidents typically took their grievances to the federal government. Furthermore, the increased opportunities for mobility during the post-war period enabled firms and individuals dissatisfied with one community to 'move on' to another. Why expend political energy to influence local government policy if the rewards were not appropriate to the task and the 'grass was greener' elsewhere?

In addition, several features of metropolitan politics made it difficult for groups outside the business community to participate in policy-making unless they made extraordinary efforts. Within local governments, 'backroom politics' became high political art, since much of their business was conducted behind the closed doors of city halls or private clubs. Local news media more often reported about colourful political personalities and shameful scandals rather than giving the basic information (such as days and times of meetings) necessary for effective participation. Finally, local government officials on the whole tended to be less dedicated than their national counterparts to make politics a vocation. Lacking the rewards of national politics, they expended little energy in sharing information with voters or soliciting their preferences about policy.[5]

By the 1980s it was increasingly clear that business leaders, allied with elected and appointed officials, ran local governments like well-tuned machines. This was specially the case when it was necessary to attract corporate investment or state and federal subsidies to protect and enhance their economic livelihood and their social prestige. These local notables bargained and compromised with other community organisations and with state and federal representatives when allocating services. In those unusual instances when groups succeeded in gaining a hearing to demand a shift in economic, social or political resources from advantaged to disadvantaged members of the local community, governments characteristically either sidestepped or avoided the issue altogether.[6]

No American community can be singled out as typical or representative of metropolitan politics and policy-making during the post-war period. However, an examination of several cases, drawn both from declining and growing regions, can illustrate the common trends and distinctive features of individual communities.

NEW YORK CITY

New York, New York: arguably the world's wealthiest city in 1945, the nation's number one metropolis tottered on the edge of bankruptcy thirty years later. New York's fiscal crisis, though more extreme than elsewhere, was a variation on a theme common to other cities in the Northeast and North Central regions. New York's near bankruptcy was rooted in its political history during the post-war period, but it also needs to be explained by the impact of its changing economic role in the American and world economy, by the influence of the federal and state governments, and by the internal social changes derived from New York's role as a haven for millions of displaced black and ethnic minorities.

New York's economic position steadily declined in comparison with the US as a whole after 1945. Like other older industrial cities, manufacturing employment sharply declined, and even its growth in finance, insurance and real estate lagged behind that of its metropolitan fringe and the nation at large. Loss of income from manufacturing, like the loss of tax-paying professional, managerial and craft workers, meant a steady decline in the city's revenue base. The loss of manufacturing jobs was not completely offset by the increase in lower paying service sector employment, a good part of which drained local revenue since it was public employment.

While New York's changing economy made it relatively vulnerable, so did its changing social composition. During the 1950s and 1960s New York attracted large numbers of low-income black and Puerto Rican families, and during the 1970s immigrants without entry documents sought New York as an alternative to their underdeveloped countries of origin. Poor families increased from just over one-third of the city's population in 1950 to almost half in 1970, at a time when the proportion of poor was falling in the US as a whole.

Business decisions led 40 per cent of the large corporations headquartered in New York in 1965 to move elsewhere by 1975. Social preferences led countless families to forsake homes in Virginia, Puerto Rico or Korea for apartments in Manhattan or Brooklyn. Decisions made by New York City political officials were the means by which local governments could cope with economic and social changes that originated elsewhere. The city government was limited in its ability to respond to these changes because of its legal and financial dependence upon the New York state government and the federal government. Business needs were often placed ahead of the needs of minorities and the poor. Elected officials, their eyes set on winning the next election, tried to ensure victory by making their record acceptable to as many voters as possible. Some of the most powerful positions in local government, however, went to appointees, and the theory of economic development of most appointed bureaucrats put them in philosophical fellowship with business interests. Furthermore, both elected officials and bureaucrats sometimes violated official ethics by indulging in New York City's lucrative, illegal, 'fee for service' tradition.

New York City politics during the post-war period gradually adapted to the increasing power of banking and real estate interests in the local economy. Business interests were not new to the city's politics. It was Lincoln Steffens who at the turn of the century described New York as 'government of the people, by the rascals, for the rich'. During the post-war period, however, bankers, builders, bond underwriters and insurance companies coalesced on behalf of property development programmes that required substantial increases in public indebtedness. Typically financed through bonds issued by special Public Authorities created by the state legislature, projects were executed free from the risk of voter rejection. Real estate firms enjoyed the enhanced property values created by projects such as the World Trade Center and extensions on the Museum of Modern Art. Banks earned interest on loans to the city, and underwriters benefited from fees collected for marketing the bonds. While business interests did not conspire with elected officials to carry out secret plans, they co-operated with leaders of organised labour and with city administrators to make property development a high priority. A business background ideally qualified one for an appointive office throughout the post-war period, and personnel regularly circulated from board rooms to administrative chambers. Furthermore, this bias in favour of business cost New York City millions of dollars in uncollected taxes, fees and fines at the very time when the price of its services skyrocketed.[7]

New York's mayors, city council members and other elected officials differed from the directors of the public authorities in one fundamental way: they owed their positions to voters. Voter accountability, while it did not sever the politicos from the property developers, linked city hall to the city's older and newer residents, to its ethnic interest groups, and to economic interest groups outside the business community.

During the administration of Mayor Robert F. Wagner, Jr. (1954–65), several groups of voters demanded changes in city policy, eventually increasing city expenditures. Wagner appeased reformers in his Democratic Party by supporting a new city charter that liberalised budgetary procedures. He followed in his father's footsteps by favouring the labour movement, and he enlisted the support of municipal employee unions by promising to listen to their demands for higher salaries. The city's budget increased at faster rates during Wagner's last administration, and when he left office New York City had a budget deficit for the first time since the Great Depression.

Mayor John V. Lindsay (1965–73), more patrician than pro-labour, won election by aligning himself with the Democratic Party reformers and attacking the leaders of civil service unions as well as the members of the municipal bureaucracy. Alert to the potential political role of the city's growing black and Hispanic population, Lindsay championed their cause while criticising the heavily Irish, Italian and Jewish-American blue-collar and white-collar municipal employees for their selfish attention to the cost of living. Although he won re-election by forming a coalition of white Liberal well-to-do voters, blacks and Puerto Ricans, Lindsay could not keep city employees from winning wage increases and pension benefits. The mayor's priorities could be seen in the increased expenditures for programmes keyed to poor minority residents versus the traditional services for home owners and white ethnics in the majority. Expenditures for higher education, which contributed to the threefold increase in black enrolments in the city university, went up 251 per cent, welfare expenditures increased 225 per cent and hospital expenses rose 123 per cent. Expenditures for police, fire, sanitation and the board of education increased an average of 66 per cent during the same 1966–71 period. The state legislature favoured Lindsay's opponents and refused to allow the city to pay for its increased expenditures by raising taxes; the city resorted to short-term borrowing. Debt service payments increased from $470 million in 1965 to $1.2 billion in 1974.[8]

During the last year of his administration, Mayor Lindsay resorted to budget manipulations to disguise the seriousness of the gap between revenue and expenditure. But long before he employed this desperate tactic, New York City tried to solve its problems by seeking state and federal relief. During the 1960s aid from New York state rose 250 per cent and federal government aid increased 706 per cent; assistance to the city from state and federal sources increased from 28 per cent of city revenue in 1959 to 47 per cent in 1969. In 1974 and 1975, with Abraham Beame in the Mayor's office, and with the national economy hit by recession, Congress and the state legislature cut their assistance to New York and the banks refused to renew their loans. New York City was saved from bankruptcy only by agreeing to restructure its municipal debt and reorder its expenditures under the direction of two quasi-public agencies: the Municipal Assistance Corporation (sometimes known as 'Big Mac') and the Emergency Financial Control Board (later simply the Financial Control Board). In 1978, Congress passed the New York City Loan Guarantee Act which established a five-year federal loan guarantee plan.

During the balance of the Beame administration (1973–7), the city adopted 'belt-tightening' measures that demonstrated how thoroughly 'the conduct of public policy in New York has increasingly come to reflect the priorities of the business community'.[9] Conservatives blamed the fiscal crisis primarily on overly liberal public employee wages or profligate welfare expenditures. The city administration under the MAC and EFCB began making massive cuts in municipal employment to show its commitment to responsible financial management. In little over a year, the city cut back its municipal payroll from 15 to 19 per cent, losing between 47,000 and 56,000 public jobs. The losses affected police, fire, sanitation and public schools; programmes that especially served blacks and Hispanics were particularly affected. During the same period (late 1974 to early 1976), the city fired half of all Spanish-surnamed workers, two of every five black male workers, and one of every three female workers. Racial minority workers were only one-third of city workers, but they accounted for almost half of the cuts. Mayor Edward Koch (1977–84), pledging to keep welfare costs low and take a hard line on crime, continued the austerity budgets and satisfied enough of the electorate to win re-election to a second term in 1981. During the Koch administration, further cutbacks in municipal jobs and services, such as the abandonment of social programmes by the federal government under President Reagan after 1980, were accompanied by tax benefits to corporations and incentives to businesses. These, mostly indirect, development policies were designed to maintain New York City's appeal as a world financial centre. Critics pointed out that the post-1975 policies contributed to a 'tale of two cities': an expanding international business capital on Manhattan Island and a shrinking city of low- and middle-income residents taxed by hardship and ignored in policy-making.[10]

SAN FRANCISCO

San Francisco, City by the Golden Gate: long celebrated as the nation's leading exponent of cultural diversity, 'Baghdad by the Bay' became the 'Manhattan of the West' during the post-war period. Internal cultural and lifestyle issues helped shape the city's politics and policy, but the dominant influences were the economic and social transformations that originated outside the city and its organised business community.

San Francisco's economy changed dramatically during the post-war period. At the end of the 1940s, six of every ten employees in the city's labour force worked either in wholesale and retail trade, manufacturing or construction. By 1977 service occupations accounted for nearly one in four. Jobs in finance, insurance, real estate, transportation, public utilities and government increased, but wholesale and retail trade employees plus manufacturing workers declined from almost half to a quarter of the labour force in 1977.

Changes in the San Francisco economy led to changes in the size and character of the city's population. Wartime migration swelled the population from about 635,000 in 1940 to over 775,000 in 1950. After the population peaked at nearly 784,000 in 1953, it gradually declined to 671,000 in 1980. San Francisco's ethnic minority population put it well ahead of the Bay Area as a whole. The white population declined from 85 per cent to 57 per cent of the total between 1950 and the 1970s, while the black share increased from 5 to 13 per cent, the Asian American from 4 to 13 per cent, and the Hispanic from about 2 to 14 per cent.

The post-1946 resettlement of San Francisco by liberal white-collar workers and non-white migrants helped to end the Republican hegemony over the city's politics. Mayors Elmer E. Robinson (1948–55) and George Christopher (1956–63) marked the end of a long Republican Party tradition. With the election of Mayor John Shelley (1963–8), San Francisco became almost a one-party city, with three Democrats to each Republican. In part this change reflected the growing non-white vote. Like Shelley, Mayors Joseph L. Alioto (1968–75), George Moscone (1976–8) and Dianne Feinstein (1978–84) were Democrats.

The impact of population resettlement on policy was limited, however, by the tendency of San Francisco's Democratic low-income non-whites to vote in smaller proportions than its conservative well-to-do citizens. Irish and Italian dominance on the Board of Supervisors and in the city hall bureaucracy declined much more slowly than the desertion of their pre-war neighbourhoods would have led one to expect. Although they constituted the city's two largest ethnic minority groups, blacks and Hispanics did not create independent and lasting political coalitions. Instead, Mayor Joseph Alioto welcomed the city's newest settlers to his coalition of labour and business, and his successors sought to cultivate a similar open-door policy. Consequently, by the end of the 1970s minorities had joined the governing coalition, but served as subordinates, not partners. Political scientist Frederick Wirt, writing in the early 1970s, referred to the inclusion of recently arrived ethnic minorities in the city's governing coalition as a 'politics of deference'.[11]

The other major aspect of San Francisco politics since the Second World War, in Wirt's terminology 'the politics of profit', represented a continuation of the campaign begun by leading corporate and banking figures before the war. They sought to take advantage of business opportunities offered by changing regional, national and international conditions. They envisioned San Francisco as the 'hub city' for bay area metropolitan co-ordination, financial headquarters for the Pacific, cultural centre for the region, and tourist mecca for the world. Their vision has directed much of the city's politics and policies since 1946.

The commitment to make San Francisco the 'hub city' of the bay area received support from the creation of specialised development agencies. These quasi-public bodies established a working coalition between the city's labour unions and elected officials. The first of these agencies, the Bay Area Council, developed out of a wartime regional planning commission. Reorganised by corporations and financial institutions in 1945 with funds from the Bank of America, American Trust Company, Standard Oil of California, Pacific Gas and Electric, United States Steel and the Bechtel Corporation, the Council and its member organisations began a drive for regional government, including the development of freeways, bridges and airports in the metropolitan area.[12]

Within San Francisco, a counterpart to the Bay Area Council began in 1956 when the Blyth–Zellerbach Committee, headed by two prominent city business leaders, endorsed the redevelopment of the wholesale produce market adjacent to the financial district. Most committee members also sat on the executive board of the Bay Area Council. They desired to make the produce market area harmonise with the more comprehensive plans for the bay area supported by the Council. In 1959, convinced that a group more independent of its member institutions and better able to attract participation from outside the business community would improve the credibility of the Bay Area Council and the Blyth–Zellerbach Committee, the latter created the San Francisco Planning and Urban Renewal Association (SPUR). In 1963, the Bay Area Council, the Blyth–Zellerbach Committee and SPUR joined with the San Francisco Convention and Visitors Bureau (CVB), a fourth quasi-public agency, to promote the hub city concept. Impetus for the CVB came from an advisory group appointed by Mayor Christopher and headed by J. D. Zellerbach of the Blyth–Zellerbach Committee. Once established, the CVB used funds from a hotel room occupancy tax to promote the city's tourist industry.

By 1980 one of the most popular tourist attractions in San Francisco was the Bay Area Rapid Transit system (BART) with its sleek futuristic-looking trains and artistically designed stations. BART began in the Bay Area Council's conviction that post-1945 metropolitan growth had created a pressing need for co-ordinated transportation services. The first step was an agreement that the San Francisco business district should be the hub of a fixed rail transit system designed to link the parts of the area. The Bay Area Council then worked with the California Legislature to create a Bay Area Rapid Transit Commission (1951) and then the Bay Area Rapid Transit District (1957). Members of the Blyth–Zellerbach Committee and the San Francisco Chamber of Commerce formed Citizens for Rapid Transit to campaign for passage of a November 1962 bond issue to finance the system. They launched a massive advertising campaign, stressing that BART would relieve traffic congestion, reduce air pollution and improve the quality of life.

San Mateo and Marin counties dropped out of the Rapid Transit District before the election, but voters in San Francisco, Alameda and Contra Costa counties approved the $792 million bond issue. Another $180 million came from Bay Bridge tolls, from a special state tax on retail sales to area residents and from the United States Department of Housing and Urban Development. With some 75 miles of track, 34 stations and the longest underwater rapid transit tube in the world, BART began regular transbay service in 1974. BART did not replace private automobiles or freeways, and residents still complained about air pollution. However, as one of the first engineering reports in the 1950s pointed out, BART was designed to complement, not replace, 'a system of freeways, expressways, and arterial highways in an area where automobile ownership per capita is very high'.

The Bay Area Council, the Blyth–Zellerbach Committee and the San Francisco Chamber of Commerce struggled in the late 1950s and early 1960s to secure public approval and support for the regional transportation integration represented by BART. The Blyth–Zellerbach Committee and SPUR also worked to gain the support of Mayors Christopher and Shelley for a programme of urban redevelopment in the south of Market area near the downtown financial district. The plan experienced considerable change between its inception in 1954 and its final approval in 1978 under the name Yerba Buena Center.

Despite endorsement by Mayors Christopher, Shelley and Alioto, planning by the San Francisco Redevelopment Agency, and support from the San Francisco Labor Council and the city's major daily newspapers and television stations, Yerba Buena Center was scaled down, redesigned and modified to include housing for displaced residents of the hotels that once filled the area. Resistance initially came from elderly residents led by George Woolf and Peter Mendelsohn, feisty (tetchy) retired labour organisers who had been active in a 1934 general strike. Eventually the group put together a coalition that included middle-income professionals from other parts of the city, public interest lawyers, and the owners of neighbourhood businesses. Federal courts supported demands for residential housing, and the plans for construction were a compromise hammered out by a Citizens Committee appointed by Mayor Moscone in 1976.

Successful resistance against the Yerba Buena Center and the eventual reform of the project through the medium of court appeals by public interest lawyers and participation on city committees by political activists demonstrated one aspect of a neighbourhood politics movement that became a widely discussed feature of San Francisco life during the post-war period. Covering a wide-ranging assortment of organisations with overlapping and sometimes opposing points of view, 'neighborhood politics' suggested that enhancement of the quality of local space should serve as the compelling rationale for political action. During 1959–66 coalitions of neighbourhood business owners and middle-income home owners successfully opposed several cross-town freeway proposals. Dubbed by the press as 'the Freeway Revolt', this coalition eventually included a majority of the Board of Supervisors and managed to halt all future freeway construction in San Francisco. In 1964, the Western Addition Community Organization, determined to protect its largely black neighbourhood against further displacement, partly succeeded in winning a battle for participation in the planning process and for replacement housing. The anti-war protests of 1967 to 1972 and the San Francisco State College strike of 1968–9 both strengthened grassroots activism in the city. Between 1969 and 1973 a coalition of environmental groups critical of what they called 'the Manhattanization of San Francisco' tried unsuccessfully to limit the height of downtown office buildings. At the same time, the city's growing homosexual community, led by populist Harvey Milk, made 'gay power' and homosexual rights the basis for a claim to greater participation in city politics.

The Hub City coalition, now with especially active support from the Building and Construction Trades Council and claiming to be on the side of growth and progress, found itself opposed by a coalition of gay activists, middle-income home owners, ethnic minorities, small business owners, environmentalists and political radicals. Their common cause grounded in mutual support for neighbourhood quality of life, they used 'popular sovereignty' as their rallying cry, organised Citizens for Representative Government in 1973, and unsuccessfully attempted to institute district election of supervisors in place of the 75-year-old at-large system. Opponents of the district measure argued that district elections would bring a return of political machines, narrow parochialism and the neglect of city-wide interests.

Between 1973 and 1980 district elections were established and then abolished during frequently bitter controversies over the philosophy of local policy-making. One newspaper columnist regarded the repeal of district elections as a shining example of political good sense: 'Perhaps the city has at last decided to put behind itself its recent passion for self-destructive special interest politics, and to behave once again in a manner befitting its stature as one of the great cities of the world.' Others disagreed, one claiming to find: 'The basic issue being whether only well heeled, well financed candidates can run for supervisor'. For both the vice-president of the San Francisco Chamber of Commerce and the secretary-treasurer of the San Francisco Labor Council, the basic issue appeared to be access to sympathetic supervisors. Speaking of the district approach, John

Crowley of the Labor Council said, 'Now, at least, we have entree to the board'. But Gregory P. Hurst of the Chamber of Commerce criticised the district board because its 'actions are clearly contrary to a healthy business climate', and he favoured repeal because 'a healthy business climate is dependent on a solid, well-run city government'.

FROSTBELT, SUNBELT AND THE SUBURBS

Case-studies of New York City and San Francisco demonstrate the ways in which business interests dominated local government policy-making after 1945. Despite the unusual strength of 'grassroots' politics emanating from San Francisco neighbourhoods, the downtown corporation-city hall connection carried the important battles. Although New York City possessed one of the most healthy systems of local electoral politics in the nation, organised business played the key role in the city's fiscal crisis. Within both San Francisco and New York political activities were limited by external economic changes and the federal and state governments. If the opportunities for growth increased due to federal and state aid (New York's loan guarantee plan and San Francisco's BART were leading examples), so did the risk of vulnerability increase due to economic dependence.

Throughout the Frostbelt, politics followed the New York and the San Francisco pattern. Whether in Pittsburgh or Detroit, Chicago or Indianapolis, Boston or St Louis, chambers of commerce, quasi-public Special Authorities and elite development committees successfully maintained the dominant role in co-operation with local government officials. When challenged by grassroots organisations or harassed by militant non-white minority groups, the business-city hall political coalitions often made places for leaders of the opposition on official deliberative bodies, but they never surrendered their controlling positions. On the contrary, they frequently discredited their critics and compromised their legitimacy. The defeat of the 1978 populist programme of Mayor Dennis Kucinich of Cleveland provided only a more dramatic example of a general phenomenon. In those communities, such as Gary, Indiana, and Newark, New Jersey, where a black politician became mayor the changing of chief executives did not diminish the power of business.

Metropolitan politics and policy-making in the Sunbelt followed the Frostbelt model in many respects. Urban areas in the South and West (with important exceptions such as San Francisco, Denver and New Orleans) experienced their greatest expansion during the post-war period. Their dependence upon the federal government and externally generated economic changes dramatised their limited power over their affairs. However, because the potential benefits of growth were so great, Sunbelt communities quickly mobilised themselves to shape growth into development. In community after community, leaders of established business firms, publishers of local newspapers and elected officials created Sunbelt counterparts to San Francisco's Bay Area Council and New York's Public Authorities. San Jose had its Progress Committee, San Antonio organised a Good Government League, Dallas formed a Citizen's Charter Association, and several dozen businessmen and politicians gathered together in the 'Phoenix 40'. With membership drawn almost exclusively from the top echelon of business, these small, cohesive, community-of-interest groups also dominated decision-making in Atlanta, Miami, Tucson, New Orleans, Dallas, Houston and Albuquerque. Members of the groups were supported by the boosterism of their newspapers. They were insulated from effective voter challenges by the at-large systems of representation (as in San Francisco) that made running for political office prohibitively expensive for members of low-income or ethnic minority groups. One critic of this Sunbelt system of governance concluded that 'to the degree that meaningful politics is practiced in these cities, it is bureaucratically orchestrated by business and government'.[13]

During the 1970s these established growth-oriented coalitions were challenged by two new social groups. One group consisted of affluent voters who had moved to the Sunbelt both for the income and for the amenities, and they demanded controls on pollution, improved services and a greater role in decision-making. They constituted a grassroots community movement that made noisy demands for political reforms. While they achieved some gains, their victories proved mainly symbolic, even in San Jose, California, where they succeeded in electing one of their own, Janet Gray Hayes, as mayor. The other group that challenged the old-established elites was composed of younger members of regional and national corporations. This was essentially a new business elite dedicated to controlled growth and anxious to preserve Sunbelt amenities by carefully planning the future allocation of local resources. 'The corporations, including the press, now advocate "good planning", instead of the unrestrained growth of the past . . . their increasingly responsible and seemingly liberal positions are, simply, good business planning.' The most serious challenges to the old elite in Sunbelt communities came not from disadvantaged groups seeking redistribution of resources; the greatest danger to the old elite came from a new generation of businessmen.[14]

The situation was much the same in America's suburban governments. Their political leaders have typically been middle-aged white males: 'local councilmen are "elite" in a very real sense'. Sharing similar class and educational backgrounds, in basic agreement about protecting their communities from undesirable physical or social changes, suburban government officials characteristically behaved more conservatively than their central city counterparts. Like the cities, suburbs had limited governmental powers, and like the cities, suburbs had little control over the economic decisions that sparked their growth during the post-war period.[15]

Policy-making in suburban governments defied all easy generalisations save one: participation was as limited as in the cities. 'Grassroots government run by automation' was the way Robert C. Wood described suburban politics in his 1958 study. Herbert J. Gans, who studied Levittown politics in the years between 1958 and 1962, discovered 'a power structure' that was 'somewhat more monolithic than those found by political scientists in established communities'. The Levitt organisation's 'imposing influence' was due partly to the newness of the community, but Levitt shared decision-making with the head of the local Democratic Party and an organised group of Catholic voters. Gans found the low rates of suburban political participation unsurprising, for the residents regarded local government's purpose as being little more than 'to protect their residential status'. Otherwise, suburbanites 'get what they want from the corporate economy' and 'from a federal government which subsidizes that economy for their benefit'.

Unlike poor people, who are increasingly dependent on government for jobs and incomes, middle class people have no need to participate or intervene, except on the rare occasions when government deprives them of goods, status, or privileges they have come to take for granted.[16]

8. Wealth and Poverty

THE coexistence of wealth and poverty after 1945 brought a central theme of American history into the post-war period. The perception of the US as a land of opportunity led many nineteenth-century observers to de-emphasise the importance of wealth among Americans. Dramatic success stories of immigrants such as Andrew Carnegie, like the modest material improvements of many families, directed attention to future possibilities rather than fear of failure. Nonetheless, throughout US history, persistence of inequality of wealth has disturbed those who literally translated Thomas Jefferson's declaration of equality. Henry George in *Progress and Poverty* (1879) argued that poverty would inevitably accompany progress unless the nation adopted his novel system of taxation. Robert Hunter in *Poverty* (1904) argued that the responsibility for most immiseration lay with the society rather than the individual, and he turned to socialism as a more likely source of equality. The 1920s brought prosperity to thousands of Americans, but many more lived on the edge of insecurity. The Great Depression showed how shallow the previous decade's prosperity had been. During the 1930s Louisiana Senator Huey P. Long excoriated the rich and demanded that they share their wealth. President Franklin D. Roosevelt, not to be outdone, criticised the country's 'economic royalists' and in 1937 demanded federal government assistance for 'the one-third of the nation ill-housed, ill-clad, ill-nourished'. The Second World War restored economic growth more effectively than FDR's New Deal, but neither the spirit of wartime solidarity nor the post-war prosperity blinded Americans to the continuing inequalities of wealth.

SOCIOLOGICAL STUDIES OF WEALTH AND CLASS

While most Americans busied themselves with making a living in the early post-war years, some professional sociologists made reputations

studying wealth and class. They discussed the extent of 'social
stratification' and debated its significance for American society.
Their academic disagreements coincided with virulent controversies
within Congress over federal economic policies, government regulation of the labour movement and government control of communism. Discussions of domestic wealth and class resonated with
special political significance during the 1940s and 1950s; looming in
the background were the international implications of what seemed to
many a test of American capitalism. Did the wealthy in the United
States maintain their places without victimising the middle and lower
orders of society? Was American society blessed with more equality
than its European allies or its communist enemies? If so, shouldn't
others follow its example? If not, wasn't the American claim to world
leadership resting upon a foundation of internal inequality that
rendered its leaders apologists for privilege?

While the Second World War and the Cold War heightened the
symbolic importance of debates about American inequality, the
controversies over wealth, economic standing and psychological
consciousness of class were a feature of sociological analysis beginning in the 1920s. In 1929, Robert S. and Helen M. Lynd published
Middletown: A Study in Modern American Culture, which reported their
study of what they considered to be a typical community during the
mid-1920s. According to the Lynds, the residents of the city (Muncie,
Indiana) divided themselves into two distinct classes defined according to occupations. Muncie's 'business class' and 'working class'
lived in dramatically distinct social, cultural and political worlds.
When the Lynds returned ten years later to examine the impact of the
Depression on Muncie, the business class still ran the city, and one
wealthy manufacturing family dominated the business class like 'a
reigning royal family'. Its ownership of wealth and its control of
investment capital allowed 'the X family' to control the community in
a way that epitomised 'the American business-class control system. It
may even foreshadow a pattern which may become increasingly
prevalent in the future as the American propertied class strives to
preserve its controls.'[1] The existence of a tenacious 'business-class
control system' did not, however, imply a flourishing belief in social
class differences or in political activities based on loyalties to one's
economic group. Residents, the poor and the wealthy alike, played
down the importance of distinctions based on wealth and emphasised

the unifying qualities of 'the Middletown Spirit' of community harmony.

Other studies at the end of the 1930s documented the coexistence of economic inequality and loyalty to community. Akron, Ohio, witnessed the nation's first sit-down strike, where workers seized control of corporate property to force management to bargain with their union. Even here, the blue-collar population respected private property and workers neither saw themselves nor wanted to be regarded as members of a separate class with particular interests.

Arthur W. Kornhauser of the University of Chicago acknowledged that 92 per cent of American families lived on incomes below $3,000 per year, while only 2.7 per cent had $5,000 or more, but he insisted that such 'objective' inequality did not translate into 'conflicting class attitudes and class antagonisms'. The upper levels of American society contained those with greater talent and ability whose families had been 'selected' over time because of energy, ambition, confidence and willingness to co-operate. The lower levels were filled with families that lacked competence and ambition. Even among the extremely wealthy and the very poor, most people could be expected to accept social conditions as they were; only the discontented at the bottom and the top of society held radical views or advocated basic social changes. Kornhauser's American society was a continuum of income groups rather than the two distinct classes of the Lynds' Muncie, but he nonetheless concluded that 'a small, top group of "capitalists" and their higher-salaried professional and white-collar associates' was 'opposed in social viewpoint to the general run of wage-earners and low-salaried groups'.[2]

By the end of the 1940s the sociological search for satisfactory generalisations about the significance of wealth in calculating social class continued along familiar lines. Katherine Archibald's study of wartime shipyard workers (1947) convinced her that most of them were 'keen-eyed enough to observe . . . wealth was the indispensable basis of privilege; it was the solid pillar about which the other attributes of the gentleman and the gentleman's life twined like decorative vines'. However, 'the shipyard worker never felt himself to be altogether and irrevocably excluded from the world of wealth and the status that wealth bestowed'. Consequently, the worker was not 'altogether ready to repudiate the hierarchical system toward whose pinnacle he looked with longing eyes'. Daniel Bell, in a 1949 article interpreted President Truman's pronouncement that Americans had 'rejected the discredited theory that the fortunes of the nation should be in the hands of a privileged few' as a sign that the US had undergone an 'Un-Marxist Revolution'. However, the nation still needed 'some new sense of civic obligation . . . that will be strong enough to command the allegiance of all groups and provide a principle of equity in the distribution of the rewards and privileges of society'.[3]

Sociologist Richard Centers, in *The Psychology of Social Class* (1949) claimed that enough disagreement about civic consciousness existed to justify a conclusion that 'Americans have become class conscious, and a part of them, calling themselves the working class, have begun to have attitudes and beliefs at variance with traditional acceptances and practices'. Walter Goldschmidt reviewed ten years of such research in 1950, and decided that the US was moving towards a 'class system', composed of four 'emerging social classes'. The great majority of Americans belonged to the middle class (some 40 per cent) and the working class, but a less affluent group, typically found in urban slums and 'the share cropper South', constituted a permanent American underclass. This submerged segment, as large as 25 per cent in some communities, lived in extreme poverty and cultural hopelessness. The American elite was the smallest and most clearly formed in the class system, but there were no sharp lines distinguishing one class from the others. Goldschmidt emphasised 'the fluidity of class position and the force of the cultural denial of class' rather than any fixity of class consciousness.[4]

Further research during the 1950s mainly confirmed previous conclusions regarding American wealth and class. All of this research suggested a hierarchical distribution of income, wealth, education, material goods, attitudes, power and prestige. Nonetheless most sociologists denied that American society rigidly divided itself into clearly demarcated classes. They preferred to stress the fluid connections between classes.

Milton M. Gordon's 1958 synthesis, like that of Walter Goldschmidt in 1950, yielded abundant evidence about the 'basic or fundamental' role of economic power in American society. Although economic, social and political factors all contributed to the hierarchical ordering of American life, 'it is quite obviously economic power which provides the means by which through successive generations particular consumption patterns may be enjoyed, occupational positions may be preempted, politico-community power may be appropriated, and status differences may be crystallized.' Gordon disagreed with Centers and argued that the 'generalized class awareness' in American society was not equivalent to class consciousness. Robert A. Nisbet, satisfied that the US had witnessed 'the decline and fall of social class' seemed willing to conclude that 'class lines recede everywhere' because 'we are living in a society governed by status, not class, values'. Vance Packard, on the other hand, argued in his popular 1959 book *The Status Seekers* that 'class lines in America are becoming more rigid, rather than withering away'.[5]

Few writers used such pessimistic language as Packard; most preferred to extol the benefits to all American social groups that accompanied 'the income revolution' of the previous twenty years. If all US families were divided into five groups according to their income, according to these analysts, the share of the top fifth declined by 12 per cent during 1935–50, while the share of the bottom fifth increased by 17 per cent. While the families at the top still received 45.7 per cent of all family income in 1950, there had been a small but definite increase in the bottom group's share. Most of the change undoubtedly came just before and during the war, mainly because mass unemployment ended while the number of working wives in low and moderate income families increased. This change was also seen in the distribution of mean family income during the period. The mean income for the bottom 60 per cent of families increased some 75 to 80 per cent, whereas the mean for the highest fifth increased only 33 per cent. Although left-wing writer Victor Perlo argued in 1954 that this presumed 'leveling' of income was more sham than substance because of various tax avoidance schemes used by the wealthy, the best evidence to date suggests that a 'Great Leveling' did take place between 1929 and 1951. It was over by 1951, however, and the distribution of income in the US has been stable ever since.[6]

THE DISCOVERY OF POVERTY

As Walter Goldschmidt's 1950 review of social class research demonstrated, American poverty did not go unnoticed during the 1950s. In 1960, however, John F. Kennedy made the rural poverty of depressed Appalachia a presidential campaign issue, and in 1962 political activist Michael Harrington dramatised the seriousness of

American poverty with his exposé *The Other America*. During the 1940s and 1950s the percentage of US families in poverty declined steadily as the economy grew. Mid-way through the 1930s some 61 million Americans, making up 51 per cent of the population, were poor, but in 1960 only 21 per cent, or 39 million people, lived in conditions incompatible with 'decency and health'. The poor and the 'near poor' together amounted to 55 million Americans, around 25 per cent of the total population. In his primary election campaign in West Virginia Kennedy faced poor families of subsistence farmers and unemployed coal miners, but he had also witnessed similar hardship in Massachusetts textile mill communities. By 1960, almost 85 per cent of the poor lived in cities or small towns, compared to only 50 per cent in 1930. The South, traditionally home to the majority of the poor, held 45 per cent of the poverty population in 1960, and 43 per cent of US farm families were poor compared to only 17 per cent of non-farm families. Michael Harrington pointed out that new groups of 'hard-core' poor existed: the aged, non-whites and broken families headed by females were becoming a larger part of the American poor. Their concentration in urban areas made their problems more visible.

The urbanisation of American poverty came during a period of increasing attention to social issues by television, and it also coincided with optimism among economists and social reformers about America's ability to end poverty altogether. CBS's television documentary *Harvest of Shame*, shown to audiences on Thanksgiving Day in 1960, dramatised the plight of poor migrant farm workers and their families. NBC's *The Battle of Newburgh* (1962) criticised the city manager of a New York community for his well-publicised attempts to remove eligible residents from the town's welfare rolls. The Ford Foundation financed a group of University of Michigan scholars which published *Income and Welfare in the United States* in 1962. The authors argued that while economic growth impressively reduced poverty, new federal government programmes in education, health, welfare, job training and tax reform were also necessary. For about $10 billion a year, or below 2 per cent of the gross national product (about one-fifth the cost of national defence), they concluded, 'poverty could be abolished easily and simply by a stroke of the pen'.[7]

In December 1962 John F. Kennedy asked the chairman of his Council of Economic Advisers for copies of Harrington's *The Other America*, and began to consider the fight against poverty as a way to extend his 'New Frontier'. By the middle of 1963 the president believed that an aggressive campaign against poverty could dramatically tie together existing economic programmes designed to strengthen the US economy by eradicating unemployment, slum housing, juvenile delinquency, adult dependency and illiteracy.

For at least a decade, federal agencies and corporate philanthropies (especially the Ford Foundation, the nation's largest) had experimented with a variety of programmes designed to alleviate such social problems. During 1963 Kennedy's staff began to prepare the data for a 'comprehensive, coordinated attack on poverty' that would be included in the administration's legislative programme for 1964. President Johnson included the idea in his own programme, and in his first State of the Union message told Congress that: 'This administration today, here and now, declares unconditional war on poverty in America.' Johnson's war on poverty captured headlines and moved the arguments of social democrat Michael Harrington on to the pages of the president's 1984 economic report. Although Harrington believed that the structure of the economy was to blame for poverty because it favoured growth at the expense of welfare, he also maintained that the poor lived in 'a separate culture . . . with its own way of life'. 'Poverty breeds poverty' according to the economic report, ensuring that 'the cruel legacy of poverty is passed from parents to children'.[8]

Despite objections by the head of the Department of Labor that breaking the 'vicious circle' of inherited poverty by providing services to children and youth would be less effective than a vigorous job-creation scheme, the administration proposal in March 1964 contained a variety of programmes. Tying them together, from the community action programme aimed at generating political initiative among the poor to the Jobs Corps intended to train youth to move into the labour force, was one, central, conservative idea. The federal government's war on poverty set out to provide opportunities to the poor which would enable them to become part of the labour force. The war on poverty did not intend to provide the poor with immediate jobs and income subsidies which would enable them to participate in the consumer economy. Unwilling to face the impact of technological change, changes in the nature of the workforce, or discrimination against minorities, women and the aged, the drafters of this legislation hoped that market decisions would create wider occupational opportunities. In August, Congress passed the Economic Opportunity Act, authorised an Office of Economic Opportunity (OEO) to administer the legislation, and budgeted $962.5 million to be spent on ten different anti-poverty programmes.[9]

For various reasons, the war on poverty proved ineffectual, if not still-born. Confusion about its goals existed from the beginning; in-fighting between the various administrative branches of the OEO quickly surfaced and never disappeared; conservatives criticised its ameliorative assumptions, as well as its bureaucratic excesses; radicals regarded it as another paternalistic palliative; state and local officials condemned what they saw as its intrusions upon local control (see Chapter 6). President Johnson, preoccupied by the Vietnam War, offered little support to the war on poverty after 1965. Congress dismantled much of the programme during the Nixon administration, and the OEO itself disappeared in 1974. Given budgets that were meagre compared to the magnitude of the problem, the OEO was destined to promise more than it could deliver, but several unexpected consequences came of its failure. The passage of anti-poverty legislation helped to establish a climate of acceptance in Congress for later health insurance and educational aid programmes for the poor, as well as the liberalisation of social security pension plans. In addition, the war on poverty and the discovery of poverty that accompanied it heightened the expectations of poor people and legitimised a groundswell of criticism directed against the power and the privileges of wealthy Americans.

THE CRITIQUE OF THE ESTABLISHMENT

The coming of the war on poverty carried the debates about wealth and class into the offices of Washington bureaucrats, and the demise of anti-poverty programmes led many social scientists to discard their earlier optimism about social reform. By the late 1970s journals such as *The Public Interest* carried tough-minded critiques of liberal schemes written by chastened poverty warriors. Neo-conservative social scientists such as Edward Banfield and Nathan Glazer regarded certain social conditions as insoluble problems, arguing that government attempts to improve society caused worse problems than the evils that prompted the programmes. Liberals and radicals took different lessons from the failure of the war on poverty. They lectured Americans about the tenacity of the wealthy, and they documented the ways in which the powerful preserved their positions and advantages at the expense of society as a whole.

Most Americans typically envied the rich and worked for wealth more often than they demanded redistribution of resources. Yet a strong tradition in American politics called out for popular accountability. Perhaps Senator Huey P. Long of Louisiana captured the American attitude best when he harangued his radio audiences about sharing the wealth and making every man a king. The popularity of Long's position owed much to the Great Depression; the same can be said of President Franklin D. Roosevelt's 1935 message to Congress on hereditary wealth. Talented individuals, according to the president, could not have earned their great fortunes without 'mass cooperation', and the wealthy consequently were indebted to the community at large. In 1939 author Gustavus Myers even suggested that the abolition of hereditary fortunes was necessary to accomplish 'that fuller economic equality toward which the spirit of the age is here progressing'.[10]

The dramatic growth in corporate concentration after the Second World War by no means implied the demise of hereditary fortunes, but criticism of unaccountable wealth focused upon corporations as well as individuals. Critics of corporate wealth contended with what historians Douglas T. Miller and Marion Nowak have described as 'the public love affair with big business' during the 1950s. A good part of this affection for corporations was actually business publicising itself. In 1956 a trade association called the Advertising Council coined the term 'people's capitalism' to describe the extensiveness of home ownership, savings accounts and corporate share holding by Americans. The phrase was included in a display of American prosperity sent around the world by the public information office of the US State Department. A *Reader's Digest* article caught the spirit of the phrase, as did other corporate spokesmen and writers, when they touted America's 'new kind of capitalism . . . capitalism for the many, not for the few'. In fact, ownership of corporate stock was restricted to a smaller percentage of the public in 1956 than it had been in 1930; only a tiny proportion of blue-collar workers (less than 1.5 per cent) owned securities, and most held less than $1000 worth. Left-wing economist Victor Perlo pointed out that any one of the nation's wealthiest families, such as the Mellons, duPonts or Rockefellers, controlled more stock than all of America's blue-collar 'people's capitalists' put together.[11]

In 1957, Perlo expanded his critique of 'people's capitalism' into a full scale muckraking book that dissected *The Empire of High Finance*. His argument proceeded from the assumption that giant concentrations of wealth and power naturally grew out of monopoly capitalism. Most Americans became dependent while 'a few hundred or at most a few thousand men of wealth determine the destinies of the nation, and are guided in so doing by the overriding principle of increasing their own profits'. Because government and the political parties had been 'submerged' into a 'corporate power structure', voters or public officials could not alter unemployment rates and plant closings. In a similar vein, sociologist C. Wright Mills complained about 'the power elite' in a book published in 1956. Mills agreed that 'the corporate rich' wielded great power, but they did so along with a 'political directorate' in government and 'warlords' who controlled the military. In Mills's version, wealthy individuals exercised power not as representatives of a capitalist class that had made government its servant, but rather their power came to them as members of 'the major institutions of modern society. These hierarchies of state and corporation and army constitute the means of power . . . command posts of modern society which offer us the sociological key to an understanding of the role of the higher circles in America.'[12]

By the 1950s, a substantial number of America's 'national upper class' had moved into high-ranking positions in corporate, government and military institutions. These were descendants of a nineteenth-century 'business aristocracy', originally centred in Philadelphia, New York or Boston, who at the turn of the century developed a keen sense of group-consciousness as immigrants became the majority in the leading cities. Mrs Astor and Ward McAlister drew up their list of 'the Four Hundred' members of Society during the 1880s, and a listing in the *Social Register* (1888) from that time on became the ticket for admission to the American upper class. Boarding schools, fashionable resorts, eastern universities and the Episcopal Church provided the institutional ties that allowed the wealthy Protestant families of particular cities to develop their national upper class. Still secure at the end of the 1950s, this national 'metropolitan upper class with a common cultural tradition, consciousness of kind, and "we" feeling of solidarity' was the nearest the US had come to producing a wealthy caste situation, with membership available only to those born into it.[13]

The national upper class provided many of the members of 'The

American Establishment' according to journalist Richard H. Rovere. Like the Power Elite of C. Wright Mills, Rovere's Establishment drew its strength from institutional bases; like the national upper class described by E. Digby Baltzell, its prestige derived from family wealth, famous universities and social exclusivity. Regardless of which party controlled Congress or which president occupied the White House, 'a more or less closed and self-sustaining institution . . . holds a preponderance of power in our more or less open society', Rovere argued. While the Establishment never controlled Congress (especially the House of Representatives), 'its influence is pervasive, and it succeeds far more often than its antagonists in fixing the major goals of American society'. Bankers, businessmen and professionals, primarily from the Northeast, comprised the nucleus of the Establishment. Both John F. Kennedy and Dwight D. Eisenhower were allowed to enter, but never reached the top ranks, whereas Adlai Stevenson and Nelson Rockefeller became leading figures. Neither doctrinaire nor monolithic, the Establishment did insist upon support for racial integration and foreign aid. On economic issues, 'A man cannot be for *less* welfarism than Eisenhower, and to be further left than Reuther is considered bad taste'.[14]

While Rovere praised the relative ideological flexibility of the Establishment, he also pointed out its penchant for selective discrimination. Southerners were shunned, for the most part, as were westerners: Texan Lyndon B. Johnson and Californian Richard M. Nixon, vice-presidents under Kennedy and Eisenhower, were outsiders. Rovere's Establishment, however, did not discriminate against Jews or Roman Catholics (except for noisy popular figures such as Bishop Fulton J. Sheen who broadcast his sermons over television). Furthermore, consistent with its disavowal of racial segregation, the Establishment regarded Baptist civil rights leader Reverend Martin Luther King, Jr. as acceptable.

While Rovere saw the Establishment as practising a relative catholicity, others charged the upper-class 'aristocracy' with protecting its privileged character. When sociologist E. Digby Baltzell published his exhaustive analysis of the national upper class in 1964, he aimed his most severe criticism at its anti-Semitism and its racist attitudes towards black Americans. No advocate of 'a more egalitarian and homogenized society', Baltzell believed nonetheless that the institutions of the 'Protestant Establishment' constituted 'vital prerequisites of a secure and organic leadership structure' for the US. But an 'authoritative aristocracy' could only flourish if 'it's membership requirements are based on talent and moral distinction rather than ethnic or racial ancestry'. Because the national upper class had enfeebled itself by evolving into 'an affluent caste', it could no longer serve as a training school for national leadership. 'Anglo-Saxonism', Baltzell concluded, 'is the greatest enemy both of our upper-class institutions and of our valuable Anglo-American traditions of democracy.'[15]

Baltzell scored the national upper class for refusing to admit Americans regardless of race, religion or economic standing. Other critics of the Establishment (the term quickly became part of American argot during the late 1960s and 1970s) attacked its effects on the quality of American life. G. William Domhoff's book *Who Rules America?* (1967) reviewed more than a decade of research and concluded that

> the income, wealth, and institutional leadership of what Baltzell calls the 'American business aristocracy' are more than sufficient to earn it the designation 'governing class' . . . this 'ruling class' is based upon the national corporate economy and the institutions that economy nourishes. It manifests itself through what the late C. Wright Mills called the power elite.

Domhoff, however, did not address the question of whether 'the role of the American upper class has been a benevolent one or a malevolent one'.[16] Other critics focused precisely upon that issue.

Veteran financial journalist and muckraking writer Ferdinand Lundberg's *The Rich and the Super Rich* (1968) became a bestseller, informing Americans they were 'nothing more than employees . . . precariously situated; nearly all of them are menials. In this particular respect', Lundberg wrote, 'Americans, though illusion-ridden, are like the Russians under Communism, except that the Russians inhabit a less technologized society and have a single employer.' College textbooks of the 1970s routinely documented the ways in which 'the class hierarchy' shaped the 'life chances' of the population. The well-to-do lived longer, stayed healthier, obtained better schooling and were more likely to finish college. People of 'higher economic and occupational levels escape arrest and conviction to a greater extent than lower-class persons even when equally guilty of crimes' according to a typical text. Corporations were increasingly criticised as the branch of the Establishment most guilty of crimes against the commons. In his introduction to *America, Inc.: Who Owns and Operates the United States* (1971), consumer activist Ralph Nader complained that 'corporate economic, product, and environmental crimes dwarf other crimes in damage to health, safety and property, in confiscation or theft of other peoples' monies, and in control of the agencies which are supposed to stop this crime and fraud.'[17]

With his well-publicised campaigns on behalf of automobile safety Nader became something of a folk hero among critics of corporate power during the 1960s. By the beginning of the 1970s, he was calling for a citizen's movement to demand that wealth be made accountable to democracy. He quoted favourably the Roman saying that: 'Whatever touches us all should be decided by all.' The critique of the Establishment gradually developed momentum and reinforced the American mistrust of private privilege during the 1960s. By the 1970s it provided an ideological rationale for several social movements aimed at changing the distribution of wealth.

THE POOR PEOPLE'S MOVEMENTS

As early as Shays' Rebellion of debtors in 1786, American history featured attempts to restrain the power of wealth. Thomas Jefferson, though a wealthy Virginia slave holder, reaffirmed the right of Revolution; his words to that effect were inscribed on the Washington DC Memorial built in his honour. Jefferson's conception of the people, however, included only property owners; like the other Founding Fathers, he had little faith in the propertyless people and slight trust in their political abilities. The Massachusetts militia decisively put down Shays' Rebellion. Nineteenth- and early twentieth-century social movements that challenged the distribution of wealth met with equally aggressive opposition. Militant actions to organise the poor during the Great Depression were less successful than the industrial union movement, but they suggested the possibilities of working directly with the residents of local communities on the basis of their common economic grievances.

Perhaps the most successful and widely imitated community organiser to emerge from the ferment of the 1930s was Saul D. Alinsky, who in 1939 helped form a People's Organization in the predominantly Catholic working-class district of Chicago, Back of the Yards. By the Second World War, this area near the stockyards had become even more notorious than it was when Upton Sinclair used it in his novel *The Jungle*. Alinsky convinced the residents of the need to settle their ethnic, religious, social and political differences in order to work together to satisfy their common needs for housing, health care and child welfare. Alinsky's basic premise was that the residents of a community needed to inform and educate themselves as they created their own local action institutions. Participation would create, and continued participation would reinforce, faith in the residents' ability to solve problems. In the process, they would discover the limits of their community's power to shape its destiny, and they would learn to identify 'those major destructive forces which pervade the entire social order'. Once a local organisation existed, it could become 'a springboard for the development of other People's Organizations throughout the nation'.[18]

Sympathetic observers, from journalists to national politicians, praised the Back of the Yards Council as a model democratic movement. Adlai Stevenson, Governor of Illinois, called the Chicago organisation the nation's best example of 'all that our democracy stands for'. Alinsky formed a non-profit organisation called the Industrial Areas Foundation and travelled throughout the US organising the poor in more than forty communities. In California, the IAF worked with Mexican-American residents of several dozen areas that later became the Community Service Organization; Cesar Chavez, the leader of the United Farm Workers, was an Alinsky protégé. His unflinching dedication to being a Radical in the Tom Paine tradition ('Let them call me rebel'), combined with his determination to create a national network of People's Organizations, brought Alinsky the enmity of conservatives. Business newspapers tried to discredit his work by associating him with the Communist Party. The editor of a religious newspaper, not without cause, argued that he was 'fomenting a political movement whose object is to establish control over urban society by raising up from its ruins a power structure dictatorship based on slum dwellers'. Between 1964 and 1971, when he published his *Rules for Radicals*, Alinsky and the IAF successfully organised a number of poor black communities in such cities as Rochester, New York and Chicago, and by the mid-1970s younger radicals were using his tactics to organise the poor throughout the US.[19]

The fact that America's central cities were increasingly the home of the nation's poorest non-whites during the 1950s and 1960s meant that community organising to secure a larger share of national resources for the urban poor overlapped with the civil rights movement (one of the subjects of the next chapter). Given the understandable community of interest between advocates of economic equality and activists for racial justice, it should be no surprise that George A. Wiley, the leader of the most extensive poor people's movement during the post-war period, began his political career as a civil rights activist. A chemistry professor at the University of Syracuse, Wiley was one of the few black PhDs working at major American universities during the early 1960s. In 1964 he left the university to become the associate director of the Congress of Racial Equality (CORE), and in 1966 he joined with disciples of Alinsky and other advocates of creating a social movement of poor welfare recipients in founding the National Welfare Rights Organization (NWRO).[20]

The NWRO grew out of an uncoordinated movement by welfare recipients who demanded increased public relief during the years of civil rights activism and mass rioting between 1963 and 1967. As welfare applicants grew impatient and angry, welfare agencies grew more accommodating. The numbers of families receiving assistance grew from 745,000 in 1960 to 1.5 million in 1968. Frances Fox Piven and Richard A. Cloward, social scientists who were also civil rights and anti-poverty activists, became convinced in 1965 that only about half the families eligible for relief were actually receiving aid. Their 'Strategy to End Poverty' had two goals. They would conduct a massive campaign to persuade poor families to overcome their aversion to being 'on the dole' and the families would launch mass protests demanding grants. Realising that severe financial pressures on city treasuries would create an urban fiscal crisis, Piven and Cloward foresaw that the federal government would be forced to assume welfare costs, hopefully establishing a national minimum income. They expected that disruptive mass protest on behalf of income grants would trigger positive federal government action. Wiley and others disagreed with the mobilise and disrupt tactic. They wanted instead to 'organize' welfare recipients who would then create institutions to lobby at the local, state and federal levels for favourable policies.

The NWRO adopted the organise-lobby tactic as its *modus*

vivendi. Noisy demonstrations became regular features of the group's seven-year existence, but they were limited in scope and subsidiary to the larger strategy of developing organisational alliances. At the high point of its work, the NWRO had some 22,000 dues-paying members; one fifth were in New York City, the remainder primarily lived in Boston, Detroit, Los Angeles and Chicago. For a variety of reasons, some related to internal administrative problems, some due to the inability of the group to expand its membership after 1969, some caused by the backlash against welfare rights in particular, the NWRO's effectiveness declined after 1971. George A. Wiley regarded the 6 million people added to relief rolls during the organisation's life and the $4 billion rise in welfare costs a tribute to the NWRO's memory. Piven and Cloward later concluded that the NWRO did not succeed in its stated objectives of creating a lasting organisation of the urban poor. They also judged the organisation a failure because it did not seize the opportunity offered by the disruptions of the mid-1960s to wrest from government 'the maximum concessions possible in return for the restoration of quiescence'.[21]

George A. Wiley resigned from the NWRO in 1973 and organised a new group called the Movement for Economic Justice. Where the NWRO had aimed to organise the very poor, the MEJ would enrol the three-fourths of Americans with family incomes below the median. The NWRO focused upon a single goal: expanding welfare benefits. The MEJ chose a larger set of issues: income redistribution, adequate jobs and tax reform. The first campaign of the new organisation was to have been built around a demand for national tax reform and federal health insurance, but Wiley died before he could begin his new campaign.

THE PROPERTY TAX REVOLT

The Poor People's Movements of the 1950s and 1960s were an attempt by the 'have-nots' to increase their share of the national wealth, but neither these social movements nor the War on Poverty created lasting results. The percentage of Americans living under poverty conditions decreased in the late 1960s and early 1970s, but by 1983 the proportion had returned to the 1965 level. The increase in families receiving welfare did not generate a decline in the incidence of dependency; by 1983 the US possessed a widely discussed 'underclass', including female-headed families who were unlikely to rise above the subsistence level. Income inequality, as mentioned above, had remained stable since 1950.

What the War on Poverty and the militant social movements of the poor did create was an unexpected backlash. To the extent that governments responded favourably to the demands of the poor for more equitable access to state-supported education, health and welfare services, they became vulnerable to criticism from taxpayers who argued that irresponsible public bureaucrats were robbing productive citizens to support indolent opportunists. Government spending increased faster during the 1960s than in the 1970s, but by the early 1970s home-owning voters had become increasingly convinced that government at all levels was doing too much. In California, this perception coincided with an inflation in the property values that led to seemingly intolerable tax increases on single family residential properties. These economic changes and social tensions led to the tax revolt of the 1970s. This was a 'revolt of the haves' determined to retain a greater share of their private wealth by limiting the taxing and spending powers of state governments.[22]

The tax revolt began in the late 1960s, but it was not until 1976 and 1977, when the New Jersey and Colorado legislatures voted to limit government spending, that it assumed the proportions of a social movement. In June 1978 California voters amended their state constitution by a two-to-one margin and cut property taxes by 57 per cent, cut the tax rate back to 1 per cent of the market value of real estate as of 1975–6, and limited the increase in value to a maximum of 2 per cent per year unless the property was resold. They required the legislature to have a two-thirds majority in order to increase state taxes. Local governments likewise could only raise special taxes if they had a two-thirds vote. California's Proposition 13 signalled similar actions across the US. In 1978, 1979 and 1980, 15 states adopted various combinations of reduced property taxes and limits on government spending. Activists demanded a constitutional amendment to limit federal spending and balance the national budget. The legislatures of 37 states responded to the pressures by cutting property taxes in 1978 and 1979. Income taxes were cut in 28 states; sales tax collections were slashed in 13 states. In all, reductions in income and sales taxes amounted to some $4 billion.

By 1981, the tax reform movement had exhausted itself and voters in some states refused to approve further reductions. Polls showed that voters wanted more efficient government budgeting and the immediate cash benefits from tax cuts rather than wanting to gut the welfare state. The California electorate rejected a 1980 proposal for further cuts by the same margin with which it had approved Proposition 13. Most voters preferred maintaining or increasing government services even at the cost of higher taxes or forgone tax cuts, but the drop in revenue triggered by the tax revolt (California was cushioned initially by the surplus in its treasury) forced both the imposition of fees and cuts in services. Homeowners in the Golden State, unless they had bought their houses after 1975, received gratifying tax relief, but business property owners obtained the greatest benefits. The share of property taxes paid by homeowners increased from 43 to 48.6 per cent in the three years after the passage of Proposition 13. As fiscal straits became apparent, public employees, educational leaders and families on public assistance girded themselves for political combat to maintain their benefits.

At the same time, the ideological fervour surrounding the urge to preserve private wealth from redistribution programmes persisted beyond the tax revolt into the social politics of the early 1980s. Like the traditionalist supporters of candidate Ronald Reagan in 1980, the most active proponents of the tax revolt saw it as a social movement aimed at restoring a fundamentalist interpretation of the role of government. According to this point of view, government had no business exploring a new frontier or building a great society. Individuals, families, churches and communities should pursue their own goals free from government guidance or regulation; the impersonal workings of the market should determine the distribution of wealth. To some extent, 'Reaganism' represented an episode in the long history of revivalistic political movements in the US. Like the abolitionist and temperance movements of the nineteenth and early twentieth centuries, it presumed to speak as the source of righteousness in a world spinning free of its moral tethers. Critics who examined the policy record of the Reagan administration, however, found the evangelistic rhetoric less significant than the punitive effects of service cutbacks for the have-nots. After two years in office, it was hard to escape the conclusion that Reagan's war against government waste was also a 'new class war' against the poor.[23]

9.   Race and Ethnicity

In October 1942, as US and British forces prepared to invade North Africa, Swedish scholar Gunnar Myrdal wrote the preface to his massive study of 'the Negro problem' in America. Because he came from a Scandinavian country with no history of black-white relations, Myrdal was an ideal director for this Carnegie Foundation project. A small army of researchers under his direction assembled the materials for what he intended to be an 'objective and dispassionate' study of all aspects of the American black experience. In fact, *An American Dilemma* exuded a passion for equality. By judging American race relations against the ideals of equality and liberty, Myrdal continued a tradition begun by the Abolitionists. By insisting upon 'the fundamental unity and similarity of mankind', Myrdal chastised Americans who mistakenly labelled Negroes a biological 'race'. By acknowledging that African ancestral and physical characteristics stigmatised American blacks 'much more ineffacebly than the yellow star is fixed to the Jew during the Nazi regime in Germany', Myrdal attested to the tenacity of American racism. Although he was 'shocked and scared to the bones by all the evils' he observed in US race relations, Myrdal was also impressed by the nation's liberalism. He saw *'fundamental changes'* under way pushing American practice closer to American ideals.[1]

When Myrdal looked at American society, he saw a populace with minds and consciences absorbed by questions of race and ethnicity. Deep historical roots nourished such preoccupations. Although the political leaders of the early American colonies came from England, the colonies and then the United States itself soon became multi-ethnic. Before the Civil War, most non-English immigrants (voluntary newcomers in contrast to the enslaved Africans) came from northern Europe. After about 1885, central, eastern and southern Europeans came in larger numbers, followed by Latin Americans after the 1930s, and Asians more recently. Since the Second World

War, the dominant tradition of insisting upon 'Anglo-Conformity' had begun to be challenged by ideas and movements demanding 'Cultural Pluralism'.

Swan's *Anglo-American Dictionary* defines 'ethnic' as an adjective pertaining to nation or race, concepts that since the Second World War have acquired an increasingly emotional charge. Within the United States, the insistence of Afro-Americans upon self-determination and appreciation of cultural heritage has stimulated a trend towards introspection and political action on the part of other groups, including so-called white ethnics such as Italian and Polish Americans.

More broadly, 'ethnic' also describes any person who differs in religion, language and culture from the original Anglo-Saxon Protestant settlers. An American ethnic would be a person who was not 'WASP-NN', that is a White Anglo-Saxon Protestant Native born of Native parents. According to this definition, about 65 per cent of the current American population would be ethnic, and the single largest minority would be WASP. Although a numerical minority, WASPs have historically wielded a disproportionate amount of power and prestige.

For white Americans since 1945, ethnic identity has been more a state of mind than an objective social category. Whether a person was a fourth-generation Irish policeman in New York, or a third-generation Hungarian scientist in Stanford, or a second-generation Mexican city councilman in San Antonio, he most probably considered himself 'ethnic' if he lived according to the cultural values and beliefs of his immigrant ancestors, or at least thought he did. It is this subjective factor that has kept the question of ethnic and cultural diversity a highly emotional and controversial issue throughout the post-war period.

Subjective factors have also been important to Afro-Americans, Mexican-Americans, Asian-Americans and American Indians, but so has the objective fact of their being people of colour. These groups have persistently been labelled inferior and subjected to prejudice and discrimination, because their physical characteristics were automatically defined as subnormal and their behaviour labelled as deviant. While Slavic peoples have experienced some stigmatising attitudes, racial stereotyping has been most harshly applied to blacks, Asians, Mexicans and American Indians, and any others considered dark-skinned people.

IMMIGRATION LAWS AND NATIVISM

Since the Great Depression, the size of the foreign-born population (and their children) has declined from about one-third in 1930 to about one-sixth in 1970. This decline in foreign-stock population was related to the restrictive immigration laws passed by Congress, beginning in the 1880s. Chinese were excluded by acts of 1882, 1894, 1902 and 1943, and Japanese by laws enacted in 1907 and 1924. The 1924 law was part of a sweeping Quota Act that limited immigrants from any country in any year to 2 per cent of the Census of 1890, a provision that reduced the numbers eligible from eastern and southern Europe. The maximum quota was set at 150,000 per year, but the western hemisphere was not included in the restriction, and Mexico and Canada continued to supply immigrants.

The Quota Law (called the Johnson Act) resulted primarily from a campaign by groups prejudiced against Roman Catholics, Jews, Asians (principally Chinese and Japanese) and Slavic peoples. This campaign sought to exclude such 'undesirables' from entry to the United States. Members of similar 'Nativist' groups (who tended to be WASPs from rural areas, small towns and cities) had played a role in American politics since the 1790s, especially in the 'Know-Nothing' or American Party of the 1850s and the American Protective Association of the 1890s. After the First World War, Nativists associated southern and eastern European immigrants with Bolshevism and 'Anti-Americanism'.

Nativism and fear of subversion led to special screening measures in the 1952 McCarran–Walter Act (passed over President Truman's veto), but the exclusion of Asian and Pacific peoples was lifted. The 1965 Immigration and Nationality Act further liberalised entry by establishing a revised quota of 170,000 for people outside the western hemisphere, with a 20,000 annual maximum plus an annual limit of 120,000 for western hemisphere immigrants. During the 1970s, the numbers of immigrants entering the US without permission, especially those from Mexico, increased to the point where proposals were introduced into Congress for substantial revisions in the laws.

ETHNIC SETTLEMENT PATTERNS BEFORE THE SECOND WORLD WAR

Large numbers (the exact figures are uncertain) of non-English immigrants greatly influenced the period before 1790. Scottish-Irish and Germans were the largest of the groups which helped create a multi-ethnic society in colonial America, making their greatest impact in Pennsylvania and Maryland (where almost all the Catholics lived). The cities tended to be more socially heterogeneous than rural areas.

The primary factor motivating immigration was the desire for a better economic and social future. Pushed out of their homelands by overpopulation, crop failures, unemployment and sometimes by political persecution, immigrants acted on information about jobs and land in the rapidly industrialising United States. During the nineteenth century, the largest groups of immigrants came from Ireland, Germany and Scandinavia. Irish immigration peaked in the late 1840s, when it amounted to 49 per cent of the total. The Irish worked on canal and railway construction, as well as in domestic service, and they settled in towns and cities along the east coast, thereby contributing greatly to the rapid urban population growth in New York and Massachusetts.

In the thirty years after the Civil War, the Germans contributed the highest numbers of immigrants. They tended to settle on farms throughout the nation, as well as in cities. Besides establishing a 'Little Germany' in New York (as early as the 1850s), they created substantial communities in Milwaukee, St Paul, St Louis, Chicago, Cincinnati and Cleveland.

Scandinavians (with Norway and Sweden the leading countries) generally settled on farms, and Wisconsin and Minnesota became the leading centres of Scandinavian-American life.

After the 1890s, immigrants came primarily from the agricultural areas of eastern and southeastern Europe. They settled, mainly as industrial workers, in factory towns and cities, and they worked as wage-earners in mining, manufacturing and unskilled labour generally.

The Italians tended to settle in New Jersey, New York and Pennsylvania (about half of the total), New England (some 15 per cent), and just under 15 per cent settled in Illinois, Indiana and Ohio. By 1930 more people of Italian stock lived in New York City than

Romans in the Eternal City. Large numbers of Italians worked the land as truck farmers or laboured in mining communities.

The Italians were but one segment of a vast turn-of-the-century immigration. The 1905–14 period saw the arrival of more than 1 million immigrants for six of the nine years, and between half and three-fourths of all newcomers were from southern or eastern Europe. According to current national boundaries, they came from Poland, Czechoslovakia, Yugoslavia, Hungary and Russia. Russia and Poland sent the largest Jewish elements. These groups settled mainly in the North Central, Northeast and Middle Atlantic states, where some cities took on a distinctive 'ethnic' character: Chicago (Poles, Bohemians, Hungarians); New York (Italians and Jews); Boston (Irish and Italian). Across the continent, in San Francisco, Irish and Italians, along with Jews from Germany, gave the City by the Golden Gate a special European ambiance that coexisted with a segregated Chinatown.

Mexicans and Asians came to the US in smaller numbers. Of the total 39.5 million immigrants between 1820 and 1951, 954,200 were Asian and 1.6 million came from Mexico. Mexicans made up large settlements in the South West and on the Pacific Coast; Asians lived mainly in the Pacific, North Central and New England states.

THE DOMINANT AMERICANS

White Americans who trace their ancestry to northern and western Europe continued to wield more power, privilege and, consequently, prestige than other ethnic groups after 1945. In political, social and cultural life, with the exceptions noted below, the highest places have been occupied by white Protestants. By the 1950s, the major nationality groups among white Protestant Americans were the English, Scotch, Welsh and Ulster Irish, the Germans, smaller groups of Scandinavians and Dutch. These groups were well assimilated by the Second World War and sociological studies of the 1950s and 1960s described how they increasingly sloughed off loyalties to ancestral homelands and replaced them with a religious identification to Protestantism.

The South, West and North Central states provided white Protestants with their strongholds in the post-war period; in these areas they comprised some two-thirds of the population. Elsewhere, particularly in central cities, they were increasingly less visible. In Middle Atlantic, Northeast and New England states, they maintained a strong presence in well-to-do suburbs and fashionable exurbia.

The roughly 15 to 20 per cent of white Americans with affiliations to Protestant churches inhabited the full range of income and class groups, and they succeeded in maintaining many of their 'national upper class' prerogatives. The preservation of privilege especially characterised members of the Episcopal Church, who during the 1960s and 1970s comprised about 3 per cent of the population. Unlike the majority of Protestants, Episcopalians remained concentrated in the urban centres of the nation's historic eastern states; fully one-third lived in cities of over a million people. Episcopalians as a group earned the highest family incomes in the US and directed leading institutions from the National Gallery to the CIA. 'What has made them so important to the country is that their set of attitudes and mores . . . has been adopted by non-Episcopalians as the standard for upper class conduct.'[2]

Episcopalian McGeorge Bundy served as special assistant for national security affairs under John F. Kennedy before going on to assume the presidency of the Ford Foundation. Both men possessed impeccable credentials: Kennedy received his education at Choate and Harvard; Bundy took his degrees from Groton and Yale. The two men became friends as well as colleagues; their backgrounds and tastes were similar. Kennedy, however, was only four generations removed from Irish Catholic immigrants, whereas Bundy's mother was a member of the Lowell family of early Massachusetts renown. Although Kennedy possessed the manners and charm of the upper class (some fellow communicants would not vote for him in 1960 because he seemed more WASP than Catholic), his ancestry barred him from the Protestant Establishment. His election to the presidency was a milestone in American social history. When poet Robert Frost, speaking at Kennedy's inauguration, adjured the new president to be more Irish than Harvard, he paid tribute to the fact that Irish Catholics had firmly established their legitimacy in the post-1945 period.

Kennedy's inauguration seemed to some observers a sign that the Irish (the vast majority of them Catholic) were losing their distinctiveness as an ethnic group as well as a symbol that they had captured the nation's highest political office. This judgement was exaggered, but it was not unreasonable given the accoutrements of advancement the Irish had earned. This 6 to 7 per cent of the American population had achieved economic and political success even prior to the Second World War. Heavily represented in public employment and blue-collar trades, the Irish also distinguished themselves at higher levels. John Kennedy's father was a millionaire banker by the age of 30 and served under Franklin D. Roosevelt as ambassador to the Court of St James. During the post-war period, Irish Americans continued to be particularly visible in national, state and local politics: Richard J. Daley, mayor of Chicago; Edmund G. Brown, senior and junior, governors of California; Hugh J. Carey, governor of New York; Mike Mansfield of Montana, Senate majority leader; Thomas P. (Tip) O'Neill, majority leader of the House of Representatives. Their early rise to prominence in the labour movement (George Meany), in business, journalism and other fields continued in the post-war period as well. Surveys during the mid-1970s ranked Irish Catholic families just below American Jewish families in average income and educational achievement.[3]

About half of world Jewry made their homes in the United States in the post-war period, and in 1977 they comprised just under 3 per cent of the population (roughly the same proportion as Episcopalians). By this time, the strong economic and cultural differences and rivalries between German and East European Jews that flourished at the turn of the century had moderated considerably without entirely fading away. After 1945, the vital awareness among American Jews of their political loyalties to Israel provided a further incentive to disregard previous class and nationality loyalties. Predominantly an urban population, two-thirds of American Jews could be found in just ten metropolitan areas in 1977 as in 1948. Los Angeles's Jewish population increased from 4.5 to 7.9 per cent during that period; Miami's share in 1977 was nearly three times that of Pittsburgh in 1948; New York, and Chicago witnessed declines, from 40 to 34.6 per cent and from 6 to 4.4 per cent respectively. A combination of low fertility rates and high rates of intermarriage with other groups during the 1960s and 1970s moved both secular scholars and Jewish leaders to predict a 'Jewish Population Erosion'. By 1979 a professor at the nation's leading Jewish university was counselling the Jewish community not to shun intermarried couples.[4]

The Jewish population in central city neighbourhoods of manufacturing-belt cities like Brooklyn, the Bronx, Cleveland and

Detroit became a smaller and smaller proportion of US Jewry during the post-war period. It was here that the largest share of poor Jews, mostly elderly, could be found in the 1970s. Like other prosperous Americans, well-to-do Jews tended to seek out the advantages of suburban living, and in some communities Jews arrived in large enough numbers to transform what had been Protestant enclaves into Jewish hamlets. In one well-studied suburb, Jews increased their share from 32 to 51 per cent of the population between 1957 and 1975. By that time, the mayor was Jewish and the schools observed the high holidays. In the early 1950s, the newcomers made themselves inconspicuous in anticipation of anti-Semitism. By the 1970s, 'a mood of Jewish affirmation and heightened Jewish ethnicity' pervaded the community.[5]

After the Second World War, some of the more tenacious institutional anti-Semitism weakened, and Jews could move in large numbers into managerial and professional occupations previously closed to them. The sons and daughters of independent city businessmen became suburban executives and white-collar workers at rates approaching three or four times the general population. Among college and university professors, between 10 and 30 per cent were Jewish, and they typically staked out the most liberal and radical political positions. A distinctively New York and Jewish literary and arts community provided post-war America with some of its most creative talent; among the best known were composer and conductor Leonard Bernstein, novelist and Nobel laureate Saul Bellow, and playwright Arthur Miller.

While New York City's Jewish population was much larger than any Jewish settlement in Israel, New York's Italian-Americans roughly equalled the number who lived in Milan. The Italians, like the Irish and the Jews, made rapid gains during the post-1945 period. Like the Jews, Italian Americans remained predominantly urban; by 1970, two-thirds lived in the Northeast, and 54 per cent could be found in 12 metropolitan areas. Outside the manufacturing belt, the largest concentrations were in the San Francisco Area and the Los Angeles–Long Beach metropolitan district. Like the Jews, Italian Americans moved to the suburbs and into white-collar, managerial and professional positions, as well as into government and the arts. By 1983, they made up 7 per cent of the population, and their median family income put them just below Jews and Irish Catholics and above most other ethnic groups. Like the Jews, Italian Americans continued to face prejudicial stereotypes, but they just as persistently rose above them. Italian Americans continued to dominate syndicated crime after 1945, but during the 1950s these organisations lost control over New York politics. On the other hand, Mario M. Cuomo, the son of parents born in the *Mezzogiorno*, was elected governor of New York, as was Richard Celeste in Ohio. With Lido (Lee) Iacocca as chairman of the Chrysler Corporation and Benjamin F. Biaggini as chairman of the Southern Pacific Corporation, there was reason to conclude that 'Italians have fully caught up with non-Italians in the upper echelons of professional and managerial occupations'.[6]

During the post-war period, the Italians and Jews, the largest of the 'white ethnic' groups who had originated in south, central and eastern Europe, moved rapidly into the major institutions of US society. The dramatic nature of the assimilation and acculturation processes became a major theme in American Jewish and Italian literature and dramatic art, from Herman Wouk's best-selling *Marjorie Morningstar* (1955) or Saul Bellow's *The Adventures of Augie March* (1953) to Mario Puzo's *The Godfather* (1969) and Martin Scorsese's *Mean Streets* (1973). One of the most emotional controversies to arise out of the assimilation process during the 1970s was the debate over the extent to which the metaphor 'the melting pot' accurately expressed the experience of these 'white ethnic' groups. Pundits offered a variety of alternative concepts: the two most frequently proferred were 'the salad bowl' and the 'stew pot'. One impassioned professor of philosophy and religion argued that the roughly 9 million Polish, Russian and Greek Americans, like the Armenians and Lebanese, the Slovenes, Ruthenians, Lithuanians, Czechs and others were 'unmeltable' and should celebrate their 'communal' identity rather than lose themselves in 'rootless' American society.[7]

THE AMERICAN MINORITIES

Although Italians, Jews and other 'white ethnics' still experienced some degree of prejudice and hostility after the Second World War, the most severe forms of discrimination continued to be directed against the traditional victims of racism: Afro-Americans, Hispanics, Asians and American Indians.

Afro-Americans consistently made up the largest minority

population in the post-war period. In 1940, just over three-fourths of the 12.8 million (9.8 per cent) black population lived in the South, where 63 per cent still resided in rural areas. Only 2.2 per cent of all blacks lived in states west of the Mississippi River outside the South. In the North and West, blacks congregated in the largest central cities. New York City was home to 17 per cent of non-southern blacks; Chicago, Philadelphia, Detroit, Cleveland and Pittsburgh made up an additional 30 per cent of the northern and western black population. Forty years later, the 26.5 million (11.7 per cent) Afro-Americans were distributed more evenly throughout the major regions. The South's share was down to 33 per cent, the North Central region had 26 per cent, followed by the Northeast with 22 per cent and the West with 19 per cent. Blacks everywhere lived mainly in the central cities (see Chapter 6).

When Myrdal puzzled over white America's 'Negro Problem' in the 1940s, he was struck by the willingness of most Americans to 'incorporate without distinction' white immigrants from all corners of the world, provided such assimilation took place 'in a distant future'. In contrast to this general enthusiasm for the eventual Americanisation of immigrants, Americans warned blacks (also Chinese and Japanese) to keep to themselves. Racial segregation governed US social relations; social contact between blacks and whites provoked outcries of 'contrary to nature' and 'detestable'.[8]

The black population moved out of southern rural counties and into central cities elsewhere in the nation in the decades after the Second World War. Its migration set in motion several developments that fed upon existing attitudes towards race relations, leading to heightened anti-black prejudice and discrimination. Their arrival in the non-southern cities made the Afro-Americans strikingly visible at the very time that the 'white ethnic' growth rate was slowing because of the discontinuance of immigration. WASP city-dwellers outside the South suddenly discovered that Afro-Americans tangibly threatened acceptable social norms. The black cityward migrants sought jobs in the very blue-collar occupations that 'white ethnics' had staked out. To these working-class hyphenated Americans, blacks were competitors, despite the fact that employers usually hired Italians, Poles and other whites first. These social responses help to account for the 'special historical experience' that distinguished the fortunes of Afro-Americans from white ethnics in the post-war period.[9]

In many respects, black-white relations seemed to edge steadily towards greater equality during the post-war years. Housing discrimination and residential segregation, once supported by both public law and private covenant, were outlawed by local, state and national statute by the 1980s. The supreme court outlawed legally segregated public education in *Brown* v. *Board of Education of Topeka* in 1954, and the Department of Justice worked to enforce this decision during the 1960s and 1970s. Employers who wanted to reject all Afro-Americans regardless of qualifications were blocked by the Civil Rights Act of 1964 and subsequent 'affirmative action' legislation. Artifacts of white supremacy taken for granted in the 1940s, such as separate entrances to public buildings, separate drinking fountains and separate seating sections in theatres, were historical curiosities to young Americans of the 1980s. American baseball in the 1970s and 1980s could scarcely be imagined without its black superstars, but the first black player, Jackie Robinson, did not set foot on a major league diamond until 1947.

Afro-Americans also seemed to be catching up with whites in the working world. Black median family income rose from 54 to 64 per cent of white families between 1950 and 1970; the median black female income soared from 40 to 92 per cent of that of white females. Black workers no longer earned less and less compared to whites as they grew older. Whites with equivalent education to blacks no longer earned higher incomes, and the percentages of blacks in clerical, managerial and professional jobs moved upwards at higher rates than those of white.

Closer examination shows that economic inequality actually decreased very little during the post-war period; the greatest changes resulted from the black movement out of the depressed agricultural South and from the impact of the business cycle on the economy. Movement into the black middle class significantly improved the lives of those individuals who experienced it, but two-thirds of them held relatively low-paying, lower echelon white-collar jobs. While black women definitely gained income in relation to white women, they often did so by working much longer hours. In addition, while black college graduates improved their positions, a much larger share of the black labour force without such educational qualifications actually lost ground relative to whites and better-off blacks. One black sociologist found 'a deepening economic schism . . . developing in the black community, with the black poor falling further and further behind middle- and upper-middle blacks'.[10]

Just as their mass migration to non-southern cities triggered economic competition and social conflict between blacks and 'white ethnics' during the 1950s and 1960s, the influx of Hispanic groups into the cities in the 1960s and 1970s generated tension between them and Afro-Americans. Hispanics were largely a rural population before the Second World War, when most were immigrants from Mexico or descendants of Mexican immigrants who came to the Southwest during the 1910–30 period. During the post-1945 period, the Mexican-American (Chicano) population swelled with continued immigration, so that by the late 1970s, in combination with Hispanic immigrants, they comprised the second largest minority group in the US. By 1980 there were some 14.6 million Hispanics (6.4 per cent) according to the Census Bureau, but other estimates ranged from 15 to 18 million. Fully 85 per cent lived in urban areas by then, with 51 per cent in the central cities. Mexican-Americans made up the largest Hispanic subgroup, followed by Puerto Ricans and Cubans. Nearly 90 per cent of the Chicanos and 60 per cent of all Hispanics lived in California, Texas, Arizona, New Mexico and Colorado. Puerto Ricans settled almost exclusively in the Northeast, particularly in New York City and Boston. Cubans (see Chapter 6) sought Florida destinations, especially Miami.

During the 1970s the Hispanic population grew by 25 per cent, compared to 12 per cent for blacks and 7 per cent for the US population as a whole. By 1980, 42 per cent of all Hispanics were under 18 years old and education emerged as a key policy issue, with various spokesmen arguing for and against bilingual instruction. Like blacks, Hispanics during the post-war period made some gains, but economic inequality persisted. By the early 1980s their median family income was just above two-thirds of the whites'; their unemployment rate was nearly double that of whites; they were two and a half times more likely to live below the government's poverty line than whites.

Asian-Americans during the post-war period generally fared better than Hispanics or blacks. Several historical factors facilitated the economic success of the Chinese and Japanese. Fierce resistance to their competition with white workers resulted in the exclusionary laws of the late nineteenth and early twentieth century; these laws put a ceiling on the size of the Asian-American population; their relatively small numbers were rigidly segregated into 'Chinatowns' and 'Little

Tokyos' where the demand for services supported the emergence of a prosperous business class; Asian-Americans also stood higher on the racial pecking order of white America than the Afro-American descendants of chattel slaves.[11]

Compared to blacks and Hispanics, the Asian-American population has remained relatively small since the Second World War. The liberalisation of the immigration laws after 1965 has contributed most to the rapid increases in population since 1940: Chinese, from 77,000 to 894,000; Japanese, from 127,000 to 791,000; Filipinos from 45,000 to 795,000. Most Asian-Americans sought homes in urban areas; this was particularly true of the Chinese. The Chinese urban population grew from 66 to 99 per cent between 1920 and 1980, whereas the Japanese living in cities increased from 55 to 89 per cent between 1940 and 1980, and by 1980 fully 89 per cent of Filipinos lived in cities. Japanese and Filipino communities continued predominantly in the West after 1945; by 1980, 77 per cent of the former and 68 per cent of the latter lived near the Pacific Coast. The Chinese population was more dispersed, although in 1980, 55 per cent lived in the West, with 25 per cent in the Northeast and 12 per cent in the South.

Prior to Pearl Harbor and their forced relocation to 'detention centers' away from the Coast, Japanese-Americans worked in fish canneries and lumber mills, and they raised nearly half of California's produce crops; they also worked in a variety of service occupations in their segregated urban communities. The disruptions of wartime relocation were severe; over 100,000 were evacuated of whom nearly two-thirds were American citizens. The financial losses to the Japanese-American community were likewise debilitating; the mean loss per family was estimated at $9,800. In the face of these hardships, the Japanese made a strong recovery during the post-war years. By means of impressively high rates of educational achievement, movement into the professions, small families, multi-income households, and their large presence in prosperous California, Japanese-Americans came to earn median family incomes 32 per cent higher than the national average and 15 per cent above the California average.[12]

While Japanese-Americans distributed themselves fairly widely throughout metropolitan areas after 1945, the Chinese continued to cluster within Chinatown settlements. In New York, the traditional Chinatown in lower Manhattan expanded and 'little Chinatowns' appeared in the borough of Queens. In San Francisco, Chinatown swallowed up part of the adjacent Italian American 'North Beach' neighbourhood. Although the Chinese, like the Japanese, managed to earn higher incomes and move into professional and scientific occupations at higher rates than the general population, immigrants during the 1970s and 1980s arrived without the education and training necessary for such achievement, at a time when the economy was lagging. Consequently, US Chinatowns continued to display traditional signs of hardship: low-paying jobs in garment factories with sweatshop conditions; high poverty rates; a high incidence of tuberculosis; teenage youth gangs made up of unemployed school dropouts.[13]

The American Indian population also experienced difficulty during the post-war period both because of a historical legacy of deprivation and because of their continuing exclusion from the mainstream economy. Between 1940 and 1980 the Indian population grew from 334,000 to 1.4 million (about 0.6 per cent of the total population). More than half of all American Indians lived in urban areas, and over half were under 20 years of age. The largest centres of urban Indian life were Los Angeles (about 50,000 in 1970), the San Francisco Area, and the Minneapolis–St Paul urban area. While Indians were probably less concentrated in segregated residential ghettoes than blacks, they were as a group continually in even worse economic circumstances. Those who did not move to cities lived in some 200 reservations. The largest groups were in Arizona, Oklahoma, New Mexico, California, North and South Dakota, Montana, Minnesota and North Carolina. About a third were Navaho, Cherokee, Sioux or Chipewa.

More than fifty Indian languages continued to exist after the Second World War, and some 300 tribes participated in various intertribal organisations. Their social and economic conditions made them the most deprived ethnic group in the United States. Average annual income during the 1970s was less than one-fourth the median for the nation, and their unemployment rate was ten times the national average. Unemployment rates for men over 16 ranged from 40 to 80 per cent on the reservations. According to some estimates, 70 per cent of all Indian housing was substandard, and the average age at death was 44 (the national average was 33 per cent higher). Their tuberculosis rate was a hundred times higher and the infant mortality rate was 50 per cent higher than the national average.

RACE, ETHNICITY AND CLASS

American Indians and Afro-Americans consistently received the fewest benefits and suffered the greatest discrimination during the post-war period. This easily documented conclusion stirred civil rights advocates to action in the 1950s and 1960s just as in earlier decades (see Chapter 10). The overlap between economic deprivation and racial subordination also spurred a long-standing debate in American society. Did the cultural heritage and the individual habits of Afro-Americans predispose them to poverty, or were these particular Americans disproportionately deprived for economic and social reasons?

Except for the most unreconstructed white supremacy advocates, few scholars or policy-makers during the post-war years boldly asserted that black poverty was caused by Afro-American culture. Many scholars even denied that blacks possessed a distinctive culture in the sense of an identifiable complex of values, beliefs and practices passed from generation to generation by social learning. Culturally, the argument went, blacks were Americans pure and simple; it was only in the social, economic and political spheres that they lived separate lives. Slavery, it was argued, was so traumatic that connections with Africa were irrevocably severed. Slavery left black Americans brutalised and without a vital cultural tradition. Abandoned by the North after the Civil War, they had been victimised by racism ever since. Those who surrendered to despair and showed no interest in working hard to achieve the American Dream had no alternatives, according to this interpretation. There was, as E. Franklin Frazier pointed out, a small 'black bourgeoisie' or 'brown middle class' which managed to avoid the worst of white prejudice and discrimination and made a modest economic success in segregated ghettoes. On the other hand, some 70 to 90 per cent of the black population were poor southern agricultural workers or part of the northern urban 'black proletariat'. It was among this black majority that black sociologist Frazier found the legacy of slavery and the later uprooting experience of northern migration most damaging. The family as an institution particularly suffered. Frazier found a terrible 'waste of human life' manifested in 'immorality, delinquency, desertions, and broken homes'. These social problems were the 'inevitable consequences of the attempt of a preliterate people, stripped of their cultural heritage, to adjust themselves to civilization'. Writing in 1948, Frazier correctly anticipated that the flight of blacks from the rural South to urban ghettoes in both South and North would continue, resulting in even more disrupted families and greater incidence of poverty. 'Of course', he concluded, 'the ordeal of civilization will be less severe if there is a general improvement in the standard of living and racial barriers to employment are broken down.'[14]

By the mid-1960s militant black scholars had challenged Frazier's equation of upward social mobility according to mainstream American values with 'civilization'. Historians argued that the economic dislocations of the Great Depression and the post-war agricultural displacement contributed more to contemporary 'social disorganization' than did the legacy of slavery. Furthermore, few could agree on the precise nature of the relationship between economic inequality and those features of ghetto society that Frazier regarded as 'waste of human life' and social-psychologist Kenneth Clark described as 'the tangle of pathology'.[15]

In 1965 these issues were addressed by President Johnson when he told the graduating class of predominantly black Howard University that he was pledging the federal government to go beyond the mere enforcement of legal rights for Afro-Americans. 'Negroes', Johnson said, 'are trapped in inherited, gateless poverty' and they needed jobs, housing and education as well as equal rights under the law. Behind the president's call for a 'more profound stage' in government intervention on behalf of black rights stood the assumption that a vicious 'circle of despair and deprivation' existed in black ghettoes. Men without stable jobs and a living wage could not be good fathers and husbands; families separated, and mothers raised children alone, often on welfare; children lacked the necessary support for successful schooling and dropped out; their subsequent lack of qualifications rendered them ineligible for well-paying jobs, and the vicious cycle continued.

Johnson's speech was written partly by Labor Department assistant secretary Daniel P. Moynihan, whose report on *The Negro Family* summarised nearly two decades of research by Frazier, Clark and others on the relationship between race, class and family poverty. The report called for federal policies 'designed to have the effect, directly or indirectly, of enhancing the stability and resources of the Negro American family'. Released to the public in August 1965, just after mass rioting broke out in the black ghetto of Watts in Los Angeles, the

Moynihan Report's most sensationalist aspects (concerning black 'family breakdown') received more press coverage than his sober statistics. The 'fundamental overwhelming fact', Moynihan emphasised in discussing 'the roots of the problem' is that *'Negro unemployment, with the exception of a few years during World War II and the Korean War, has continued at disaster levels for 35 years'* (emphasis in original).

Civil rights activists divided in their reactions to the report. Some saw it as a restatement of familiar data and hoped to use it to wrest economic reform policies from the government; others found the discussion of black family problems patronising and its lack of distinction between different classes of 'the Negro family' dangerous. The editor of the magazine *Commonweal* was troubled for similar reasons. While he generally agreed that Moynihan had performed a service by raising such a controversial subject, he also thought that liberals usually ignored the subject of the Negro family for good reasons. Problems such as desertion, delinquency, dropouts and drug addiction 'can be used by racists to suggest the basic inferiority of the Negro and his inability to build a firm family foundation'. Moynihan himself took pains to deny any 'genetic differential' between blacks and whites and argued that it was 'American society' that 'impairs the Negro potential'.

Lyndon Johnson's Howard University speech did not lead to programmes designed to induce the kinds of changes in American capitalism necessary for full employment. In the 1970s liberals such as Moynihan moved towards conservatism and counselled the nation to wean its expectations that the government could solve long-standing social and economic inequities. Policy analyst Edward C. Banfield argued that most Americans, having shorn themselves of virulent racism, judged each other more according to class than to racial criteria: 'Much of what appears (especially to Negroes) as race prejudice is really class prejudice, or at any rate, class antipathy.' Blacks were disproportionately lower class, and Banfield regarded lower-class poverty as by and large the consequence of 'deeply ingrained habits' that were 'inwardly caused, and improvements in external circumstances are likely to affect it gradually if at all'.[16] At the same time, other liberals moved towards more radical analyses and a growing cadre of Marxist-inspired social scientists connected the accumulating evidence of increasing immiseration to the slipping position of American business in the world economy. Black political theorist and activist Manning Marable argued that the 'strongest roots of Black poverty were anchored firmly in the capitalist market-place'. To historian and critic Irving Howe:

> The central problems of our society have to do, not with ethnic groupings, but with economic policy, social rule, class relations. They have to do with vast inequities of wealth, with the shameful neglect of a growing class of subproletarians, with the readiness of policy-makers to tolerate high levels of unemployment.[17]

10.   The Struggle for Civil Rights

THE dramatic rise and gradual decline of militant mass action on behalf of civil rights distinguishes the post-war years from earlier periods, but political struggles between competing ethnic groups have always played a central role in American history. The battles between the haves and the have-nots, from the attempts by Philadelphia shoemakers to organise in the 1790s to the southern textile worker union campaigns of the 1970s, have periodically disrupted American society. But the 1970s also witnessed emotional campaigns by white ethnics intent upon keeping blacks out of their predominantly white suburbs. Throughout American history, competing ethnic groups have used political parties and interest groups to build, maintain and enhance their access to power, privilege and prestige. Because the dominant citizens have been WASP Americans, civil rights have been instrumental to minority group members seeking jobs, housing, education, and health and welfare services. Because the nation's values and institutions are descended from the Anglo-American political tradition, civil rights have protected the ability to vote, to hold office, to serve on juries and the enjoyment of full citizenship. Since 1945 the struggle for black civil rights has involved the largest numbers of Americans and has served as a model for other ethnic minorities, as well as women, homosexuals and other self-defined groups claiming collective grievances. Attempts to widen the practice of a group's citizenship rights, however, are rooted in nineteenth-century American history.

THE PERIOD BEFORE 1945

Because of the regional diversity of the nation and the decentralised character of the federal system of government, much of the substance of civil rights politics emerged during conflicts between ethnic and class groups at the local and state level. During the nineteenth century, Irish and German Catholic working-class immigrants frequently differed with well-to-do Protestants over how far the civil rights of a particular group should be tolerated in the making of public policy. The newcomers wanted liberal immigration laws; the natives preferred restriction and a lengthy naturalisation period. The recent settlers demanded poor relief and tax-supported schools for religious groups; the more established Protestants wanted fiscal conservatism rather than expensive charity and they feared the purported influence of the pope over American Catholics. WASPs argued that the language of instruction in public schools should be English and the curriculum should assume the importance of more guidance according to 'Anglo-Conformity'; immigrants from Bavaria wanted their children to learn German in school, and they had no desire to wean their offspring away from their cultural heritage. Similar conflicts over the legality of saloons and beer gardens, definitions of public morality, and the policy of the US government towards liberal or revolutionary movements in Europe marked the nineteenth and early twentieth centuries.

If the civil rights of immigrants proved a source of political controversy, so did the legal standing of slaves and former slaves. The disruption of the political system in the 1850s and the Civil War itself demonstrated that differences of opinion over slavery and its future growth could not be contained within political parties. Abolitionists, including black leader Frederick Douglass, uncompromisingly insisted that slaves were human beings, not property. Either the Constitution should be amended to provide all black people with full citizenship rights, or a higher moral law should govern race relations.

Post-Civil War politics were continually beset by racial and ethnic controversy. In the South, white supremacy grew in political strength as the civil rights guaranteed in the 13th, 14th and 15th amendments to the Constitution were effectively stymied by the mid-1880s. The supreme court's *Plessy* v. *Ferguson* decision (1896) ruled that separate facilities for blacks did not violate Constitutional equality of the races. The Jim Crow system of racial discrimination constrained blacks to subordinate roles and enforced a double standard of citizenship. In the North, black-white relations were equally governed by caste-like principles of racial segregation and dual citizenship.

Outside the South, especially in the manufacturing belt, class conflict frequently coincided with ethnic conflict. In state legislatures, Irish Catholic Democrats representing heavily white ethnic constituencies fought for laws that later became the foundation of the post-1945 welfare state. They backed business regulation laws, pension and social security measures, factory reform acts, protective legislation for women and children at work, progressive tax increases and reapportionment of state legislatures aimed at ending the rural (Protestant) control of urban policy-making. In city councils, a succession of neighbourhood and ward politicians – Irish, Italian, Slavic, and later black and Puerto Rican – worked to improve their group's situation. They resisted attempts by WASP reformers to trim city services in the name of fiscal accountability and to sever policy-making from electoral control by increasing the power of administrative government. The Irish Catholic and white ethnic 'bosses' who directed urban political machines need not be romanticised. They were not public-spirited Robin Hoods protecting the immigrant poor from the native rich. On the other hand, the WASP reformers of city government acted out of self-interest as well as a concern for governmental efficiency. For both bosses and reformers, civil rights meant enhanced economic opportunities, more secure social benefits and greater enjoyment of cultural liberties.

Political rivalries between dominant white Protestants and ethnic immigrant Americans and their offspring continued to be important during the 1910s and 1920s. Catholics and Jews moved slowly into local and national positions of power and influence. Catholics and Jews also continued to attract hostility, and they faced a variety of barriers to full participation in American life. More severe restrictions upon citizenship were reserved for blacks.

The late 1930s witnessed the beginnings of change. The New Deal brought welfare services and government positions to blacks; more aggressive leaders came to the forefront of the established Negro rights organisations; militants of the political left made common cause with black activists. The cumulative effect of these developments fell far short of substantial victories for the cause of black civil rights, but 'something vital did begin in the thirties. Negro expectations rose; black powerlessness decreased; white hostility diminished.'[1]

FROM 1940 TO 1960

Only a miniscule proportion of the 12.8 million black Americans belonged to civil rights organisations during the early 1940s. The largest of the two major groups was the National Association for the Advancement of Colored People (NAACP). Founded in 1909, the NAACP had 481 branch offices in 1940 and drew its 85,000 members from the upper echelons of the black community. The National Urban League (1910), more a social service agency dedicated to helping newcomers adjust to city life than a protest organisation, had some 26,000 members in 46 branches. During the year that Hitler occupied Paris and blitzed London, the NAACP, backed by the Negro press, published an eight-point civil rights programme based on the assumption that the federal government should aggressively promote racial equality. They addressed several measures specifically to conditions in the South, where three-fourths of the black population still lived in 1940: legislation against lynching; laws ending peonage and debt slavery for tenant farmers and share croppers; enfranchisement of southern blacks. The 2.8 million blacks who lived in the North and West (90 per cent in cities) would also benefit from the other NAACP demands: equitable treatment in court, and fair distribution of public education funds; abolition of segregated public facilities; equality of opportunity in the workplace, and abolition of differential pay rates for blacks and whites doing the same work; equal access to labour unions and collective bargaining.

The possibility of US entrance into the Second World War lent a special urgency to the NAACP's demand for black equality. Once again, Afro-Americans would be expected to sacrifice their lives for their country, but only as second-class citizens in segregated units doing the dirtiest and most menial work. When the heads of the NAACP and the Urban League, along with the militant president of the Brotherhood of Sleeping Car Porters, A. Philip Randolph, met with Franklin D. Roosevelt and asked him to write an executive order desegregating the armed forces, they were rebuffed. The president, afraid of a backlash from white southern voters, refused to accommodate the leaders of Negro organisations with relatively few members and minimal political clout. Worse yet, the administration released a public statement implying that the black leaders had endorsed the continuation of segregation at the meeting with the president. Stung by the seeming betrayal and disillusioned with the practice of holding polite but pointless meetings, Randolph (long an advocate of mass militancy and a supporter of socialism) called in 1941 for a March on Washington. He promised to bring 100,000 determined blacks to the Capitol unless the president issued an executive order requiring that all federal government agencies and defence industries should hire blacks on a non-discriminatory basis. Six days before the scheduled march, Roosevelt signed Executive Order 8802 banning employment discrimination because of race, creed, colour or national origin. A temporary Fair Employment Practices Committee (FEPC) was also established to investigate complaints and resolve grievances arising out of the new hiring rules. While Executive Order 8802 declined to address the issue of segregation in the armed forces, it did pledge the federal government to definite action on behalf of equal employment opportunity. Randolph cancelled the March on Washington, but the threat (some called it a 'magnificent bluff') proved effective. One newspaper concluded that the episode demonstrated that 'only mass action can pry open the iron doors that have been erected against America's black minority'.[2]

The 1941 March on Washington movement showed how effective mass militancy and unrelenting pressure on the federal government could be, even as a threat. The establishment of the Congress of Racial Equality (CORE) in 1943 showed that American black activists were borrowing theories and techniques from overseas struggles for human rights in their fight for civil rights. Inspired by A. Philip Randolph's militancy, by Gandhi's tactics of non-violent direct action, and by the Quaker belief in witnessing, CORE operated primarily in northern and border state cities. It was not a mass membership organisation, but it made some progress in challenging segregation in restaurants, swimming pools and other local public facilities during its first decade.

CORE's limited success provided small comfort in the early post-war years compared to the setbacks symbolised by the expiration of the temporary FEPC, the lynchings of black veterans, and the attacks by white mobs on black neighbourhoods. Most white Americans were opposed to racial equality and preoccupied with re-establishing their own private, segregated lives. The interracial 'journey of reconciliation' sponsored by CORE in 1947, during which a small band of intrepid activists practised non-violent direct action and challenged segregated travel in several border states, went largely unnoticed. The Congress, immune to pressure from civil rights organisations, filibustered to death the bill for a permanent FEPC in 1946, and declined to strike down the poll tax in southern states or to pass anti-lynching legislation. Former NAACP secretary W. E. B. DuBois and world-famous actor and singer Paul Robeson were harassed by federal government agencies because of their sympathies with the socialist principles of the Soviet Union. Robeson, considered a 'Communist dupe', had his passport cancelled by the State Department in 1950. The NAACP, CORE and A. Philip Randolph continued to lobby the White House, however, and President Truman responded with several positive symbolic actions. He appointed a Civil Rights Committee whose 1947 report, *To Secure These Rights*, called for strong federal government leadership in the complete elimination of racial segregation and positive action towards equality of opportunity. In 1948, Truman called upon Congress to pass a ten-point programme that followed the 1940 NAACP proposal and became the basic minimum standard for civil rights legislation during the following two decades.

New York and several other northern industrial states passed FEPC acts by 1950, but Congress during the late 1940s and early 1950s did little to favour the cause of civil rights. Despite the co-ordinated lobbying efforts of the AFL, the CIO, the NAACP and the other black organisations, plus church and other minority associations, the 1950 FEPC bill was defeated. On the other hand, Truman nudged the armed services towards desegregation by a series of presidential orders, and created a new executive branch agency (continued by President Eisenhower in 1953) that monitored the enforcement of anti-discrimination clauses in federal contracts. The most encouraging signs of progress during this period, however, were federal court decisions.

Refusing to despair at the slow pace of improvement, the NAACP doggedly pursued the goal of equality under the law. With financial support from thousands of middle- and upper-class business and professional people, predominantly graduates of Negro colleges and members of established Protestant churches in southern towns and northern cities, the NAACP attorneys, notably Thurgood Marshall, successfully battled against legal segregation. In 1944 the supreme court in *Smith* v. *Allwright* abolished Democratic Party primary elections restricted to whites, and in 1950 the court rejected segregated dining cars on southern trains, ended segregated education at the University of Oklahoma, and ordered the University of Texas Law School to admit a black student to its regular programme.

Emboldened by its effectiveness between 1944 and 1950, the NAACP decided in 1951 to launch an all-out attack on segregated public education. Encouraged by the supreme court's insistence that while separate educational facilities were legal, they had to be equal (hence states could be forced to increase their spending on all-black schools), the NAACP challenged the entire concept of separate and equal schooling. Using a variety of evidence, including social science research that blamed the low self-esteem and retarded educational and mental development of black children on segregated education, the NAACP sued five school boards in South Carolina, Virginia, Delaware, Washington, DC, and Kansas. On 17 May 1954 Chief Justice Earl Warren announced the unanimous decision that 'Separate educational facilities are inherently unequal' thereby putting the prestige of the supreme court behind two propositions that were to shape the struggle for civil rights from the 1950s through to the 1970s. The first was that racism needed to be attacked in the South initially and only later in the North, where presumably it was more benign. This assumption blocked the US from realistically confronting civil rights as a national problem and contributed both to Southern defensiveness and northern chauvinism. The second principle that *Brown* v. *Board of Education of Topeka* fostered was the mistaken belief that equal educational opportunity offered a 'quick fix' for the nation's race relations problems. Historian J. Harvie Wilkinson III is persuasive in arguing that the decision was 'humane, among the most humane moments in all our history' as well as 'a great political achievement'. On the other hand, 'the nation learned . . . that public schools were not the panacea and that the problem existed beyond the south'.[3]

The supreme court complicated the difficult problems of implementing the *Brown* decision by ruling that local communities would be allowed to desegregate their schools according to the ambiguous criteria of 'all deliberate speed'. President Eisenhower refused to counsel southern communities to follow the law of the land; Congressional opponents of the decision vowed to resist its implementation; recalcitrant state and local governments passed legislation limiting its effect; Governor Faubus of Arkansas dramatically resisted federal orders to desegregate Central High School in Little Rock.

The 'massive resistance' to court-ordered public school integration also stimulated the revitalisation of the Ku Klux Klan and the organisation of White Citizens' Councils and local vigilante groups who used intimidation and violent demonstrations to discourage blacks from attending integrated classes. The optimism expressed by Walter White, head of the NAACP, when he exclaimed that the court's decision was 'a miracle' and 'a day of jubilation' proved unfounded, for in 1960 only one-sixth of 1 per cent of southern black students attended desegregated schools.

The massive resistance campaign against the implementation of the *Brown* decision accomplished more than the maintenance of segregated southern public education. The vigorous and widespread violation of the Constitution by white supremacists helped to convince large numbers of law-abiding middle-class Afro-Americans that mass militancy was needed in the struggle for racial justice. The terrorist tactics and the violent harassment of small children by vociferous White Citizen's Councils contributed to the popularization of non-violent direct action as a tool of peaceful protest on the part of respectable black church members. In 1955 and 1956 virtually the entire black population of Montgomery, Alabama, with 27-year-old Baptist minister Martin Luther King, Jr. at the head of their Montgomery Improvement Association, participated in a 381-day boycott of the transportation system and succeeded in forcing the city to desegregate its buses. In 1958 and 1959 student members of CORE and NAACP launched boycotts and sit-in demonstrations aimed at desegregating public facilities, and in February 1960 middle-class students from predominantly black North Carolina Agricultural and Technical College set in motion a nationwide direct action protest movement when they sat down at their local Woolworth lunch counter and refused to leave until served.

THE YEARS OF MILITANCY, 1960–8

The sit-in demonstrations of 1960 eventually drew students in their tens of thousands, black and white, into spontaneous non-violent mass protests against segregation. In spite of the usually violent white reactions, the students persisted. Their real goal, as activist Ella Baker described it during the organisation of the Student Nonviolent Coordination Committee (SNCC) in 1960 was 'more than a hamburger' and encompassed nothing less than 'full equality' in all institutions of American life. The passage by Congress of civil rights legislation in 1957 and 1960 undoubtedly contributed to the rising sense of impatience within the southern black communities, as did the anti-colonial movements in Africa, but it was the determined mass activism of the Montgomery bus boycott and the student sit-in demonstrations that more than any other single factor inspired a new spirit of militancy on behalf of black civil rights. When John Lewis, a divinity student and later head of SNCC, first heard the news of the Greensboro events, he 'began to think right away about it happening in Atlanta. . . . It was a sense of duty, you had an obligation to do it, to redeem the city.' Atlanta Baptist minister Martin Luther King, Sr. remarked that: 'The low-down Negroes are getting tired. . . . They just aren't going to take it like they always have before.'⁴

Like SNCC, the Southern Christian Leadership Conference (SCLC) was the product of the new mass militancy. Buoyed by the success at Montgomery and undeterred by the bombing of four churches and the houses of two ministers, Martin Luther King, Jr. met with black clergymen and activists from over two dozen communities. This group decided to combine religious pacifism and militant protest in an organisation that would represent southern blacks from all stations in life. By 1961 SCLC, SNCC and CORE were all involved – sometimes harmoniously, often with overt differences in programme and style – in mass protests involving sit-in demonstrations, 'freedom rides' challenging segregation in bus terminals, and boycotts against discriminatory businesses. In 1962 mass protest in Albany, Georgia, failed to dislodge discrimination from the city's institutions. One participant in the Albany movement (it struggled on until 1968) concluded that 'Albany was successful only if the goal was to go to jail'. In 1963, on the other hand, mass protest achieved a compromise agreement in Birmingham, Alabama, between the city and SCLC. Martin Luther King, Jr. called the settlement 'the most magnificent victory for justice we've seen in the Deep South'. Besides the release of all jailed demonstrators and the setting up of regular communication between black and white leaders, the agreement included desegregation of lunch counters, rest rooms, fitting rooms and drinking fountains of downtown stores and the hiring of black department store clerks. Inspired by the SCLC's victory, achieved in the face of police chief 'Bull' Connor's fire hoses and police dogs, protestors in 186 American cities carried out 758 demonstrations in which nearly 15,000 were arrested in the ten weeks following Birmingham. Veteran activist Bayard Rustin announced to the nation that 'Negro masses are no longer prepared to wait for anybody; not for elections, not to count votes, not wait on the Kennedys or for legislation, nor, in fact, for Negro leaders themselves'.[5]

John F. Kennedy, more favourably disposed by philosophy and temperament than Dwight Eisenhower to place the presidency on the side of full citizenship rights for blacks, took office in 1961. Robert F. Kennedy, as attorney general, was even more sympathetic to the civil rights movement. But both brothers acted only after carefully calculating the political risks and benefits that presidential action might bring to JFK's and the Democratic Party's future strength. Kennedy came into office with the slimmest of voter approval margins, and like previous Democratic Presidents Roosevelt and Truman, was aware of the potential damage that southern Democrats could do to his overall legislative programme. While Kennedy's belief in eventual equality for Afro-Americans moved him to approve federal intervention against the worst of the violence by white mobs, his lack of sympathy with the increasingly uncompromising nature of the black movement led him to counsel moderation. Both the president and the attorney general went along with the Federal Bureau of Investigation's (mistaken) argument that the SCLC was influenced by the Communist Party and they authorised personal and electronic surveillance of Martin Luther King, Jr. The brothers had also decided by the summer of 1963 that strong presidential leadership was necessary to end racial disorder, maintain black confidence in government effectiveness, satisfy white liberal demands for justice and fulfil their own moral belief in racial justice.

In May 1963 Kennedy altered his earlier practice of making only half-hearted attempts to enforce educational desegregation when he refused to allow Governor George Wallace to bar the door of the University of Alabama to black students. In June the president repudiated an earlier, weak, proposal in favour of the strongest civil rights bill ever sent to Congress. White supremacist Mississippi Senator James Eastland called the measure a 'complete blueprint for a totalitarian state', but it was still too weak for some liberals in

Congress. In July JFK overcame his initial misgivings about a proposed March on Washington set for late August and told reporters he looked forward to it as part of an American tradition of assembly for 'a redress of grievances'. On 28 August almost 250,000 marched in Washington, including some 75,000 whites. They joined Joan Baez in singing 'We shall overcome', and heard Martin Luther King, Jr. describe his dream of racial equality and announce his determination that 'we will not be satisfied until justice rolls down like the waters and righteousness like a mighty stream'.

Kennedy's death on 22 November 1963 did not halt the civil rights movement. In fact, the widespread public outrage over the assassination lent support to the drive to pass the slain president's Civil Rights Bill. In the middle of 1964 Lyndon Johnson signed a measure that outlawed most discrimination in public accommodations, allowed the federal government to deny funds to public agencies that ignored the law, prohibited employers and unions from discriminating, established an Equal Employment Opportunity Commission, committed the government to provide technical and financial help to communities trying to integrate their schools, and set up a Community Relations Service. The following August, Congress passed the Voting Rights Act of 1965 which abolished literacy tests and other barriers to black suffrage and allowed federal officers to supervise voter registration. By the end of 1965, it appeared that mass militancy combined with federal government activism had carried out a 'Second Reconstruction' which 'swept aside the last vestiges of legal discrimination and segregation and ended black disenfranchisement'.[6]

Actually, the situation was more complex. The 1964 Civil Rights Bill passed in the House only after a long and sometimes bitter debate, while in the Senate, die-hard opponents tried as in the past to kill the measure with a filibuster. For the first time during debate on a civil rights bill cloture (a rule that closes debate) was enforced. Within the South, as CORE and SNCC workers discovered when they tried to register voters in 1964 and 1965, attempts to turn legal guarantees into community practices often provoked murderous violence. The beatings, jailings and killings suffered by non-violent young civil rights activists gradually turned many of them into embittered advocates of aggressive counterforce 'by any means necessary'. When President Johnson refused to unseat the regular, segregationist, white Mississippi delegation to the 1964 Democratic

Party convention in favour of the Mississippi Free Democratic Party group that more accurately represented the state's black population, he strengthened the hands of those who counselled against compromise. Black racial chauvinism increasingly became the common denominator of the most militant civil rights activists. Stokely Carmichael and H. Rap Brown of SNCC and Floyd McKissick of CORE introduced the slogan 'Black Power'. The SCLC and the NAACP continued to support non-violent interracial co-operation, but Martin Luther King, Jr. moved further to the political left and called for basic economic and social changes in the US. During 1967, King condemned the US as 'the greatest purveyor of violence in the world today' because of its conduct of the Vietnam War. By the time of his murder in April 1968, King had lost influence with Black Power advocates because they regarded his militancy as still incomplete. Liberals, by contrast, became uncomfortable with his argument that economic and political immiseration at home was supported by violent imperialism abroad.

The Nation of Islam, best known to white Americans through the charismatic Malcolm X, had long preached black separatism and pride in blackness, and excoriated 'the devil white man' for his violent oppression of black society. But large-scale advocacy of Black Power, linked to criticism of US foreign policy, was a new development that troubled most Americans. Moderate leaders Roy Wilkins and Whitney Young of the NAACP and the Urban League dissociated themselves from the anti-draft and war-resistance positions of SNCC, CORE, SCLC. Some liberals took comfort in Malcolm X's move away from black chauvinism when he formed the Organization of Afro-American United after his break with Elijah Muhammad and the Nation of Islam. Others pointed to Malcolm's assassination by Black Muslim followers in 1965 as evidence of the poisonous influence of 'reverse racism'. Other whites who looked askance at intensified militancy and were repelled by black rage reasoned that the recent gains should have given blacks more satisfaction.

The combined effect of voter registration drives and new federal laws and supreme court decisions did bring impressive changes in the South. In Selma, Alabama, for example, black registration increased from 10 per cent to more than 60 per cent; where 24 per cent of black Alabamans were registered in 1964, the proportion rose to 57 per cent in 1968; only 7 per cent of Mississippi blacks were registered in 1964, but 59 per cent signed up in 1968. In the South as a whole from 1964 to

1968, the number of black registered voters rose from 1 to 3.1 million.

The conservatives who disingenuously asked 'what more do blacks want?' mistakenly believed that southern black masses were not satisfied with voting rights and the desegregation of public facilities. Like most Americans, conservatives were shocked by the spontaneous ghetto riots outside the South, from Los Angeles to Newark, between 1965 and 1968, and they angrily demanded a return to law and order. Liberals who earnestly prescribed massive government programmes to relieve ghetto poverty, create jobs, build public housing and speed up school integration mistakenly believed that the ghetto rioters were the poorest of the poor, moved to desperation by their misery alone. In fact, the rioters represented a cross-section of their communities, were working-class people more often than the down-and-out, believed in the civil rights movement, and wanted a larger piece of the American socio-economic pie. The rioters correctly judged southern mass militancy and civil disorder to have been an effective political strategy. They 'chose to protest by rioting . . . because they had no other viable strategy of change and because the struggle for equality in the South had changed the psychology of the Northern ghetto'.

By 1967 and 1968, however, the political climate for federal co-operation had grown cool, and the civil rights movement – divided within and under attack from the FBI and local police departments – grew increasingly fragmented and ineffective. As the rhetorical demand for Black Power grew more shrill, the political effectiveness of the white backlash grew stronger. The Fair Housing Act of 1968 outlawed racial discrimination in the rental and sales of residences, but it included an anti-riot clause as well. The favourable showing of independent candidate George Wallace, and the election of Richard M. Nixon to the presidency in 1968 symbolised the demise of the campaign for black equality and the beginning of more than a decade of defensive struggles to maintain the gains of the 'Second Reconstruction'.

THE PERIOD SINCE 1968

Nixon knew that Alabaman Wallace's appeal to white 'rednecks' had given him as many votes in the North as in the South, and the president played upon the widespread resentment and fear of black

activism by standing firm against further federal civil rights legislation. Thinking ahead to the 1972 election and hoping to increase
Republican Party support below the Mason–Dixon line, the Nixon
administration convinced Congress of the need to take the pressure off
the South by relaxing enforcement of voting rights and by extending
voting rights regulations in the North. Arguing for a policy of
'cooperation rather than coercion', the Nixon administration informed the nation that busing children to integrate schools was
undesirable, schools should be in the business of 'education not
integration', and the Justice Department should relax the enforcement of desegregation. Going well beyond the recommendation of
sociologist Daniel P. Moynihan, one of his key domestic advisers, who
advocated 'benign neglect' of all issues involving race relations,
Nixon actually aggressively pruned back federal guarantees of
equality in housing, employment, education and voting rights.
Gerald Ford, who assumed the presidency after Nixon's resignation,
though less decisive, was equally unfriendly to the cause of civil
rights.

In addition to opposing federal supports for civil rights, the Nixon
and Ford administrations turned to a time-honoured proposal 'to
curb black militancy and tame the ghetto': black capitalism. This
gambit had been used by philanthropist Andrew Carnegie at the turn
of the century when he financed the National Negro Business League
and other groups associated with Booker T. Washington. In 1968
Nixon reminded the nation that 'People who own their own homes
don't burn down their neighborhoods', and he proposed that a
partnership between business and government should facilitate the
development of black business by offering indirect subsidies and loans
to hopeful black entrepreneurs. The president upstaged black
nationalists by arguing that 'black pride, black jobs, black opportunity, and yes, black power' would be more likely to come from free
enterprise than through fire in the streets.

By the late 1970s, nearly 200,000 black enterprises were operating
in the US, but four out of five shared common characteristics that
rendered them incapable of providing a strong economic foundation
for achieving further civil rights gains. Besides being almost entirely
proprietorships owned by single individuals, they were under-
capitalised, mostly in human services and retail trade, averaged
between $3,000 and $15,000 annually in gross receipts, and three-
fourths of them failed within three years. 'Economically and politi-

cally, these Blacks are essentially workers who are attempting to become small business persons, struggling against massive odds to leave the ranks of the proletariat.'[7]

While fledgling black capitalists de-emphasised legislation and lobbying in favour of building economic clout during the 1970s, black politicians fought to stem the tide of reaction that threatened the success of the 1960s. In 1970 the nine black members of the House of Representatives organised the Congressional Black Caucus and began, as 'a new kind of black leadership by committee', to re-establish a civil rights agenda in the national capitol. Nixon initially refused to meet with the group, and the Caucus gained an audience only after it had boycotted the president's State of the Union message in 1971. Even then, Nixon relegated the group's legislative recommendations to a study committee, and the Caucus supported liberal Democrat George McGovern in the 1972 election. Two Black Caucus members, John Conyers, Jr. (Democrat from Detroit) and Ronald V. Dellums (Democrat from Oakland, California) were outspoken critics of the Vietnam War. Conyers, the first black member of the House Judiciary Committee, played a leading role in the 1974 impeachment hearings against Nixon. Andrew Young (elected to the House in 1972 from an Atlanta district) was the first black Congressman from the Deep South since 1898. Like his fellow black Caucus members, Young fought to end the Vietnam War in 1973 and 1974 and to extend the Voting Rights Act in 1975.

In the decade following the passage of the Civil Rights Act of 1964, the number of blacks elected to the House of Representatives increased from 5 to 17; the total number of black public officials increased from 103 to 3,503. While the increases were an important gain, blacks still constituted less than 1 per cent of all US public officials in 1975: 55 per cent were in the South, which made up 61 per cent of all black mayors and 44 per cent of all black legislators and executives. The number of black mayors grew from 48 in 1970 to 135 in 1975; most were in small towns, but blacks presided over city hall in Newark, Detroit and Gary, Indiana. The numbers of black judges appointed also increased, by 18 between 1963 and 1969 and by 20 between 1969 and 1975 (compared to the 17 appointed between 1901 and 1963). Virtually all the nation's black politicians, with Atlanta's Andrew Young in the vanguard, supported Georgia Democrat Jimmy Carter for the presidency in 1976. Blacks showed somewhat less interest in the presidential election than whites; 49 per cent of the black voting-age population turned out on election day compared to 61 per cent for whites. Blacks, however, almost unanimously preferred the Democratic candidate; 94 per cent of black voters cast their ballots for Carter.

Andrew Young's arguments that Carter 'is a product of the Southern church and knows the language and culture of the black community' helped to enlist prominent black leaders to his candidacy. Operation Big Vote, a national campaign to register black voters, took place at athletic events in the Houston Astrodome and in the outlets of the McDonald's Hamburger chain. In thirteen states, including those with substantial numbers of electoral votes such as Texas, New York, Pennsylvania and Ohio, the black vote pushed Carter to victory over Ford. Having worked hard for Carter's election, black leaders were disappointed when a second New Deal for blacks did not appear in his legislative programme. More interested in balancing the federal budget than in rejuvenating the Second Reconstruction, Carter also placed defence spending above the social welfare and education needs of low-income Americans. By the end of Carter's first year in office, the economic situation of blacks looked worse than at any time since the recession of the late 1950s. There was grim truth in the pundits' description of Jimmy Carter as simply a 'second-hand Ford' and at the meeting of the heads of fifteen black organisations in July 1977, former Carter supporters accused him of 'callous neglect' towards civil rights and the economic needs of black Americans. Black Georgia Congressman Julian Bond decided that 'we voted for a man who knew the words to our hymns, but not the numbers on our paychecks'.

Black leaders' disappointment with Carter's performance was understandable given their high expectations during his campaign. Some critics, however, disapproved of both the president and the black leaders; they argued that both parties ignored several developments that made the civil rights struggle of the late 1970s more complex than earlier periods. First, the lagging economy dramatically showed that black Americans occupied just as dependent a position as they always had; long-term improvement required basic types of economic reforms that had never been attempted. Second, the fact that the Democratic Party could rely on the black vote meant that it could dispense with special rewards for its delivery, though Carter, in fact, appointed more black judges and more black federal officials than his predecessors. Third, achievement of the legal guarantees that followed passage of the Civil Rights and Voting Rights legislation of 1964 and 1965 pushed the struggle for equality on to more ambiguous terrain; disputes over employment rights, school busing and special admission programmes for minorities seeking higher education generated a good deal more ambivalence than earlier debates over segregation and the right to vote. The debate over a national urban policy during the first half of the Carter administration (1977–9) showed how complex the politics of civil rights had become.

Carter appointed Patricia Roberts Harris, the former dean of the predominantly black Howard University's law school and a Democratic Party activist, as secretary of the Department of Housing and Urban Development. Immediately upon taking office, and even before the Senate confirmed her appointment, Harris announced to the press that the Carter administration would make a special effort to aid distressed central cities and their poor black populations. The White House, she said, was now occupied by 'a friend of the cities'. Both the US Conference of Mayors and the National Urban League, taking the president's announced position as an accurate guide to his intentions, began lobbying. The Urban League's July 1977 Annual Conference was devoted to 'Revitalizing Our Cities' and the president, as well as Secretary Harris, the heads of the Labor and Health, Education, and Welfare Departments, and the director of the Equal Employment Opportunity Commission, reassured the black organisation that their fears of the administration not living up to its campaign promises were unfounded. In September, Carter met with the Congressional Black Caucus and promised the group that full employment legislation and central city economic revitalisation programmes, both of which would increase black opportunities, were high priorities for his administration.

The president unveiled his 'New Partnership to Conserve America's Communities' in late March 1978, after consultation with the Urban League and the Black Caucus. Secretary Harris of Housing and Urban Development supervised the drafting of the 'National Urban Policy'. However, it was a compromise document that offered more to the banking constituents of the Treasury Department than to the black organisations that spoke for distressed black populations in declining central cities and poor ethnic neighbourhoods in Sunbelt metropolitan areas. Critics pointed out that less than 10 per cent of the $8.3 billion suggested for the first two years was intended for social services and other programmes for low-income families; 75 per cent of the proposed spending was to go directly or indirectly to business. Presumably, the incentives offered would stimulate investment and the benefits, including jobs, would 'trickle down' to the needy. The $3 billion proposed for public works grants, a measure that would have created jobs, was deleted by Congress in January 1979, as was a $400 million proposal for urban revitalisation grants. By the spring of 1979 the combined impact of Congressional hostility to the urban policy and administration cuts on other social service programmes had led one urban economist to declare that 'The heyday of urban policy' was 'the period just before the announcement of the Carter urban program'. Vernon Jordan, president of the Urban League, criticised the president for pushing the black population to 'the brink of disaster'.[8]

The failure of the Congressional Black Caucus and the Urban League to make the National Urban Policy into a tool for the advancement of black economic opportunity was regarded by critics on the left as proof of the limits of politics in 'racist/capitalist America' and by conservatives as a proper defeat of a potentially wasteful government programme. The major black organisations became increasingly balkanised in the late 1970s. The NAACP, the Urban League, SCLC, the Congressional Black Caucus, and People United to Serve Humanity (PUSH), the latter headed by the Rev. Jesse Jackson, a former lieutenant of Martin Luther King Jr., all differed in their diagnoses of the leading problems.

Black leaders had reason to doubt the efficacy of Democratic promises. Many were sceptical of Andrew Young's assurance that civil rights demonstrations were unnecessary 'when you can pick up a phone and call someone'. The black electorate, however, acted according to Young's prescription that 'Politics is the civil-rights movement of the 1970s'. In the 1980 election, black voters (7 per cent of the total electorate compared to 11 per cent of the population) gave 85 per cent of their votes to Carter; in the South, only 10 per cent of the blacks voted for Reagan compared to 70 per cent of southern white voters. One political scientist read the voting returns as evidence that 'As a group [blacks] are more nearly isolated now than they have been since at least the beginning of the civil rights revolution in the 1950s'.[9]

Ronald Reagan's policies toward civil rights were consistent with his conservative beliefs in self-reliance and his desire to lessen America's dependence upon government programmes. No more a 'racist' than Carter or Ford, the former governor of California was taken aback by the vehemence with which some black leaders attacked him in 1981 when the Treasury and Justice Departments began to relax the enforcement of school desegregation. The 1980 Republican Party platform condemned busing children to equalise educational opportunity, but it also promised that its candidate would be 'shoulder to shoulder with black Americans' in their fight against 'vestiges' of racial oppression. However, the president's willingness to intervene to preserve the tax-exempt status of segregated colleges appeared to one Justice Department official who resigned in protest as 'emasculating the civil rights laws as we know them'. In 1982, Reagan's unwillingness to assume leadership in the civil rights cause became even more clear when he only minimally supported Congress' second extension of the 1965 Voting Rights Act.[10]

Reagan's positions on civil rights provoked cries from the president of the Urban League that the president 'provided aid and comfort to the racists in our midst'. Black conservatives, however, such as the president's Secretary of Housing and Urban Development Samuel Pierce and the Hoover Institution economist Thomas Sowell, took a more benign view of the situation. Immediately after Reagan's election, Sowell, the nation's most prominent black neo-classical economic theorist, convened 125 black leaders in San Francisco. Reagan advisers Ed Meese and Milton Friedman attended as special guests, and the group plotted a course for black conservatives during the 1980s. 'The meeting', wrote political scientist Manning Marable,

> marked a significant turning point for national Black politics, for it dramatized and made public the severe contradictions on major political, economic and educational issues which divided the members of the Black elite. By the autumn of 1981, differences within the elite had become so intense that any possibility of building a consensus position on major public policy issues was lost.

On 27 August 1983 nearly 300,000 supporters of civil rights celebrated the twentieth anniversary of the 1963 Washington March by attending a demonstration in the nation's capitol. Some journalists saw the event as evidence of a revival of the political left and mass militancy. Others pointed out the severe divisions within the black community that made the 1980s different from the 1960s. The well-publicised refusal of several prominent black leaders to participate in the 1983 demonstration for 'jobs, peace, and freedom' lent weight to Marable's conclusion that 'the goals of the Civil Rights Movement . . . have been abandoned by major sectors of the Black elite'.[11]

11. Cultural Politics

COMMITMENTS to religious world views, codes of moral behaviour, and visions of future social order have frequently moved Americans to political action. Rooted in attachments to values and beliefs, such cultural energies have periodically equalled economic self-interest or ethnic loyalty as motivating forces of public life. Cultural politics provoked crusades against libertines and saloons in the nineteenth century and counter-attacks against teetotallers and Prohibition during the 1920s. During the interwar years, heated controversies over the teaching of scientific theories of biological evolution in public schools divided some American communities more irrevocably than class conflict or ethnic competition.

Since 1945 groups insisting upon the ascendancy of their particular values and beliefs have pursued the power to implement their preferences by public propaganda campaigns, legislative lobbying, litigation and protest demonstrations. Cultural conservatives and anti-communist nationalists from the late 1940s to the mid-1960s sought to preserve their version of an ideal America from the taint of socialist and anti-capitalist doctrines. Standing Tom Paine on his head, they argued that eternal vigilance against liberal legislation and revolutionary ideology was the necessary price for protecting American liberties. The 1960s and 1970s also witnessed a political turmoil generated by advocates of a 'counterculture', by feminists and by proponents of homosexual rights. These three social movements demanded public acceptance and legal guarantees of radical changes in male and female social roles and sexual practices. The reformers and radicals touched off an energetic counter-attack by conservatives determined to hold the line against the drastic and immoral changes they perceived in American society and the unacceptable expansion of governmental powers. By the 1980s, as more and more Americans of all persuasions sought greater measures of personal fulfilment, debates over cultural preferences increasingly motivated political controversies.

POST-WAR CONSERVATISM AND THE RADICAL RIGHT

Conservatism in the early post-war years owed as much to the reaction against the New Deal as to the attraction of Edmund Burke's philosophical tradition. Critics of federal economic and social welfare legislation of the 1930s demanded a return to *laissez faire* practices in industrial relations to begin the restoration of personal liberty. Government activism, according to this argument, fostered an unhealthy dependence upon the state that sapped the initiative and enterprise from American citizens. Opponents of the Democratic Party coalition (labour, white ethnic urban workers and black voters) opposed President Truman's civil rights and full employment legislation and demanded that the Republican Party should devote itself to minimal government. Conservatives wanted an independent Congress, dominated by WASP business-oriented advocates of free enterprise rather than a strong president of liberal persuasion. In their reckoning, state and local governmental autonomy was more compatible with individual rights than a strong central government. States rights, local control, personal liberty and preservation of traditional moral values: these were the values of the conservative critics of post-war liberalism.

From the conservative point of view, as articulated in journals such as *Human Events* and the *American Mercury*, Democratic Party public officials who pushed for further federal social and economic policies were counterfeit liberals. True liberalism regarded government regulation and social policy planning as a misuse of state power. To the extent that such statist imperatives became an integral feature of American institutional life conservatives sensed an ominous similarity between the US and the Soviet Union. Displeased with the Second World War alliance between the two nations, influential spokesmen for the right warned of Russia's alleged appetite for territory in eastern Europe after the armistice. Horrified by the Soviet Union's atheistic communism, Roman Catholic leaders and Catholic Poles, Hungarians, Czechs and Slovaks inveighed against 'Godless Russia'. Former President Herbert Hoover, an indefatigable campaigner for conservatism, saw 'Communism and Creeping Socialism sweeping over Europe' in 1945. In the tense atmosphere of the late 1940s, as the two giant powers settled into a Cold War stance, true liberalism (conservatism) and true Americanism (patriotic nationalism) provided the ideological rationale for the preservation of seemingly endangered American liberties.

Support for conservatism came from groups and individuals representing a wide spectrum of regional, religious, ethnic and class positions. Pundits and journalists during the late 1940s and 1950s, and social scientists during the 1960s, were quick to generalise about the 'social base' of the political right. Many of these early assessments have since been discredited, but several conclusions can be made with relative confidence. In the decade after the war most Americans were too absorbed in their personal and family lives to give more than passing attention to the putative dangers of creeping socialism and collectivism. The controversies over cultural conservatism and Americanism were thus pressing issues primarily for political officials and party activists, publicists and leaders of interest groups, and journalists. Republicans were more likely to vote for conservatives than Democrats; upper-middle-class small businessmen and independent professionals from small cities and towns, and farmers, typically took the more conservative positions, and they were often joined by blue-collar white ethnic residents of metropolitan areas. Catholics, like Protestants, were divided on domestic cultural issues as well as on questions of anti-communist foreign policy, whereas on both counts Jews presented a relatively united front against the right. Finally, while the Democratic and Republican parties both contained a large and varied constituency, it seems clear that 'the Republican right was the principal voice of independent capitalism'.[1]

Few episodes during the immediate post-war years illustrated the complex nature of conservatism as clearly as McCarthyism. The term 'McCarthyism' was frequently on the front pages of American newspapers from early 1950 to the end of 1954. It came to signify all of the disruptive consequences to public life occasioned by charges made by Wisconsin Senator Joseph R. McCarthy of communists in high federal government positions. Although they were vague, contradictory, and unsubstantiated, conservative Republicans in Congress seized upon McCarthy's charges in order to weaken the Democratic administration and pave the way for a Republican victory in 1952. Investigative hearings into McCarthy's charges did not turn up communist cadres committing treason and espionage, but they did allow Anti-New and Fair Deal critics to pillory the Democrats for enhancing US vulnerability to external threat and internal subversion. Although McCarthy's Wisconsin constituency provided him with little more than a perfunctory majority in his re-election, and although Republican President Eisenhower (after 1952) did not sanction McCarthy's demogogic tirades against 'atheistic Communism', the Senator received vigorous support from numerous veterans' organisations and from right-wing Congressmen and the press. During most of his four years in the national spotlight, public opinion polls showed that more Americans disliked his crude, blustering campaign against communism than approved of his activities. Except for a brief period in 1954 (just prior to his demise), Republicans were about evenly divided in their opinion of the Senator, and Democrats, by a two to one margin, opposed him. McCarthy was of Irish Catholic background, and those Catholics of Irish and Italian background who regarded 'Joe' as a heroic defender of Americanism probably did so out of their pride in being sufficiently Americanised to be able to defend *their* country against dangerous outsiders. However, Catholics did not support McCarthy *en masse*; like Protestants, they were divided along party lines, and the Catholic press and the Catholic hierarchy were also divided.[2]

McCarthy's ability to capture national attention was due more to the fact that his rhetoric and bombast fitted the Truman administration's (1945–52) mould of official anti-communism than to any upsurge of conservative mass activism. Having paved the way for 'Redbaiting' and 'guilt by association' during the 1948 election campaign against Progressive Party candidate Henry Wallace, Truman and his appointees by 1950 had already familiarised journalists and the reading public with dire warnings against 'Reds, phonies, and parlor pinks'. During McCarthy's four years of flailing away at supposed saboteurs, the press routinely sensationalised his activities and consistently overestimated his support among the public. McCarthy's Congressional colleagues, as well as Presidents Truman and Eisenhower, refused directly to criticise his public speeches or his Senatorial investigations. It was the live television coverage of McCarthy's investigation of communism in the US Army that provided the Senate with an excuse to condemn him. Emboldened by their sense that McCarthy's vulgar behaviour on national television would disgust the viewers, Democrats and moderate Republicans overcame their fear of his power and censured him for breaking Senate rules and bringing their institution into disrepute.[3]

McCarthy's personal decline did not signal the demise of conservatism. In fact, right-wing Republican Senators voted solidly against his censure, and as large a segment of the public voiced a favourable opinion of him at the time of his censure as had for most of his career. However, conservatives did lose some of their most prestigious national leaders by the mid-1950s; General MacArthur had returned to private life and Robert A. Taft ('Mr. Republican') died in 1953. The Democratic Party strengthened its hold on national politics, made itself the majority party by the late 1950s, and recaptured the White House in 1960. The Democrats were a divided party, however. Deep South Democrats opposed the supreme court's *Brown* decision in 1954 and condemned President Eisenhower's decision to send the National Guard to force the integration of Little Rock's high school in 1957. By 1963, when John F. Kennedy was beginning to use the presidency to advocate civil rights legislation, Democratic white supremacists had discovered common conservative ground with Sunbelt residents who worshipped *laissez-faire* economic liberalism along with God, country and order.

Republican Senator Barry Goldwater emerged as the national spokesman for conservatism during the first half of the 1960s. As a department store owner from Phoenix, Arizona, Goldwater became well-known by calling for a restoration of honesty in local government, a state right-to-work law, and the dismantling of federal economic regulations and social service agencies. Elected to the Senate in 1950, Goldwater campaigned against creeping socialism by denouncing Walter Reuther of the United Auto Workers as an advance agent of international communism. The Senator won re-election in 1958, a year when Republicans suffered heavy losses, and became both the leader of the Republican right in Congress and the chairman of the Senate Republican Campaign Committee.

In 1960, Goldwater published *The Conscience of a Conservative*, expressing his concern that 'in spite of a Conservative revival among the people the radical ideas that were promoted by the New and Fair Deals under the guise of Liberalism still dominate the councils of our national government'. Goldwater's book was ghost-written by L. Brent Bozell, a former aide and speech writer for Joseph R. McCarthy and brother-in-law of William F. Buckley, conservative ideologue and publisher of the right-wing journal *National Review*. Clarence Manion, a member of the national council of the John Birch Society, a group considered by some to be 'the spearhead of the Radical Right', assisted with the book's publication. By 1964, three and a half million copies had been sold, and Goldwater gathered around himself the leading lights of the nation's conservative intelligensia. The Senator's intellectual supporters were joined by the adherents of a variety of conservative organisations between 1960 and 1964. The John Birch Society, named in memory of a US intelligence agent supposedly murdered by Chinese communists, claimed to have some 4,000 local chapters containing 75,000 to 80,000 members nationwide. Over 200 radio stations broadcast the sermons of the Rev. Billy James Hargis of the anti-communist Christian Crusade and the preaching of the Rev. Carl McIntyre against modernism and liberalism. The Washington, DC, organisation, Liberty Lobby, distributed its *Liberty Letter* to about 175,000 readers, and a Florida physician established Let Freedom Ring, a recorded message from the John Birch Society that could be dialled on the telephone, in over 100 major cities.[4]

Goldwater increased his national popularity among conservatives in the South and southern California by declaring himself unfriendly to the federal government's imposition of desegregation and civil rights for blacks, by taking a militant stand against 'international communism', and by calling for states' rights and an end to 'the welfare state'. Nelson Rockefeller, the leader of the moderate Republicans, alienated conservative delegates to the 1964 Republican Party nominating convention by fathering a child with his second wife (he was divorced), and the strength of Goldwater's zealous supporters among party activists and his victory in the California primary made him the Republican candidate. If his campaign was the high point of national exposure to conservative rhetoric (Goldwater insisted upon the legitimacy of right-wing 'extremism in the defense of liberty'), his defeat with not even 39 per cent of the electoral vote showed the limits of the conservative ideological appeal. He won only in Mississippi, South Carolina, Alabama, Louisiana and Georgia (all Deep South states) and in his own Arizona. He won in only 4 of the 61 metropolitan areas that contained 44 per cent of the American population: Birmingham and Mobile, Alabama, Tulsa, Oklahoma and Jacksonville, Florida. He also lost the non-metropolitan voters outside the South. The Goldwater defeat was accurately interpreted as in part a repudiation of cultural conservatism and patriotic nationalism.

THE YOUTH REVOLT AND THE COUNTER-CULTURE

Americans born between the attack on Pearl Harbor and the Korean War came of age betwen 1958 and 1968. Regardless of their class, ethnic or regional situation, this age group experienced their childhood and adolescent years at a time of rising expectations rooted in the nation's unprecedented economic prosperity. The vast majority of this group, black and white, wealthy and poor, southern and northern, fit themselves into conventional roles according to models provided by families, schools, churches and synagogues, and communities. A minority, however, rejected material progress as well as the work ethic of their parents, demanded the right to indulge in instinctual gratification through drugs and sexual experimentation, and pursued a vision of communal harmony that ran counter to the American mainstream by establishing unconventional lifestyles. This 'counterculture' was not synonomous with the New Left, an equally protean group that supported 'participatory democracy' and called for an immediate end to all forms of inequality and injustice. But the press and television, bored with the anti-communist crusades of the previous decade, frequently collapsed the differences as they avidly recorded the tirades of leaders of the 'New Left' on college campuses and photographed the colourfully-dressed 'hippies' of San Francisco's Haight-Ashbury neighbourhood.

The black college students who sparked the direct action of the southern civil rights movement demanded fundamental changes in the political relations of their communities. They did not seek the cultural transformation of the South, nor did they expect American society to undergo a mutation in values and beliefs leading to the rapid erosion of racial prejudice. Nonetheless, the commitment of the early civil rights movement to morality above expediency, justice over compromise, and love over hatred, powerfully influenced large numbers of impressionable young Americans born between 1940 and 1950. Those most affected by the idealistic vision of immediate racial justice were undoubtedly the well-to-do offspring of liberal parents. Such parents had educated their children to expect a continuation of the economic and social aims of the New and Fair Deal, and these children attended colleges and universities in record numbers during the 1960s. Most college students during the 1960s did not participate in either New Left groups or the counter-culture, but the leading members of both movements were relatively affluent white children pushing their parents' liberalism further rather than working-class and ethnic-minority students trying to achieve the American dream of material success for the first time.

The activists organised mass protest demonstrations, the concept borrowed from the civil rights movement, to dramatise their rejection of the traditional political culture that stressed pragmatism, compromise and accommodation. These events brought together tens of thousands of students and young people on the fringe of the New Left and the counter-culture, as well as hundreds of full-time political radicals and members of communal 'families' living in unconventional households. Carefully staged, artfully executed, and exhaustively chronicled by the media, the Anti-Vietnam War, pro-Native American and other mass protests of the 1963–70 period were part political revival meeting, part circus, part Rock concert, part psychedelic 'happening'. While the media exaggerated their political impact as routinely as it had the speeches of Joe McCarthy, it accurately observed that the 'New American Revolution' seemingly under way in the streets and parks of New York City, Boston, Chicago, San Francisco, Madison, Wisconsin, Berkeley, California, and Woodstock, New York, aspired to be a noisy challenge to the traditional American culture.

Cultural revolutionaries generally lacked the toughness of vision demonstrated during the 1960s by a political pragmatist such as Walter Reuther of the United Auto Workers, and they were unwilling to labour patiently like Saul Alinsky organising the poor in gritty working-class neighbourhoods. Blocked by what one doting, 'over-thirty', professor described as 'these apocalyptic yearnings that beset our young' from the kinds of practical activities that would have been necessary to wage a *kulturkampf* against the dominant values, some of the young radicals cavorted through the streets playing at 'political theater' and acted out episodes of 'revolution for the fun of it'. Others, possibly envious of the professed revolutionary commitment of Black Power groups, applauded sentiments such as those of Black Panther Party officer Bobby Seale, who with all due earnestness informed his University of California audience that: 'Life, liberty, and the pursuit of happiness don't mean nothing to me if I can't go home and feel safe with my wife in bed replenishing the earth.' Some, following neo-Freudians such as Norman O. Brown, neo-Marxists such as Herbert Marcuse, and revolutionaries such as Che Guevara and Ho Chi Mihn, pursued bloody vendettas against the Establishment by robbing banks and killing police officers in the name of the Revolution. The less fortunate died in accidental bomb explosions or in shoot-outs with police. Still others made one-time Harvard University psychotherapist Timothy Leary their spiritual guide to the 'Holy City that lies beyond technocracy' and practised 'the politics of ecstasy' by 'living high' on hallucenogenic drugs.[5]

By 1969 and 1970, with crowds of youth celebrating the dawn of a new culture at the Woodstock Rock Festival and fortyish Yale professor Charles Reich proclaiming 'the greening of America', the New Left and the counter-culture were already disappearing as identifiable social movements. However, many of the values honoured by the young rebels and their imitators pervaded their thinking as they grew older along with the 1960s. The communications media, hungry for sensationalism, ceaselessly covered the self-conscious and sometimes exhibitionist activities of the radicals, revolutionaries, hippies and Yippies (Youth International party). Film producers turned out worshipful adulations of the tribulations of idealistic youths and gently-wrought parodies of the battle between the children and the parents. By the end of the decade, the surface phenomena of the counter-culture were widely disseminated throughout the society. Main Street matrons wore bell-bottomed blue jeans to PTA meetings; suburban housewives listened to the music of The Grateful Dead as they drove to the supermarket; Wall Street brokers wore their hair a bit longer and their neckties wider; well-to-do middle-aged metropolitan parents smoked marijuana at cocktail parties; members of discussion groups at churches and synagogues put their chairs in a circle, expressed their feelings about love and intimacy, personal relationships and crises of identity, and 'opened up to one another' as they explored the difficulties of 'being their own person'. The absorption of counter-culture argot accompanied the rapid spread of its music, clothing and attitudes towards personal relationships; this process seemed complete when President Nixon used the phrase 'New American Revolution' to describe his domestic legislative programme in 1971. During the middle and late 1970s New Left and counter-culture influences also contributed to a variety of community political movements focused on improving the access of citizens to public services and on increasing the 'quality of life'.

THE FEMINIST MOVEMENT

The revival of the movement for the rights of women during the 1960s was based on the steady growth of both single and married women in the labour force and the growing proportion of women high school and college graduates, stimulated by the struggle for civil rights, and aided by federal government equal employment legislation and favourable court decisions. Feminism also drew inspiration from countless numbers of small groups of women in thousands of communities whose 'consciousness raising' sessions generated mutual support that sustained the drive for gender equality in their personal lives. Never a homogeneous political phenomenon that spoke in one voice, resurgent feminism was, like the civil rights struggle, an internally divided social movement that continued to change its strategies and tactics during the 1960s and 1970s.

The cause of equal rights for women languished during the 1940s. After several episodes of fiery militancy during the antebellum period and the Progressive Era, feminists could point to the 1920 passage of national women's suffrage as proof of equal political participation. But by the late 1940s and 1950s the vast majority of American women were more involved in homemaking and raising families than in further agitation for the extension of women's rights into the workplace, the government office and the family situation itself. This period was not entirely 'bleak and lonely' for the 1,000 or so active members of the National Woman's Party (NWP), who had developed a well-established national organisation that provided a sense of continuity with the earlier militant period and a hope for the future. In the 1940s and 1950s, the NWP doggedly pursued its goal of a constitutional amendment that would declare the legal inviolability of equal rights for women. But numerous other women's organisations opposed an Equal Rights Amendment (ERA), during these years, and a large and focal segment of the established women's groups dissociated themselves from explicitly 'women's' issues and the term 'feminist' in order to avoid being dubbed political extremists or social failures. The president of one of the largest national organisations declared that 'selfish, strident feminism' was a relic from the past as quaint as high button shoes, and the League of Women Voters discussed whether they should change their name to the 'League of Active Voters'.[6]

If the older middle- and upper-class women's organisations were deeply divided over agitation for female equality as an appropriate activity, the more recently organised industrial labour unions were becoming bureaucracies with few positions for the activist women who had walked the picket lines and mobilised the women's auxiliaries of the late 1930s. Working-class and middle-class women who went out to work during the 1950s regularly took home smaller paycheques than men doing similar jobs, and typically received minimal assistance in household and child-raising duties from their husbands. Unlike married women who remained within the home, working women were less economically dependent upon their husbands. But the male-female wage differential, combined with the fact that with a divorce or husband's death child-rearing fell disproportionately upon the woman, meant that for the majority of women marriage was an economic decision as well as a culturally approved personal choice.

Not surprisingly, the expression of relative deprivation in personal and occupational success was first expressed by college graduates, accomplished career women in professions dominated by men. Betty Friedan, author of the best-selling *The Feminine Mystique* (1963) was a case in point. Educated at prestigious Smith (women's) College and a successful writer and editor, Friedan dissected 'the problem that has no name' (the yearning for an identity beyond the nursery, the kitchen and the supermarket) and recommended that women should adopt 'a new life plan' (a purposeful life in the public sphere). Her book resonated among hundreds of thousands of women and became a classic of American cultural criticism. But some critics (usually male) wondered why a woman like Friedan (didn't she have everything already?; why was she complaining?) was so unhappy with her life. Captives of the cultural conditioning that taught women to define their personal identities with the roles of mother, wife and housekeeper, these critics of the emerging feminist argument were unable to see how women's experiences in the 'heterosocial' world of college, university and office provoked their discontent. Trained by education to excel at academic work but also taught to practise traditional feminine skills, middle- and upper-class women chafed at being restricted to the latter. Recruited into professional occupations and expected to produce at rates equivalent to their male colleagues, they bristled when addressed as 'girls' and resented lower salaries. Enjoying the opportunities provided by their economic remuneration, women in the labour force – and those with relatives and friends in the labour force – logically compared themselves with their more independent husbands and male colleagues rather than with the dependent situations of full-time working-class housewives.[7]

Even before Friedan published her book, Presidents Kennedy and Johnson and their Democratic Congresses facilitated the emergence of the feminist movement by a combination of personal leadership and legislative enactments. Although JFK did not appoint more women to federal positions than Truman or Eisenhower, he did endorse the ERA and in 1961 established a Presidential Commission on the Status of Women. The Commission investigated employment discrimination against women in government and private industry, and its work facilitated the passage of a 1963 Equal Pay Act covering federal employees. The Commission's report, released shortly after the massive civil rights demonstration in Washington, put the prestige of the federal government at the service of 'widening the choices for women beyond their doorstep', and by the middle of 1964, 21 states had established commissions on the status of women.

Lyndon Johnson, moved in part by the influence of his strong-willed mother and the example of his active and accomplished wife, and in part by the opportunity to extend his reputation beyond that of Kennedy, made women's rights a policy issue of high priority during his first year in office. With great fanfare, LBJ announced a campaign to hire women in high federal offices, and in October 1964 he announced that 'the doors of public service' had opened to admit 1,600 women, including two ambassadors, members of the Atomic Energy Commission, the Interstate Commerce Commission, an assistant secretary of agriculture, and a director of the Import-Export Bank. When a conservative southerner added an amendment to the Civil Rights Act of 1964 calling for the prohibition of sex discrimination in private employment (in the mistaken belief that the majority of Congress would then defeat the entire measure), Johnson supported it, calling for 'equal opportunity for all our citizens regardless of their sex or their religion or their race'. The passage of this unprecedented federal guarantee of women's employment rights led Esther Peterson, director of the Women's Bureau and assistant secretary of labor, to exclaim that the nation was witnessing a 'sudden jump through many stages of history'.[8]

The passage of the anti-sex discrimination clause of the Civil Rights Act suggested to feminists like Betty Friedan an opportunity to link their cause to that of black civil rights. In 1966 Friedan and a small group of like-minded activists formed a National Organization of Women (NOW). NOW was soon dubbed the women's counterpart of the NAACP because of its commitment to further legislation and litigation on behalf of women's rights. At the same time, younger women, often college students who had experienced their first taste of politics in the civil rights movement and were disgusted with their 'second class citizenship' in the male-dominated councils of SNCC and other New Left organisations, began to drift towards a more militant form of feminism: women's liberation.

Impatient with the legalistic strategies of NOW and unwilling to adopt pragmatic tactics to monitor the implementation of equal employment legislation, advocates of women's liberation called for a 'personal politics'. All aspects of daily life would be subjected to thorough-going scrutiny according to the criteria of gender equality. While long-term economic and political goals were still high on their agenda, these radical feminists also insisted that friendships, love relationships, family life and workplace activities must immediately be purged of 'sexism'. By the beginning of the 1970s, this left-wing branch of the new feminism had pushed the more staid supporters of NOW to adopt a more aggressive strategy, including a drive to broaden membership by recruiting ethnic-minority and working-class women. Meanwhile, the women's liberation movement, in a manner reminiscent of the far left in the civil rights movement, fractured into subgroups devoted to specialised causes such as Revolutionary Marxism and lesbian separatism. Aware that their fervid protests against the symbols of 'patriarchy' made good copy and dramatic television, overnight celebrities such as Kate Millet, author of *Sexual Politics* (1970) and groups like the Women's Liberation Front, proudly wore workmen's overalls, refused to 'make up' in order to appeal to men, and flaunted their newly fashioned 'women's culture'. Robin Morgan, author of *Sisterhood is Powerful* (1970), destroyed the decorum of the 1968 Miss America contest by disrupting the Atlantic City proceedings. The members of the Women's International Terrorist Conspiracy from Hell (WITCH) specialised in 'staging dramatic happenings such as a coven of witches dancing down Wall Street on Halloween to hex the financiers'.[9]

HOMOSEXUAL RIGHTS AND GAY LIBERATION

If 'women's lib' struck a raw spot on the nation's cultural nervous system, it was nothing compared to the emotions generated by the emergence of the gay liberation movement in the years after 1969. The constraints upon public agitation for changes in sexual mores were if anything much more powerful than those that limited women's rights. Religious traditions, law codes, medical lore and conventional wisdom proscribed homosexuality as sinful, criminal, pathological and ridiculous. Those who dared to violate the norms were subject to a range of consequences from harassment to prison terms and personal disgrace. Despite the strength of disapprobation that existed throughout the nation, several traditional centres of cosmopolitan urbanity – New York and San Francisco in particular – permitted a relatively tolerant environment for the thousands of homosexuals and lesbians whose sexual coming of age had coincided with the mass military mobilisation of the Second World War. In these and other large cities the immediate post-war years witnessed the quiet establishment and growth of 'urban gay subcultures' that dramatically contrasted with the more secretive sexual lifestyles necessary in other parts of the nation.

In 1950 the first American organisation dedicated to the protection of homosexual rights was formed in Los Angeles. Named the Mattachine Society after a mysterious group of masked medieval figures thought to be homosexuals, the organisation was founded by several members of the Communist Party who met while working on the 1948 presidential campaign of Progressive Party candidate Henry Wallace. Originally founded by homosexuals as a buffer against the accelerating anti-communist movement and against the tendency to identify radicals and 'sexual perverts' as coequal devils threatening American culture, the society gradually repudiated radicalism in favour of political respectability. By the end of the 1950s the Mattachine Society (purged of its radical founders), ONE, Inc. (a group that published a magazine fostering an attitude of 'defiant pride'), and the Daughters of Bilitis (a lesbian group founded in San Francisco in 1955) were the motive force behind a national homophile movement. More accommodationist than ONE, which addressed itself only to other homosexuals, the other two groups adopted a moderate political strategy. They tried, according to John D'Emilio, 'to diffuse social hostility as a prelude to changes in law and public polity'.[10]

During the late 1950s and early 1960s internal differences kept the homophile movement from unifying nationally, while increased police harassment kept abreast of the expanding gay subculture centred in taverns and bars. As early as 1959, in San Francisco, a mayoral candidate tried to embarrass his incumbent opponent by accusing him of permitting the city to become 'national headquarters of the organized homosexuals in the United States'. But the attacks of the early 1960s, coming as they did at the time of the civil rights movement, served only to stimulate a new militant consciousness among San Francisco homosexuals. In 1961 Jose Sarria campaigned for the San Francisco Board of Supervisors as a homosexual rights advocate. In the following three years the city's activists organised three new groups; the League for Civil Education; the Society for Individual Rights; the Council on Religion and the Homosexual. Similar changes were occurring in New York City, and by the middle of the decade, the numbers of gay taverns in both cities were increasing. In 1966 the representatives of 15 local groups met in Kansas City and formed the National American Conference of Homophile Organizations.

During the late 1960s the homophile organisations gained the support of the American Civil Liberties Union. Reversing its earlier policy of refusing to consider homosexual practices as a subject of civil rights, the ACLU now led the defence of homosexuals and lesbians against employment discrimination, unfair and unequal law enforcement, harassment of individuals and raids upon gay bars. After 1967 the organisations themselves, encouraged by this and other such alliances, and influenced by the New Left and the women's liberation movement, experienced tensions between militant and moderate factions. By the end of the decade over 5,000 men and women belonged to the various groups. This was a number large enough to suggest the potential of organised politics on behalf of the cause of homosexual rights, but it was the first years of the 1970s that witnessed the birth of a truly mass movement among homosexuals and lesbians that made the nation aware of their insistent demand for equality.

THE REVIVAL OF THE RIGHT

Given the way that the press and relevision lavished attention on the counter-culture, the New Left, the feminist movement and the homosexual rights campaigns, it was not surprising that uncritical viewers in the US as well as America-watchers abroad were tempted to conclude that the nation was experiencing a cultural metamorphosis. In reality, the country's traditional values stood firmly in place. The relatively conservative Judeo-Christian moral values of the majority of the population were if anything more tightly held as 'middle America' braced itself against the media-induced fear of rampant divorce, reckless 'abortion on demand', raging epidemics of communicable disease following the loosening of sexual mores, and repulsive interracial marriages. More careful observers, such as Ben J. Wattenberg and Richard M. Scammon (*The Real Majority*, 1970), cautioned against hasty generalisations about changes in the nation's cultural preferences. The overwhelming defeat in 1972 of Democratic Party candidate George McGovern, proponent of a 'new politics' dedicated to equal rights for ethnic groups, women and homosexuals, as well as disengagement from international competition with communist revolutionaries, supported the thesis that cultural conservatism and patriotic nationalism remained a potent force.

By the middle of the 1970s grass-roots 'right to life' organisations had mobilised to protest against the 1973 *Roe* v. *Wade* supreme court decision that held state laws prohibiting abortion to be unconstitutional. At the same time, conservative women, inspired by long-time activist Phyllis Schlafly (*The Power of the Positive Woman*, 1977), organised a highly successful campaign against ratification of the Equal Rights Amendment that Congress had passed in 1972. In 1974 several conservative activists in Washington organised the Committee for the Survival of a Free Congress, and in 1975 the National Conservative Political Action Committee began to finance the election campaigns of conservative candidates. Richard Viguerie, a Louisiana-born Catholic who ingeniously used computerised lists of voters for direct mail advertising and solicitation for conservative campaigns, and Paul Weyrich, creator of the Heritage Foundation (1973), an information clearing house for right-wing causes, worked with other strategists to link the 'pro-family' groups with the anti-communist and anti-labour organisations among Republican Party conservatives. Viguerie's political career began with the 1952

Eisenhower campaign, and his heroes, because of their uncompromising defence of America, were 'the two Macs' (Senator Joseph McCarthy and General Douglas MacArthur). Weyrich, who like Viguerie grew up in a blue-collar working-class family, was fond of quoting MacArthur's 'There is no substitute for victory' as the political philosophy of the New Right.[11]

Joining forces with conservative evangelical groups such as the Rev. Jerry Falwell's Moral Majority and with pro-family groups like Phyllis Schlafly's Eagle Forum, the Washington organisations (receiving impressive financial support from anti-union business leaders like Joseph Coors) helped to defeat more than a dozen liberal Democratic Party senators and representatives in the 1978 and 1980 elections. Ronald Reagan's comfortable presidential victory in 1980 also benefited from such conservative support. The Republican Party's promise in its 1980 platform to seek a constitutional amendment banning most abortions pleased the traditionalist Catholics and fundamentalist Protestants who agitated for the 'rights of the unborn'. Conservatives were also pleased with the growing rifts in feminist ranks. By 1983 an increasing number of prominent women were publicly stating that while they agreed with feminist goals they disavowed feminism because of its 'image of a narrow, negative fringe group'. Younger women, part of 'the post-feminist generation', rejected the 'incredible bitterness' they saw in the 1960s and 1970s activists; one secretary declared that while she certainly wanted equal rights, she would never consider herself a 'women's libber'. On the other hand, Dr Sally Ride, the first woman astronaut, proudly credited the women's movement for helping her get 'where I am today'.[12]

According to conservatives, the values and beliefs of counter-culture adherents, feminists, political radicals and sexual libertarians were all too pervasive in the nation's largest metropolitan areas in the early 1980s. Activists therefore supported what Burton Yale Pines called a 'traditionalist movement . . . sweeping grass roots America'. The cultural movements that challenged traditional morality had in no way displaced the older Judeo-Christian cultural practices of the nation.[13] But the very fact that behavioural practices heretofore deemed abhorrent could now be seriously discussed as part of a viable lifestyle symbolically challenged older definitions of acceptable conduct. On the other hand, gone too were the days of the 1960s and early 1970s which could be characterised as a 'one-sided cold war in which counterculture, ultraliberal and other anti-traditionalist forces employed classic salami tactics, cutting away at traditionalist positions a slice at a time'. Perhaps the nation *was* 'heading back to basics' in the 1980s, with organised conservatism 'challenging liberalism on every major front and ending the liberal monopoly of the agenda setting process'.[14] If this assessment seemed correct, it was partly because of the political activities of such 'traditionalist' interest groups, but only the future could tell whether the old guard would make better use of cultural politics than its liberal opponents.

Notes and References

1. BUSINESS

1. Thomas C. Cochran, *Business in American Life: A History* (New York: McGraw-Hill Book Company, 1972), pp. 312–13. Robert L. Heilbroner, *The Economic Transformation of America* (New York: Harcourt Brace Jovanovich, 1977), pp. 214–15.

2. Charles E. Lindblom, *Politics and Markets: The World's Political-Economic Systems* (New York: Basic Books, 1977), pp. 172–9.

3. Hugh S. Norton, *The Employment Act and the Council of Economic Advisers, 1946–1976* (Columbia, SC: University of South Carolina Press, 1977), p. 96.

4. Ibid., 99.

5. Alfred C. Neal, *Business Power and Public Policy* (New York: Praeger, 1981), p. 23. Leonard Silk and Mark Silk, *The American Establishment* (New York: Basic Books, 1980), p. 252.

6. Gabriel Kolko, *Main Currents in Modern American History* (New York: Harper and Row, 1976), p. 314.

7. *New York Times*, 18 March 1979. *San Francisco Examiner*, 25–27 November 1980.

8. Paul A. C. Koistenen, *The Military-Industrial Complex: A Historical Perspective* (New York: Praeger, 1980), p. 99. Jacques S. Gansler, *The Defense Industry* (Cambridge, Mass: MIT Press, 1980), pp. 12, 21.

9. Murray L. Weidenbaum, *The Future of Business Regulation* (New York: Amacom Press, 1979), p. 172.

10. Mark V. Nadel, *Corporations and Political Accountability* (Lexington, Mass.: D. C. Heath and Company, 1976), p. 77.

11. Quoted in V. O. Key, Jr., *Politics, Parties, and Pressure Groups*, fifth edition (New York: Thomas Y. Crowell, 1964), p. 88.

12. Sarah McCally Morehouse, *State Politics, Parties and Policy* (New York: Holt, Rinehart and Winston, 1980), pp. 107–13.

13. Robert L. Lineberry and Ira Sharkansky, *Urban Politics and Public Policy*, third edition (New York: Harper and Row, 1978), p. 104.

14. Norman Podhoretz, 'The New Defenders of Capitalism', *Harvard Business Review*, 59, 2 (March–April 1981), p. 105. Peter L. Berger, 'New Attack on the Legitimacy of Business', *Harvard Business Review*, 59, 5 (September–October 1981), 89.

2. LABOUR

1. John T. Dunlop, 'The Development of Labor Organization: A Theoretical Framework', in *Insights into Labor Issues*, eds Richard A. Lester and Joseph Shister (New York: Macmillan, 1948), p. 180. Henry C. Simons, 'Some Reflections on Syndicalism', *Journal of Political Economy* (March 1944), quoted in Charles Craypo, 'The Decline of Union Bargaining Power', in *New Directions in Labor Economics and Industrial Relations*, eds Michael J. Carter and William H. Leahy (Notre Dame and London: University of Notre Dame Press, 1981), p. 107.

2. John Kenneth Galbraith, *American Capitalism: The Concept of Countervailing Power* (Boston: Houghton Mifflin, 1956), p. 105.

3. A. H. Raskin, 'Frustrated and Wary, Labor Marks Its Day', *New York Times*, 5 September 1982, section 3, p. 1.

4. Sidney Lens, 'The American Labor Movement: Out of Joint with the Times', *In These Times*, 14–18 February 1981, p. 12. Michael Harrington, 'Toward Solidarity Day II', *Democratic Left* (September–October 1982), 3–4.

5. John Barnard, 'American Workers, the Labor Movement, and the Cold War, 1945–1960', in *Reshaping America: Society and Institutions 1945–1960*, eds Robert H. Bremner and Gary W. Reichard (Columbus: Ohio State University Press, 1982), p. 138.

6. Quoted in John Barnard, *Walter Reuther and the Rise of the Auto Workers* (Boston: Little, Brown, 1983), p. 102.

7. Howell John Harris, *The Right to Manage: Industrial Relations Policies of American Business in the 1940s* (Madison: University of Wisconsin Press, 1982), pp. 118–25.

8. Ibid., p. 127.

9. Doris McLaughlin and Anita L. W. Schoomaker, *The Landrum–Griffin Act and Union Democracy* (Ann Arbor: University of Michigan Press, 1979), pp. 180–1.

10. Philip Shabecoff, 'N.L.R.B. Bill: The Battle Rages On', *New York Times*, 9 October 1977, section 3, p. 2.

11. For a typical argument on the need for co-operation, see A. H. Raskin, 'Changing Face of Industrial Relations', *San Francisco Examiner*, 26 March 1982, section B, p. 3.

12. The term 'factories in the field' comes from Carey McWilliams' *Factories in the Fields* (Boston: Little, Brown, 1939).

13. I. Herbert Rothenberg and Steven B. Silverman, *Labour Unions: How to Avert Them, Beat Them, Out-Negotiate Them, Live With Them, Unload Them* (Elkins Park, Pa: Management Relations, 1973).

14. Derek C. Bok and John T. Dunlop, *Labor and the American Community* (New York: Simon and Schuster, 1970), Chapter 1, 'Trade Unions and Public Opinion', pp. 11–63. George Gallup, 'Biggest Anti-Union Feeling in 45 Years, Gallup Poll Says', *San Francisco Chronicle*, 18 September 1981, section 1, p. 8.

15. Quoted in Marten Estey, *The Unions: Structure, Development, and Management*, third edition (New York: Harcourt Brace Jovanovich, 1981), p. 41.

16. Bok and Dunlop, *Labour and the American Community*, p. 457.

17. 'Poll Discounts Labor's Power', *New York Times*, 21 June 1983.

3.   THE CHANGING NATURE OF WORK

1. *Business Week*, 1 June 1981, 86. John Gunther, *Inside USA* (New York: Harper and Brothers, 1947), p. 615.

2. Quoted in Eli Ginzberg and George J. Vojta, 'The Service Sector of the U.S. Economy', *Scientific American*, 244, 3 (March 1981), 50.

3. Constance Bogh Dicesare, 'Changes in the Occupational Structure of U.S. Jobs', *Monthly Labor Review*, 98, 3 (March 1975), 24–34.

4. Thomas M. Stanback, Jr. *et al.*, *Services: The New Economy* (Totowa, NJ: Allanheld, Osmun, 1981), pp. 2, 71.

5. Andrew Levison, *The Working-Class Majority* (New York: Penguin Books, 1974), p. 25.

6. William H. Chafe, *The American Woman: Her Changing Social, Economic, and Political Role, 1920–1970* (New York: Oxford University Press, 1972), p. 219. Mary P. Ryan, *Womanhood in America: From Colonial Times to the Present*, third edition (New York: Franklin Watts, 1983), pp. 278–82, 317–21.

7. *The Mechanization of Work (A Scientific American Book)* (San Francisco: W. H. Freeman, 1982). S. A. Levitan and C. M. Johnson, 'The Future of Work: Does it Belong to Us or to the Robots?' *Monthly Labor Review*, 105, 9 (September 1982), 10–14.

8. Michael Burawoy, *Manufacturing Consent: Changes in the Labor Process under Monopoly Capitalism* (Chicago: University of Chicago Press, 1979), p. 199. Erik Olin Wright and Joachim Singelmann, 'Proletarianization in the Changing American Class Structure', *American Journal of Sociology*, 88 (Supplement 1982), S198.

9. Ely Chinoy, *Automobile Workers and the American Dream* (Boston: Beacon Press, 1955), p. 124.

10. C. Wright Mills, *White Collar: The American Middle Classes* (New York: Oxford University Press, 1956), pp. 232–3.

11. Angus Campbell, *The Sense of Well-Being in America: Recent Patterns and Trends* (New York: McGraw-Hill, 1981), p. 120.

12. George Ritzer, *Working: Conflict and Change*, second edition (Englewood Cliffs, NJ: Prentice-Hall, 1977), p. 409.

4.   REGIONAL METAMORPHOSIS

1. This section relies heavily upon Harvey S. Perloff *et al.*, *Regions, Resources, and Economic Growth* (Baltimore: Johns Hopkins University Press, 1960); see also Carl Abbott, *The New Urban America: Growth and Politics in Sunbelt Cities* (Chapel Hill: University of North Carolina Press, 1981).

2. John Herbers, 'Studies Find Dispersal of Industries in North Accelerated in 1970s', *New York Times*, 21 September 1980, p. 1.

3. Alfred J. Watkins and David C. Perry, 'Regional Change and the Impact of Uneven Urban Development', in *The Rise of the Sunbelt Cities*, eds David C. Perry and Alfred J. Watkins, vol. 14, *Urban Affairs Annual Reviews* (Beverly Hills: Sage, 1977), p. 43.

4. Martha E. Palmer and Marjorie N. Rush, 'Houston', in *Contemporary Metropolitan America*, vol. IV, *Twentieth Century Cities* (Cambridge Mass.: Ballinger, 1976), p. 135.

5. James L. Clayton, 'The Impact of the Cold War on the Economies of California and Utah, 1946–1965', *Pacific Historical Review*, XXXVI (1967), 449–73.

6. State of California, Department of Economic and Business Development, Office of Economic Policy, Planning and Research, 'The Effect of Increased Military Spending in California', typescript, 19 May 1982. Data on Defense Spending in the 1970s and 1980s come from this report.

7. Clayton, 'Impact of the Cold War', 462.

8. John Herbers, 'In Many Ways, Regions of U.S. Grow More Diverse', *New York Times*, 26 August 1982, p. 1. Robert Lineberry, 'Sunbelt, Frostbelt – So What?' *Urban Affairs Quarterly*, 16, 1 (September 1980), 124.

5.   SUBURBAN AMERICA

1. Peter O. Muller, *Contemporary Suburban America* (Englewood Cliffs, NJ: Prentice-Hall, 1981), p. xi.

2. Ibid., p. 82.

3. Kenneth T. Jackson, 'The Spatial Dimensions of Social Control: Race, Ethnicity, and Government Housing Policy in the United States, 1918–1968', in Bruce M. Stave (ed.), *Modern Industrial Cities: History, Policy, and Survival* (Beverly Hills: Sage, 1981), p. 93.

4. Thomas M. Stanback, Jr. and Richard V. Knight, *Suburbanization and the City* (Montclair, NJ: Allanheld, Osmun, 1976), p. 26.

5. William Severini Kowinski, 'The Malling of America', *New Times*, 1 May 1978, p. 34.

6. 'Many Companies Shift to Suburbs: Former Bedroom City Turning into a Major Center for Offices', *Los Angeles Times*, Part ix, Sunday 20 July 1980, p. 2.

7. John Keats, *The Crack in the Picture Window* (Boston: Houghton Mifflin, 1956), p. xi.

8. William H. Whyte, Jr., *The Organization Man* (New York: Simon and Schuster, 1956), pp. 286–7, 404.

9. Ibid., p. 404.

10. Bennett M. Berger, *Working-Class Suburb: A Study of Auto Workers in Suburbia* (Berkeley: University of California Press, 1960), pp. 89–90.

11. Herbert J. Gans, *The Levittowners: Ways of Life and Politics in a New Suburban Community* (New York: Pantheon Books, 1967), p. 419.

12. Scott Donaldson, *The Suburban Myth* (New York: Columbia University Press, 1969), pp. 83–90.

13. Gans, *Levittowners*, p. 416.

14. Robert W. Lake, *The New Suburbanites: Race and Housing in the Suburbs* (New Brunswick, NJ: Center for Urban Policy Research, 1981), p. 240.

15. Muller, *Contemporary Suburban America*, pp. 90–1.

16. Frederick C. Klein, 'Urban Irony: Some Integrated Towns Draw Fire for Efforts to Keep Racial Balance', *Wall Street Journal*, 8 January 1979, 14.

17. Robert Reinhold, 'U.S. Backed Chicago Test Offers Suburban Life to Ghetto Blacks', *New York Times*, 22 May 1978.

18. David Moberg, 'Little Progress in Integrating Suburbs', *In These Times*, 1 February 1977, 6.

6. THE CITIES

1. This discussion of US cities follows Thomas M. Stanback *et al.*, *Services: The New Economy* (Totowa, NJ: Allanheld, Osmun, 1981), pp. 99–102.

2. George Sternlieb and James Hughes, 'The Changing Cities – What is Happening and Why?' in *How Cities Can Grow Old Gracefully* (Washington, DC: US Government Printing Office, 1977), p. 3. J. E. Gibson, *Designing the New City: A Systemic Approach* (New York: John Wiley, 1977), p. 33.

3. The interpretation here follows the argument of R. D. Norton, *City Life-Cycles and American Urban Policy* (New York: Academic Press, 1979) particularly Chapter 4 'City Borders and the Timing of Urban Development'.

4. Morton Grodzins, *The Metropolitan Area as a Racial Problem* (Pittsburgh: University of Pittsburgh Press), p. 1.

5. Todd Gitlin and Nanci Hollander, *Uptown: Poor Whites in Chicago* (New York: Harper Colophon, 1970), p. xvii.

6. William Serrin, 'Hamtramck Is Losing a Plant – and More', *New York Times* 16 December 1979. Ivar Peterson, 'Company Towns Without Companies Lack Remedies', *New York Times*, 30 November 1980. Peter T. Kilborn, 'The Twilight of Smokestack America', *New York Times*, Sunday 8 May 1983.

7. Larry H. Long and Donald C. Dahmann, 'The City-Suburban Income Gap: Is It Being Narrowed by a Back-to-the-City Movement?' (Bureau of the Census, March 1980), quoted in Jane Newitt, 'Behind the Big-City Blues', *American Demographics*, 5 (June 1983), 28.

8. Robert Lindsey, 'California Becoming a New Melting Pot', *New York Times*, 23 August 1981, 14.

9. George Volsky, 'Miami – Gateway to the Latin Dollar', *New York Times*, 14 August 1977. Herbert Burkholz, 'The Latinization of Miami', *New York Times Magazine*, 21 September 1980, 46. Reginald Stuart, 'Economic Troubles of Miami's Blacks is Major Issue Facing Prospering City', *New York Times*, 16 January 1983.

10. Theodore J. Lowi, 'The State of Cities in the Second Republic', in John P. Blair and David Nachmias (eds), *Fiscal Retrenchment and Urban Policy* (Beverly Hills: Sage, 1979), pp. 47–8. William K. Stevens, 'Texas Isn't So Rich – It Only Seems That Way', *New York Times*, 20 May 1979.

11. Carl Abbott, *The New Urban America: Growth and Politics in Sunbelt Cities* (Chapel Hill: University of North Carolina Press, 1981), p. 254.

12. Quoted in Mark I. Gelfand, *A Nation of Cities: The Federal Government and Urban America, 1933–1965* (New York: Oxford University Press, 1975), p. 295.

13. Quoted in H. V. Savitch, *Urban Policy and the Exterior City: Federal, State and Corporate Impacts on Major Cities* (New York: Pergamon, 1979), p. 167.

14. Art Harris, 'Portman's Sky-High Philosophy', *San Francisco Examiner*, 30 March 1976, p. 20.

7. METROPOLITAN POLITICS

1. Robert L. Lineberry and Ira Sharkansky, *Urban Politics and Public Policy*, second edition (New York: Harper and Row, 1974), p. 57.

2. Robert A. Dahl, *Who Governs: Democracy and Power in an American City* (New Haven: Yale University Press, 1961). For a critical analysis of Dahl's conclusions, see G. William Domhoff, *Who Really Rules? New Haven and Community Power Reexamined* (Santa Monica: Goodyear, 1978).

3. Floyd Hunter, *Community Power Structure: A Study of Decision Makers* (Garden City: Anchor Books, 1963 originally published 1953). M. Kent Jennings came to different conclusions about Atlanta. See his *Community Influentials: The Elites of Atlanta* (New York: Free Press of Glencoe, 1964).

4. Domhoff, *Who Really Rules*, p. 13.

5. The interpretation here follows the argument of Paul E. Peterson, *City Limits* (Chicago: University of Chicago Press, 1981), pp. 109–30.

6. Ibid., pp. 41–65.

7. Jack Newfield and Paul DuBrul, *The Abuse of Power: The Permanent Government and the Fall of New York* (New York: Penguin Books, 1977), 80–7, 106–8. William K. Tabb, *The Long Default: New York City and the Urban Fiscal Crisis* (New York: Monthly Review Press, 1982), p. 23.

8. Martin Shefter, 'New York City's Fiscal Crisis: The Politics of Inflation and Retrenchment', *The Public Interest*, 48 (Summer 1977), 98–127, at 106–7.

9. Ibid., 113.

10. Tabb, *The Long Default*, pp. 89–106.

11. Frederick M. Wirt, *Power in the City: Decision-Making in San Francisco* (Berkeley: University of California Press, 1974), pp. 338, 340.

12. J. Allen Whitt, 'Can Capitalists Organize Themselves?' in G. William Domhoff (ed.), *Power Structure Research* (Beverly Hills: Sage, 1980), p. 109.

13. Murray Bookchin, 'Toward a Vision of the Urban Future', in David C. Perry and Alfred J. Watkins (eds), *The Rise of the Sunbelt Cities*, (Beverly Hills: Sage, 1977), p. 265.

14. Philip J. Trounstine and Terry Christensen, *Movers and Shakers: The Study of Community Power* (New York: St. Martin's Press, 1982) p. 190.

15. Thomas P. Murphy and John Rehfuss, *Urban Politics in the Suburban Era* (Homewood, Ill.: Dorsey Press, 1976), p. 55. John C. Bollens and Henry J. Schmandt, *The Metropolis: Its People, Politics, and Economic Life*, fourth edition (New York: Harper and Row, 1982), p. 122.

16. Robert C. Wood, *Suburbia: Its People and Their Politics* (Boston: Houghton Mifflin, 1958), p. 197. Herbert J. Gans, *The Levittowners: Ways of Life and Politics in a New Suburban Community* (New York: Pantheon Books, 1967), pp. 358–9.

8. WEALTH AND POVERTY

1. Robert S. Lynd and Helen Merrell Lynd, *Middletown in Transition* (New York: Harcourt, Brace and World, 1937), p. 77.

2. Arthur W. Kornhauser, 'Analysis of "Class" Structure of Contemporary American Society – Psychological Bases of Class Divisions', in George W. Hartmann and Theodor Newcomb, *Industrial Conflict: A Psychological Interpretation* (New York: Cordon, 1939), p. 262.

3. Daniel Bell, 'America's Un-Marxist Revolution', in Reinhard Bendix and Seymour Martin Lipset, *Class, Status and Power: A Reader in Social Stratification* (New York: The Free Press, 1953), pp. 163, 172. Katherine Archibald, 'Status Orientations Among Shipyard Workers', in ibid, pp. 400–1.

4. Richard Centers, *The Psychology of Social Classes: A Study of Class Consciousness* (New York: Russell and Russell, 1961, originally 1949), p. 218. Walter Goldschmidt, 'Social Class in America – A Critical Review', *American Anthropologist*, 52 (October–December 1950), 494–5. For recent sociological research that reaffirms the conclusions of Centers' book, see Mary R. Jackman and Robert W. Jackman, *Class Awareness in the United States* (Berkeley: University of California Press, 1983).

5. Milton M. Gordon, *Social Class in American Sociology* (Durham: Duke University Press, 1958), p. 236. Robert A. Nisbet, 'The Decline and Fall of Social Class', *Pacific Sociological Review*, II (Spring 1959), 17. Vance Packard, *The Status Seekers* (New York: David McKay, 1959), p. 8.

6. Herman P. Miller, *Income of the American People* (New York: John Wiley, 1955), pp. 109–12. Jeffrey G. Williamson and Peter H. Lindert, *American Inequality: A Macroeconomic History* (New York: Academic Press, 1980), pp. 82–92.

7. James N. Morgan, Martin H. David, Wilbur J. Cohen and Harvey E. Brazer, *Income and Welfare in the United States* (New York: McGraw-Hill, 1962), p. 3.

8. James L. Sundquist, *Politics and Policy: The Eisenhower, Kennedy, and Johnson Years* (Washington, DC: Brookings Institution, 1968), p. 140.

9. James T. Patterson, *America's Struggle Against Poverty: 1900–1980* (Cambridge, Mass.: Harvard University Press, 1981), pp. 133–41.

10. Gustavus Myers, *The Ending of Hereditary American Fortunes* (New York: Julian Messner, 1939), p. 381.

11. Douglas T. Miller and Marion Nowak, *The Fifties: The Way We Really Were* (Garden City, NY: Doubleday, 1977), pp. 112–13.

12. C. Wright Mills, *The Power Elite* (New York: Oxford University Press, 1956), p. 5. Victor Perlo, *The Empire of High Finance* (New York: International Publishers, 1957), p. 13.

13. E. Digby Baltzell, *Philadelphia Gentlemen: The Making of a National Upper Class* (New York: The Free Press, 1958), p. 389.

14. Richard H. Rovere, *The American Establishment and Other Reports, Opinions and Speculations* (New York: Harcourt, Brace and World, 1962), pp. 3, 11.

15. E. Digby Baltzell, *The Protestant Establishment: Aristocracy and Caste in America* (New York: Vintage Books, 1966 originally 1964), p. 382.

16. G. William Domhoff, *Who Rules America?* (Englewood Cliffs, NJ: Prentice-Hall, 1967), pp. 156, 161.

17. Ferdinand Lundberg, *The Rich and the Super-Rich* (New York: Bantam Books, 1968), p. 3. Kurt B. Mayer and Walter Buckley, *Class and Society*, third edition (New York: Random House, 1970), pp. 79–80. Morton Mintz and Jerry S. Cohen, *America Inc.: Who Owns and Operates the United States* (New York: Dial Press, 1971), p. 13.

18. Saul D. Alinsky, *Reveille for Radicals* (Chicago: University of Chicago Press, 1946), p. 86.

19. Robert Bailey, Jr., *Radicals in Urban Politics: The Alinsky Approach* (Chicago: University of Chicago Press, 1974), p. 1.

20. This section draws upon Nick Kotz and Mary Lynn Kotz, *A Passion for Equality: George A. Wiley and the Movement* (New York: W. W. Norton, 1977), and Frances Fox Piven and Richard A. Cloward, *Poor People's Movements: Why They Succeed, How They Fail* (New York: Vintage Books, 1979).

21. Piven and Cloward, *Poor People's Movements*, p. 353.

22. The term 'revolt of the haves' is that of Robert Kuttner. See his *Revolt of the Haves: Tax Rebellions and Hard Times* (New York: Simon and Schuster, 1980). This section relies upon Kuttner and David O. Sears and Jack Citrin, *Tax Revolt: Something for Nothing in California* (Cambridge, Mass.: Harvard University Press, 1982).

23. Reaganism is discussed in James Q. Wilson, 'Reagan and the Republican Revival', in *Commentary*, 70 (October 1980), 25–32. Details on cuts to public services can be found in Laurence I. Barrett, *Gambling With History: Reagan in the White House* (Garden City, NY: Doubleday, 1983), pp. 401–14, and Frances Fox Piven and Richard A. Cloward, *The New Class War: Reagan's Attack on the Welfare State and Its Consequences* (New York: Pantheon Books, 1982).

9.   RACE AND ETHNICITY

1. Gunnar Myrdal, *An American Dilemma: The Negro Problem and Modern Democracy* (New York: Harper and Row, 1962 originally 1944), pp. lxi, 115.

2. Kit and Frederica Konolige, *The Power of Their Glory: America's Ruling Class: The Episcopalians* (New York: Wyden Books, 1978), p. 29.

3. Richard D. Alba and Gwen Moore, 'Ethnicity in the American Elite', *American Sociological Review*, 47 (1982), 382.

4. Stephen Steinberg, *The Ethnic Myth: Race, Ethnicity, and Class in America* (Boston: Beacon Press, 1981), pp. 69–71.

5. Marshall Sklare and Joseph Greenblum, *Jewish Identity on the Suburban Frontier: A Study of Group Survival in the Open Society*, second edition (Chicago: University of Chicago Press, 1979), p. 403.

6. Stephen S. Hall, 'Italian-Americans: Coming Into Their Own', *New York Times Magazine*, 15 May 1983, 31. Humbert S. Nelli, *From Immigrants to Ethnics: The Italian Americans* (New York: Oxford University Press, 1983), pp. 187, 191.

7. Michael Novak, *The Rise of the Unmeltable Ethnics: Politics and Culture in the Seventies* (New York: Macmillan, 1973), p. 54.

8. Myrdal, *American Dilemma*, p. 53.

9. Stanley Lieberson, *A Piece of the Pie: Blacks and White Immigrants Since 1880* (Berkeley: University of California Press, 1980), pp. 363–83.

10. Michael Reich, *Racial Inequality: A Political-Economic Analysis* (Princeton: Princeton University Press, 1981), pp. 28–9, 31, 74. William Julius Wilson, *The Declining Significance of Race: Blacks and Changing American Institutions*, second edition (Chicago: University of Chicago Press, 1980), p. 152.

11. Lieberson, *A Piece of the Pie*, p. 368.

12. Thomas Sowell, *Ethnic America: A History* (New York: Basic Books, 1981), p. 177.

13. James W. Vander Zanden, *American Minority Relations*, fourth edition, (New York: Alfred A. Knopf, 1983) pp. 259–60.

14. E. Franklin Frazier, *The Negro Family in the United States*, revised and abridged edition (New York: Citadel Press, 1948), pp. 367–8.

15. This section is based on the materials collected in Lee Rainwater and William L. Yancey, *The Moynihan Report and the Politics of Controversy* (Cambridge, Mass.: MIT Press, 1967), pp. 66, 81, 149.

16. Edward C. Banfield, *The Unheavenly City Revisited: A Revision of The Unheavenly City* (Boston: Little, Brown, 1974), p. 143.

17. Manning Marable, *How Capitalism Underdeveloped Black America* (Boston: South End Press, 1983), p. 59. Irving Howe, 'The Limits of Ethnicity', *New Republic*, 25 June 1977, p. 19, quoted in Steinberg, *The Ethnic Myth*, p. 261.

10. THE STRUGGLE FOR CIVIL RIGHTS

1. Harvard Sitkoff, *A New Deal for Blacks: The Emergence of Civil Rights as a National Issue*, Vol. I, *The Depression Decade* (New York: Oxford University Press, 1978), pp. 34, 330–1.

2. Quoted in Jervis Anderson, *A. Philip Randolph: A Biographical Portrait* (New York: Harcourt, Brace and Jovanovich, 1973), p. 260.

3. J. Harvie Wilkinson III, *From Brown to Bakke: The Supreme Court and School Integration: 1954–1978* (New York: Oxford University Press, 1979), pp. 39, 57.

4. Harvard Sitkoff, *The Struggle for Black Equality: 1954–1980* (New York: Hill and Wang, 1981), pp. 86–7.

5. Quoted in Thomas R. Brooks, *Walls Come Tumbling Down: A History of the Civil Rights Movement, 1940–1970* (Englewood Cliffs, NJ: Prentice-Hall, 1974), p. 209.

6. Sitkoff, *Struggle*, p. 165.

7. Thomas L. Blair, *Retreat to the Ghetto: The End of a Dream?* (New York: Hill and Wang, 1977), p. 165. Manning Marable, *How Capitalism Underdeveloped Black America* (Boston: South End Press, 1983), p. 156.

8. Marc A. Weiss and Erica Schoenberger, 'Carter Throws Peanuts to Cities', *In These Times*, 28 February–6 March, 1979.

9. Walter Dean Burnham, 'The 1980 Earthquake: Realignment, Reaction, or What', in Thomas Ferguson and Joel Rogers (eds), *The Hidden Election: Politics and Economics in the 1980 Presidential Campaign* (New York: Pantheon, 1981), p. 105.

10. Laurence I. Barrett, *Gambling With History: Ronald Reagan in the White House* (Garden City, NY: Doubleday, 1983), pp. 422–3, 418.

11. Marable, *Black America*, pp. 172, 193.

11. CULTURAL POLITICS

1. Michael W. Miles, *Odyssey of the American Right* (New York: Oxford University Press, 1980), p. 45.

2. Ibid., pp. 123–47, 208–21. Donald F. Crosby, SJ, *God, Church, and Flag: Senator Joseph R. McCarthy and the Catholic Church, 1950–1957* (Chapel Hill: University of North Carolina Press, 1978), pp. 228–51.

3. Robert Griffith and Athan Theoharis, *The Specter: Original Essays on the Cold War and the Origins of McCarthyism* (New York: New Viewpoints, 1974), pp. 276–80. David M. Oshinsky, *A Conspiracy So Immense: The World of Joe McCarthy* (New York: The Free Press, 1983), p. 472–94.

4. Barry Goldwater, *The Conscience of a Conservative* (Shepherdsville, Kentucky: Victor Publishing, 1960), foreword. Benjamin R. Epstein and Arnold Foster, *The Radical Right Report on the John Birch Society and Its Allies* (New York: Random House, 1967), pp. 3–15.

5. Theodore Roszak, *The Making of a Counter Culture: Reflections on the Technocratic Society and Its Youthful Opposition* (Garden City, NY: Anchor Books, 1969). My interpretation of the youth revolt and the counter-culture is indebted to Joseph Conlin, *The Troubles: A Jaundiced Glance Back at the Movement of the Sixties* (New York: Franklin Watts, 1982).

6. Quoted in Leila J. Rupp, 'The Survival of American Feminism: The Women's Movement in the Postwar Period', in *Reshaping America: Society and Institutions, 1945–1960*, eds Robert H. Bremner and Gary W. Reichard (Columbus: Ohio State University Press, 1982), p. 42.

7. The term 'heterosocial' is from Mary P. Ryan, *Womanhood in America: From Colonial Times to the Present*, third edition (New York: Franklin Watts, 1983), pp. 305–17. This section draws on Ryan's discussion of feminism.

8. Patricia G. Zelman, *Woman, Work, and National Policy: The Kennedy–Johnson Years* (Ann Arbor: UMI Research Press, 1982), p. 57.

9. June Sochen, *Movers and Shakers: American Women Thinkers and Activists, 1900–1970* (New York: Quadrangle/New York Times, 1973), p. 259.

10. John D'Emilio, *Sexual Politics, Sexual Communities: The Making of a Homosexual Minority in the United States, 1940–1970* (Chicago: University of Chicago Press, 1983), p. 109. This section draws upon D'Emilio's work and Toby Marotta, *The Politics of Homosexuality* (Boston: Houghton Mifflin, 1981).

11. This section relies upon Alan Crawford, *Thunder on the Right: The 'New Right' and the Politics of Resentment* (New York: Pantheon Books, 1980); Richard A. Viguerie, *The New Right: We're Ready to Lead* (Falls Church, Va.: Viguerie Company, 1981); Connie Paige, *The Right to Lifers: Who They Are, How They Operate, Where They Get Their Money* (New York: Summit Books, 1983).

12. Susan Bolotin, 'Voices from the Post-Feminist Generation', *New York Times Magazine*, 17 October 1982, 28, 107. Letty Cottin Pogrebin, 'Hers', *New York Times*, 22 September 1983, p. 18. Betty Friedan, *The Second Stage* (New York: Summit Books, 1981).

13. University of Washington sociologists conducted a nationwide survey between 1975 and 1982 that provided overwhelming evidence about the continued strength of pre-counter-culture values and behaviour. See Philip Blumstein and Pepper Schwartz, *American Couples: Money, Work, Sex* (New York: William Morrow, 1983), pp. 47–8, 188–9, 302–6, 318–30.

14. Burton Yale Pines, *Back to Basics: The Traditionalist Movement That Is Sweeping Grass-Roots America* (New York: William Morrow, 1982), pp. 308, 331.

Bibliography

Carl Abbott, *The New Urban America: Growth and Politics in Sunbelt Cities* (Chapel Hill: University of North Carolina, 1981).

Saul D. Alinsky, *Reveille for Radicals* (Chicago: University of Chicago Press, 1946).

Jervis Anderson, *A. Philip Randolph: A Biographical Portrait* (New York: Harcourt, Brace and Jovanovich, 1973).

Robert Bailey, Jr., *Radicals in Urban Politics: The Alinsky Approach* (Chicago: University of Chicago Press, 1974).

E. Digby Baltzell, *Philadelphia Gentlemen: The Making of a National Upper Class* (New York: The Free Press, 1958).

E. Digby Baltzell, *The Protestant Establishment: Aristocracy and Caste in America* (New York: Vintage Books, 1966).

Edward C. Banfield, *The Unheavenly City Revisited: A Revision of The Unheavenly City* (Boston: Little, Brown, 1974).

John Barnard, *Walter Reuther and the Rise of the Auto Workers* (Boston: Little Brown, 1983).

Laurence I. Barrett, *Gambling With History: Reagan in the White House* (Garden City, NY: Doubleday, 1983).

Reinhard Bendix and Seymour Martin Lipset (eds), *Class, Status and Power: A Reader in Social Stratification* (New York: The Free Press, 1953).

Bennett M. Berger, *Working-Class Suburb: A Study of Auto Workers in Suburbia* (Berkeley: University of California Press, 1960).

John P. Blair and David Nachmias (eds), *Fiscal Retrenchment and Urban Policy* (Beverly Hills: Sage, 1979).

Thomas L. Blair, *Retreat to the Ghetto: The End of a Dream?* (New York: Hill and Wang, 1977).

Derek C. Bok and John T. Dunlop, *Labor and the American Community* (New York: Simon and Schuster, 1970).

John C. Bollens and Henry J. Schmandt, *The Metropolis: Its People, Politics, and Economic Life*, fourth edition (New York: Harper and Row, 1982).

Robert H. Bremner and Gary W. Reichard (eds), *Reshaping America: Society and Institutions, 1945–1960* (Columbus: Ohio State University Press, 1982).

Thomas H. Brooks, *Walls Come Tumbling Down: A History of The Civil Rights Movement, 1940–1970* (Englewood Cliffs, NJ: Prentice-Hall, 1974).

Michael Burawoy, *Manufacturing Consent: Changes in the Labor Process Under Capitalism* (Chicago: University of Chicago Press, 1979).

Angus Campbell, *The Sense of Well-Being in America: Recent Patterns and Trends* (New York: McGraw Hill, 1981).

Peter N. Carroll, *It Seemed Like Nothing Happened: The Tragedy and Promise of America in the 1970s* (New York: Holt, Rinehart, and Winston, 1982).

Michael J. Carter and William H. Leahy (eds), *New Directions in Labor Economics and Industrial Relations* (Notre Dame and London: University of Notre Dame Press, 1981).

Richard Centers, *The Psychology of Social Classes: A Study of Class Consciousness* (New York: Russell and Russell, 1961).

William H. Chafe, *The American Woman: Her Changing Social, Economic, and Political Role, 1920–1970* (New York: Oxford University Press, 1972).

Ely Chinoy, *Automobile Workers and the American Dream* (Boston: Beacon Press, 1955).

Peter Clecak, *Radical Paradoxes: Dilemmas of the American Left, 1945–1970* (New York: Harper Torchbooks, 1973).

Peter Clecak, *America's Quest for The Ideal Self: Dissent and Fulfillment in the 60s and 70s* (New York: Oxford University Press, 1983).

Thomas C. Cochran, *Business in American Life: A History* (New York: McGraw-Hill, 1972).

Joseph Conlin, *The Troubles: A Jaundiced Glance Back at the Movement of the Sixties* (New York: Franklin Watts, 1982).

Alan Crawford, *Thunder on the Right: The 'New Right' and the Politics of Resentment* (New York: Pantheon Books, 1980).

Donald F. Crosby, SJ, *God, Church, and Flag: Senator Joseph R. McCarthy and the Catholic Church, 1950–1957* (Chapel Hill: University of North Carolina Press, 1978).

Robert A. Dahl, *Who Governs: Democracy and Power in an American City* (New Haven: Yale University Press, 1961).

John D'Emilio, *Sexual Politics, Sexual Communities: The Making of a Homosexual Minority in the United States, 1940–1970* (Chicago: University of Chicago Press, 1983).

G. William Domhoff, *Who Rules America?* (Englewood Cliffs, NJ: Prentice-Hall, 1967).

G. William Domhoff, *Who Really Rules? New Haven and Community Power Reexamined* (Santa Monica: Goodyear, 1978).

G. William Domhoff (ed.), *Power Structure Research* (Beverly Hills: Sage, 1980).

Scott Donaldson, *The Suburban Myth* (New York: Columbia University Press, 1969).

Benjamin R. Epstein and Arnold Foster, *The Radical Right Report on the John Birch Society and Its Allies* (New York: Random House, 1967).

Marten Estey, *The Unions: Structure, Development, and Management*, third edition (New York: Harcourt Brace Jovanovich, 1981).

Thomas Ferguson and Joel Rogers (eds), *The Hidden Election: Politics and Economics in the 1980 Presidential Campaign* (New York: Pantheon, 1981).

E. Franklin Frazier, *The Negro Family in the United States*, revised and abridged edition (New York: Citadel Press, 1948).

Betty Friedan, *The Second Stage* (New York: Summit Books, 1981).

John Kenneth Galbraith, *American Capitalism: The Concept of Countervailing Power* (Boston: Houghton Mifflin, 1956).

Herbert J. Gans, *The Levittowners: Ways of Life and Politics in a New Suburban Community* (New York: Pantheon Books, 1967).

Mark I. Gelfand, *A Nation of Cities: The Federal Government and Urban America, 1933–1965* (New York: Oxford University Press, 1975).

J. E. Gibson, *Designing the New City: A Systematic Approach* (New York: John Wiley, 1977).

Todd Gitlin and Nanci Hollander, *Uptown: Poor Whites in Chicago* (New York: Harper Colophon Books, 1970).

Barry Goldwater, *The Conscience of a Conservative* (Shepherdsville, Kentucky: Victor Publishing, 1960).

Milton M. Gordon, *Social Class in American Sociology* (Durham: Duke University Press, 1958).

Robert Griffith and Athan Theoharis, *The Specter: Original Essays on the Cold War and the Origins of McCarthyism* (New York: New Viewpoints, 1974).

Morton Grodzins, *The Metropolitan Area as a Racial Problem* (Pittsburgh Press, 1958).

John Gunther, *Inside USA* (New York: Harper and Brothers, 1947).

Howell John Harris, *The Right to Manage: Industrial Relations Policies of American Business in the 1940s* (Madison: University of Wisconsin Press, 1982).

George W. Hartmann and Theodore Newcomb, *Industrial Conflict: A Psychological Interpretation* (New York: Cordon Company, 1939).

Robert L. Heilbroner, *The Economic Transformation of America* (New York: Harcourt Brace Jovanovich, 1977).

Floyd Hunter, *Community Power Structure: A Study of Decision Makers* (Garden City, NY: Anchor Books, 1963).

Mary R. Jackman and Robert W. Jackman, *Class Awareness in the United States* (Berkeley: University of California Press, 1983).

M. Kent Jennings, *Community Influentials: The Elites of Atlanta* (New York: The Free Press of Glencoe, 1964).

Marty Jezer, *The Dark Ages: Life in the United States, 1945–1960* (Boston: South End Press, 1982).

Ira Katznelson, *City Trenches: Urban Politics and the Patterning of Class in the United States* (New York: Pantheon Books, 1980).

John Keats, *The Crack in the Picture Window* (Boston: Houghton Mifflin, 1956).

V. O. Key, Jr., *Politics, Parties, and Pressure Groups*, fifth edition (New York: Thomas Y. Crowell, 1964).

Paul A. C. Koistinen, *The Military-Industrial Complex: A Historical Perspective* (New York: Praeger, 1980).

Gabriel Kolko, *Main Currents in Modern American History* (New York: Harper and Row, 1976).

Kit Konolige and Frederica Konolige, *The Power of Their Glory: America's Ruling Class, The Episcopalians* (New York: Wyden Books, 1978).

Nick Kotz and Mary Lynn Kotz, *A Passion for Equality: George A. Wiley and the Movement* (New York: W. W. Norton, 1977).

Robert Kuttner, *Revolt of the Haves: Tax Rebellions and Hard Times* (New York: Simon and Schuster, 1980).

Lawrence Lader, *Power on the Left: American Radical Movements Since 1946* (New York: W. W. Norton, 1979).

Robert W. Lake, *The New Suburbanites: Race and Housing in the Suburbs* (New Brunswick, NJ: Center for Urban Policy Research, 1981).

Richard A. Lester and Joseph Shister (eds), *Insights Into Labor Issues* (New York: Macmillan, 1948).

Andrew Levison, *The Working-Class Majority* (New York: Penguin Books, 1974).

S. A. Levitan and C. M. Johnson, 'The Future of Work: Does it Belong to Us or to the Robots?' *Monthly Labor Review*, 105 (September 1982).

Stanley Lieberson, *A Piece of the Pie: Blacks and White Immigrants Since 1880* (Berkeley: University of California Press, 1980).

Charles E. Lindblom, *Politics and Markets: The World's Political-Economic Systems* (New York: Basic Books, 1977).

Robert L. Lineberry and Ira Sharkansky, *Urban Politics and Public Policy*, third edition (New York: Harper and Row, 1978).

Ferdinand Lundberg, *The Rich and the Super-Rich* (New York: Bantam Books, 1968).

Robert S. Lynd and Helen Merrell Lynd, *Middletown in Transition* (New York: Harcourt, Brace and World, 1937).

Doris McLaughlin and Anita L. W. Schoomaker, *The Landrum–Griffin Act and Union Democracy* (Ann Arbor: University of Michigan Press, 1979).

Carey McWilliams, *Factories in the Fields* (Boston: Little Brown, 1939).

Manning Marable, *How Capitalism Underdeveloped Black America* (Boston: South End Press, 1983).

Toby Marotta, *The Politics of Homosexuality* (Boston: Houghton Mifflin, 1981).

Kurt B. Mayer and Walter Buckley, *Class and Society*, third edition (New York: Random House, 1970).

The Mechanization of Work, A Scientific American Book (San Francisco: W. H. Freeman, 1982).

Michael W. Miles, *The Odyssey of the American Right* (New York: Oxford University Press, 1980).

Douglas T. Miller and Marion Nowak, *The Fifties: The Way We Really Were* (Garden City, NY: Doubleday, 1977).

Herman P. Miller, *Income of the American People* (New York: John Wiley, 1955).

C. Wright Mills, *The Power Elite* (New York: Oxford University Press, 1956).

C. Wright Mills, *White Collar: The American Middle Classes* (New York: Oxford University Press, 1956).

Morton Mintz and Jerry S. Cohen, *America, Inc.: Who Owns and Operates the United States* (New York: Dial Press, 1971).

Sarah McCally Morehouse, *State Politics, Parties and Policy* (New York: Holt, Rinehart, and Winston, 1980).

James N. Morgan, *et al.*, *Income and Welfare in the United States* (New York: McGraw-Hill, 1962).

Peter O. Muller, *Contemporary Suburban America* (Englewood Cliffs, NJ: Prentice-Hall, 1981).

Thomas P. Murphy and John Rehfuss, *Urban Politics in the Suburban Era* (Homewood, Ill.: Dorsey Press, 1976).

Gustavus Myers, *The Ending of Hereditary American Fortunes* (New York: Julian Messner, 1939).

Gunnar Myrdal, *An American Dilemma: The Negro Problem and Modern Democracy* (New York: Harper and Row, 1962).

Mark V. Nadel, *Corporations and Political Accountability* (Lexington, Mass.: D. C. Heath, 1976).

Alfred C. Neal, *Business Power and Public Policy* (New York: Praeger, 1981).

Humbert S. Nelli, *From Immigrants to Ethnics: The Italian Americans* (New York: Oxford University Press, 1983).

Jack Newfield and Paul DuBrul, *The Abuse of Power: The Permanent Government and the Fall of New York* (New York: Penguin Books, 1977).

Hugh S. Norton, *The Employment Act and the Council of Economic Advisers, 1946–1976* (Columbia, SC: University of South Carolina Press, 1977).

R. D. Norton, *City Life-Cycles and American Urban Policy* (New York: Academic Press, 1979).

Michael Novak, *The Rise of the Unmeltable Ethnics: Politics and Culture in the Seventies* (New York: Macmillan, 1973).

David M. Oshinsky, *A Conspiracy So Immense: The World of Joe McCarthy* (New York: The Free Press, 1983).

Vance Packard, *The Status Seekers* (New York: David McKay, 1959).

Connie Paige, *The Right to Lifers: Who They Are, How They Operate, Where They Got Their Money* (New York: Summit Books, 1983).

James T. Patterson, *America's Struggle Against Poverty: 1900–1980* (Cambridge, Mass.: Harvard University Press, 1981).

Victor Perlo, *The Empire of High Finance* (New York: International Publishers, 1957).

Harvey S. Perloff, *et al.*, *Regions, Resources, and Economic Growth* (Baltimore: Johns Hopkins University Press, 1960).

David C. Perry and Alfred J. Watkins (eds), *The Rise of the Sunbelt Cities* (Beverly Hills: Sage, 1977).

Paul E. Peterson, *City Limits* (Chicago: University of Chicago Press, 1981).

Kevin P. Phillips, *Post-Conservative America: People, Politics, and Ideology in a Time of Crisis* (New York: Vintage Books, 1982).

Burton Yale Pines, *Back to Basics: The Traditionalist Movement That Is Sweeping Grass Roots America* (New York: William Morrow, 1982).

Frances Fox Piven and Richard A. Cloward, *Poor People's Movements: Why They Succeed, How They Fail* (New York: Vintage Books, 1979).

Frances Fox Piven and Richard A. Cloward, *The New Class War: Reagan's Attack on the Welfare State and Its Consequences* (New York: Pantheon, 1982).

Lee Rainwater and William L. Yancey, *The Moynihan Report and the Politics of Controversy* (Cambridge, Mass.: MIT Press, 1967).

Michael Reich, *Racial Inequality: A Political-Economic Analysis* (Princeton: Princeton University Press, 1981).

George Ritzer, *Working: Conflict and Change*, second edition (Englewood Cliffs, NJ: Prentice-Hall, 1977).

Theodore Roszak, *The Making of a Counter Culture: Reflections on the Technocratic Society and its Youthful Opposition* (Garden City, NY: Anchor Books, 1969).

I. Herbert Rothenberg and Steven B. Silverman, *Labor Unions: How to Avert Them, Beat Them, Out-Negotiate Them, Live with Them, Unload Them* (Elkins Park, Pa.: Management Relations, 1973).

Richard H. Rovere, *The American Establishment and Other Reports, Opinions, and Speculations* (New York: Harcourt, Brace and World, 1962).

Mary P. Ryan, *Womanhood in America: From Colonial Times to the Present*, third edition (New York: Franklin Watts, 1983).

H. V. Savitch, *Urban Policy and the Exterior City: Federal, State and Corporate Impacts on Major Cities* (New York: Pergamon, 1979).

David O. Sears and Jack Citrin, *Tax Revolt: Something for Nothing in California* (Cambridge, Mass.: Harvard University Press, 1982).

Leonard Silk and Mark Silk, *The American Establishment* (New York: Basic Books, 1980).

Harvard Sitkoff, *A New Deal for Blacks: The Emergence of Civil Rights as a National Issue. Volume I. The Depression Decade* (New York: Oxford University Press, 1978).

Harvard Sitkoff, *The Struggle for Black Equality: 1954–1980* (New York: Hill and Wang, 1981).

Marshall Sklare and Joseph Greenblum, *Jewish Identity on the Suburban Frontier: A Study of Group Survival in the Open Society*, second edition (Chicago: University of Chicago Press, 1979).

June Sochen, *Movers and Shakers: American Women Thinkers and Activists, 1900–1970* (New York: Quadrangle/New York Times, 1973).

Thomas Sowell, *Ethnic America: A History* (New York: Basic Books, 1981).

Thomas M. Stanback, Jr. *et al.*, *Services: The New Economy* (Totowa, NJ: Allanheld, Osmun, 1981).

Thomas M. Stanback, Jr. and Richard V. Knight, *Suburbanization and the City* (Montclair, NJ: Allanheld, Osmun, 1976).

Bruce M. Stave (ed.), *Modern Industrial Cities: History, Policy, and Survival* (Beverly Hills: Sage, 1981).

Stephen Steinberg, *The Ethnic Myth: Race, Ethnicity, and Class in America* (Boston: Beacon Press, 1981).

James L. Sundquist, *Politics and Policy: The Eisenhower, Kennedy, and Johnson Years* (Washington, DC: The Brookings Institution, 1968).

William K. Tabb, *The Long Default: New York City and the Urban Fiscal Crisis* (New York: Monthly Review Press, 1982).

Philip J. Trounstine and Terry Christensen, *Movers and Shakers: The Study of Community Power* (New York: St. Martin's Press, 1982).

Jules Tygiel, *Baseball's Great Experiment: Jackie Robinson and his Legacy* (New York: Oxford University Press, 1983).

James W. Vander Zanden, *American Minority Relations*, fourth edition (New York: Alfred A. Knopf, 1983).

Richard A. Viguerie, *The New Right: We're Ready to Lead* (Falls Church, Va.: Viguerie Company, 1981).

Murray L. Weidenbaum, *The Future of Business Regulation* (New York: Amacom Press, 1979).

William H. Whyte, Jr., *The Organization Man* (New York: Simon and Schuster, 1956).

J. Harvie Wilkinson III, *From Brown to Bakke: The Supreme Court and School Integration, 1954–1978* (New York: Oxford University Press, 1979).

Jeffrey G. Williamson and Peter H. Lindert, *American Inequality: A Macroeconomic History* (New York: Academic Press, 1980).

William Julius Wilson, *The Declining Significance of Race: Blacks and Changing American Institutions*, second edition (Chicago: University of Chicago Press, 1980).

Frederick M. Wirt, *Power in the City: Decision-Making in San Francisco* (Berkeley: University of California Press, 1974).

Alan Wolfe, *America's Impasse: The Rise and Fall of the Politics of Growth* (New York: Pantheon Books, 1981).

Robert C. Wood, *Suburbia: Its People and Their Politics* (Boston: Houghton Mifflin, 1958).

Patricia G. Zelman, *Women, Work, and National Policy: The Kennedy–Johnson Years* (Ann Arbor: UMI Research Press, 1982).

Index